# Obsessive-Compulsive Disorder:

## Etiology, Phenomenology, and Treatment

**Caleb W. Lack, Editor**

**Foreword by Dean McKay**

Obsessive-Compulsive Disorder: Etiology, Phenomenology, and Treatment.

Published by *Onus Books*

Onus Books, Fareham, UK

Printed by Lightning Source International

Cover design: Caleb W. Lack

Trade paperback ISBN: 978-0-9926000-5-1

OB 09/13

## *Acknowledgements*

This book would not have been possible without the support of my family and colleagues. I would specifically like to express appreciation to my parents, Johnny and Patty Lack, who have been an unwavering source of strength for me to draw upon. Special thanks are also due to Ms. Amanda Beck, who helped with the copyediting of the chapters in this book. Finally, I greatly appreciate the time and efforts which all of the chapter authors put forth, resulting in a wonderful introduction to Obsessive-Compulsive Disorder.

# CONTENTS

# Where We Are and
# Where We Can Go

## Dean McKay

As any reader of this text will quickly appreciate, obsessive-compulsive disorder (OCD) is a highly complex and heterogeneous condition. Individuals with severe symptoms suffer additional complications including ancillary mood problems, social and occupational disability, and often long and frustrating treatment histories marked by limited successes or improvements followed by return of symptoms. The arrival of a text that highlights the current state of psychological, pharmacological and family interventions is a welcome addition to the available literature.

While it could be easily taken that the outlook for OCD sufferers is bleak, particularly given my opening paragraph, there are actually well established and highly effective interventions for OCD. Treatment guidelines emphasize specific psychosocial interventions, namely exposure with response prevention (ERP) and cognitive therapy. Selective serotonin reuptake inhibitors (SSRIs) are considered first line pharmacological agents. These two broad treatment approaches are not new. A meta-analysis of ERP of treatment trials first appeared in 1987 (Christensen et al., 1987). A meta-analysis of SSRIs first appeared in 1995 (Greist et al., 1995). However, sufferers continue to struggle to find competent providers who can offer these procedures. This is the real challenge facing the field – how do we ensure that individuals with OCD receive proper treatment?

The limited dissemination of medically appropriate treatment for OCD stems, in part, from the problems in diagnosing the condition. While the criteria for OCD are fairly clear, client presentation of symptoms often fails to neatly comport to the criteria. Consider the following relatively common presentation: a client has to repeatedly check to be sure that she did not inadvertently molest a child after visiting a fast-food restaurant where children where dining. In her presentation, she reports acute distress and has trouble describing the intrusive thoughts as rightly originating in her mind rather than as a psychotic experience. This client could very easily end up with a diagnosis in the psychotic disorders. Taken further, assume this hypothetical client correctly receives a diagnosis of OCD; she could, however, end up prescribed antipsychotic medication as a first line due to presumed cognitive difficulties. This kind of diagnostic scenario is not an uncommon occurrence and can ultimately serve to delay proper treatment delivery.

In the psychosocial treatment realm, the problems involve the aforementioned diagnostic errors, and are compounded by reluctance on the part of many providers to conduct ERP. Specifically, ERP involves provoking discomfort in clients, albeit when done properly this discomfort is temporary, and leads to longer term and profound symptom relief. It is this short term distress provocation, however, that causes clinicians discomfort as there are numerous mistaken assumptions about the consequences of causing anxiety in session including fear of litigation (Richard & Gloster, 2007), contrary theoretical position (Wachtel, 1995), a feeling that causing distress is contrary to the clinician's personal identity (McKay & Ojserkis, in press), and embracing a 'spun-glass theory of mind' (Meehl, 1973). All of these preconceived notions serve as potent barriers to treatment delivery.

Fortunately, there are efforts afoot to alleviate this problem. The one that is most promising and having significant impact is the initiative by the International Obsessive Compulsive Disorder Foundation (IOCDF) called the Behavior Therapy Training Institute (BTI). This program intensively trains practicing licensed clinicians in ERP, and has several follow-up consultations to ensure that they are implementing the procedure properly. There have been approximately one thousand clinicians trained in this program as of this writing (March 30, 2014).

# Future Directions

Whereas there are effective treatments, but not yet fully disseminated, research continues on the basic mechanisms underlying the disorder. This line of inquiry has been far more limited in scope. The psychological mechanisms underlying the condition have not been conclusive. There is mixed support for the concept of inflated responsibility, overestimation of threat, and perfectionism, to name just three prominent cognitive components hypothesized to account for the condition. On the biological side, the findings have been similarly disappointing. While the serotonin hypothesis is a prominent model purported to account for the disorder, the findings have been far from conclusive and certainly not unique to the condition as serotonin has been implicated in virtually all other psychopathological states. Genetic research, often hailed as the domain sure to unlock the mysteries of how to quickly and efficiently treat the condition, has produced more heat than light. On this last note, a recent meta-analysis (Taylor, 2013) showed limited gene-specific associations for OCD, and what little support was found was also not consistent with hypothesized models of the disorder. At the same time, a genome-wide association study of OCD (Stewart et al., 2013) failed to show specific genetic associations with expected genes; the genes identified were extremely small in magnitude of association and also were not in line with existing biological models of the condition.

In light of these findings, consider the radical alternative: what if OCD as currently described is simply not a valid disorder? It would not be outrageous to make such a claim. The contemporary psychopathology classification system is not ordered based on an underlying theory of behavior and emotional disorders. Instead, it is a checklist of symptoms that are conferred upon by a committee of experts on the condition. Recent years have witnessed substantial refinements that could allude to what constitute valid dimensions of the disorder. For example, hoarding was recently reclassified as a separate disorder within a broader class of obsessive-compulsive related disorders in the DSM-5 (Pertusa et al., 2008, 2010). What if it turned out that other symptom domains were also sufficiently different from each other that it appeared each was a unique syndrome? If this were in fact the case, it would require a substantial re-organization of how biological models account for the disorder, or in this case disorders.

At the present time, it appears that we have a set of interventions that are generally effective at providing substantial relief for OCD. The challenge that is facing the profession is how to ensure that people who suffer from obsessive-compulsive symptoms receive appropriate care, a daunting prospect at the present time. As you hold this volume, it is anticipated that we are coming another step closer to ensuring more individuals with OCD receive effective care.

## References

Christensen, H., Hadzi-Pavlovic, D., Andrews, G., Mattick, R., 1987. Behavior therapy and tricyclic medication in the treatment of obsessive-compulsive disorder: A quantitative review. *Journal of Consulting and Clinical Psychology* *55*, 701-711.

Greist, J.H., Jefferson, J.W., Kobak, K.A., & Katzelnick, D.J. (1995). Efficacy and tolerability of serotonin transport inhibitors in obsessive-compulsive disorder: A meta-analysis. *Archives of General Psychiatry, 52,* 53-60.

McKay, D. & Ojserkis, R. (in press). Exposure in experiential context: Imaginal and in vivo approaches. In N. Thoma & D. McKay (Eds.), *Working with Emotion in Cognitive Behavioral Therapy: Techniques for Clinical Practice.* New York, NY: Guilford.

Meehl, P.H. (1973). Why I do not attend case conferences. In P.E. Meehl, *Psychodiagnosis: Selected Papers (pp. 225-308).* Minneapolis, MN: University of Minnesota Press.

Pertusa, A., Frost, R.O., Fullana, M.A., Samuels, J., Steketee, G., Tolin, D.F., Saxena, S., Leckman, J.F., Mataix-Cols, D., 2010. Refining the diagnostic boundaries of compulsive hoarding: A critical review. *Clinical Psychology Review 30,* 371-386.

Pertusa, A., Fullana, M. A., Singh, S., Alonso, P., Menchon, J. M., Mataix-Cols, D., 2008. Compulsive hoarding: OCD symptom, distinct clinical syndrome, or both? *American Journal of Psychiatry 165,* 1289-1298.

Richard, D. C. S., & Gloster, A. T. (2007). Exposure therapy has a public relations problem: A dearth of litigation amid a wealth of concern. In D. C. S. Richard, & D. Lauterbach (Eds.), *Comprehensive handbook of the exposure therapies* (pp. 409–425). New York, NY: Academic Press.

Stewart, S.E., Yu, D., Scharf, J.M., Neale, B.M., Fagerness, J.A., Mathews, C.A., Arnold, P.D., Evans, P.D., et al. (2013). Genome-wide association study of obsessive-compulsive disorder. *Molecular Psychiatry, 18,* 788-798.

Taylor, S. (2013). Molecular genetics of obsessive-compulsive disorder: A meta-analysis of association studies. *Molecular Psychiatry, 18,* 799-805.

Wachtel, P. (1995). *Psychoanalysis, behavior therapy, and the relational world.* Washington, DC: American Psychological Association.

*CW Lack*

# Introduction

This book aims to provide a concise reference to the current state of the scientific and clinical knowledge on Obsessive-Compulsive Disorder (OCD). It is broadly divided into two parts. The first half of the book concentrates on understanding the disorder better, while the second half focuses on the effective and evidence-based treatment of OCD.

My colleagues and I start in Chapter One with a broad overview of how OCD is currently conceptualized and then move into Chapter Two with an examination of what causes OCD, relying on a multi-level explanation that accounts for evolutionary, biological, psychological, and social influences. Adam Lewin and his colleagues then use Chapter Three to break OCD, as a whole, down into the different types of symptoms we see and explain both what they look like and what impact that has on treatment. Chapter Four has Monnica Williams and Ashleigh Steever providing a thorough survey of what the literature says about how OCD manifests itself across different cultures.

The second half of the book begins with Eric Storch and his colleagues in Chapter Five reviewing the most effective psychosocial treatment for OCD, cognitive-behavioral therapy incorporating exposure with response prevention. Next we have psychiatrists Erika Nurmi and Roy Eyal detailing pharmacological treatment options in Chapter Six. In Chapter Seven, Heather Yardley leads a team examining the frontiers of treatment options that, while not well-established yet, show great promise. In our concluding Chapter Eight, Gary Geffken and associates take a look at a crucial aspect of treatment success – the involvement of the family.

It is my hope that this book will prove useful not only to those new to the mental health field, but also those established professionals who are nonetheless new to the incredibly interesting problem we call OCD. With that said, on to the chapters!

Caleb W. Lack, Ph.D.

# Chapter One

# What is Obsessive-Compulsive Disorder?

Caleb W. Lack & Sean McMillan

Obsessive-compulsive disorder (OCD) is a mental disorder that is primarily diagnosed based upon the presence of *obsessions* and/or *compulsions* (Diagnostic and Statistical Manual of Mental Disorders, Fifth Edition; American Psychiatric Association, 2013). The *DSM-5* defines obsessions as "recurrent and persistent thoughts, urges, or images that are experienced as intrusive and unwanted" and compulsions as "repetitive behaviors or mental acts that an individual feels driven to perform in response to an obsession or according to rules that must be applied rigidly" (APA, 2013, p. 237).

Far from being odd or unusual experiences, most people have experienced non-clinical levels of obsessions and compulsions at some point in their lives (Abramowitz et al., 2014). Obsessing over an upcoming event (e.g., an exam), worrying that you forgot to lock the front door or turn off the stove before leaving for a trip, always having your desk organized in a specific way, and performing superstitious behaviors (e.g., always wearing a particular sports jersey on days that your favorite sports team plays) are examples of some minor obsessions and compulsions. Insignificant obsessions and compulsions are harmless and can actually prove to be beneficial to individuals. Ritualistic behaviors (i.e., compulsions), such as taking time to organize one's desk at the start or end of a workday can create a sense of relief and reduce anxiety. This may be why routines and rituals are extremely common in the population, from sleeping in the same position every night to buttoning your shirt in a particular fashion (Kanner, 2005). Much like many other cognitions and behaviors, obsessions and compulsions only become problematic when they are carried out excessively, irrationally, for unreasonable amounts of time, to a level that causes significant distress to the person, or when they hinder daily living (Lack, 2013).

This chapter will focus on defining obsessions and compulsions, the disorder that arises from their presence, how that disorder has changed across time in diagnostic nosologies, controversies over its classification, epidemiology, and a brief overview of the problems it can cause for individuals.

# A Brief History of OCD

References to symptoms of what we now call obsessive-compulsive disorder date back hundreds of years to the 17th century. From Lady Macbeth's excessive handwashing to Martin Luther's excessive scrupulosity, case studies and reports from history make it clear that OCD has been with the human species for a very long time (Krochmalik & Menzies, 2003). Attempts at systematic research on OCD began in the early 1800s, when it was often considered a form of insanity, although this gradually developed into "insanity with insight" as it was acknowledged that persons suffering from OCD did not have the disconnect from reality seen in psychosis (Salzman & Thaler, 1981). A more contemporary understanding began by the early 19th century, with several psychological frameworks for understanding why people had OCD competing for attention. Sigmund Freud's hypotheses regarding obsessional thoughts battled Pierre Janet's views of abnormal personality in the minds of clinicians (Boileau, 2003). Although influencing later conceptions, these have fallen by the wayside as new perspectives on OCD have developed in the last century, particularly the criteria as outlined in two distinct diagnostic manuals.

*Classification of OCD in the DSM*

As diagnostic nosologies for mental disorders were developed in the 20th century, two systems rose to prominence. The Diagnostic and Statistical Manual for Mental Disorders, published by the American Psychiatric Association, is currently the most widely-used manual by mental health clinicians to define the symptoms of what are variously called mental disorders, mental illness, or psycholopathology, including OCD, in the United States. It is currently on its fifth revision, which contained some major changes in how OCD is conceptualized compared to prior versions.

In the DSM-IV-TR (APA, 2000), OCD was classified as an anxiety disorder (as it was in all prior versions). In the DSM-5 (APA, 2013), OCD has been removed from the anxiety disorders and placed alongside body dysmorphic disorder, trichotillomania or hair-pulling, hoarding, and excoriation or skin-picking in a new section titled Obsessive-Compulsive and Related Disorders. The DSM-5 notes, however, that the Obsessive-Compulsive and Related Disorders section was purposefully placed right after the Anxiety Disorders section because "there are close relationships between the anxiety disorders and some of the obsessive-compulsive and related disorders (e.g., OCD)" (American Psychiatric Association, 2013). Even with that in consideration, it was and remains a highly controversial decision to remove OCD from the Anxiety Disorders and create a new category that it apparently exemplifies.

To illustrate the controversy, an international survey involving 187 authors of OCD research articles was conducted to determine how the authors felt about OCD being relocated from the Anxiety Disorders section to a different section (Mataix-Cols et al., 2007). Roughly 60% of those who answered the survey endorsed OCD being moved for the DSM-5. Survey respondents comprising the 60% most commonly reported basing their decision on the finding that obsessions and compulsions, instead of anxiety, make up the central traits of OCD. Respondents that opposed the move frequently stated that they arrived at their opinion based on the evidence that OCD and the other anxiety disorders benefit from comparable treatment methods and typically are comorbid. Intriguingly, there was a significant difference in opinion between psychiatrists (where 75% supported the change) and other health professionals (where only 40–45% supported the change). Although covering the complete controversy and issues surrounding OCD's classification is outside of the scope of this chapter, interested readers can refer to Leckman et al. (2010), Stein et al. (2010), and Storch et al. (2008) for differing perspectives on this issue and a review of the literature.

A section change was not the only OCD-related change given consideration when the DSM-5 was being developed. Changing of the wording in the diagnostic criteria for OCD was also debated and, in fact, the DSM-5 has different wording for OCD diagnostic criteria than the DSM-IV-TR. For example, in item 1 under Obsessions the word "impulses" (DSM-IV-TR) was changed to "urges" (DSM-5). Although "impulse" and "urge" both effectively represent the seemingly uncontrollable drive associated with obsessions, "impulse" obliquely makes reference to impulse control disorders, which may confuse or influence clinicians and lead them to make an inaccurate diagnosis (Leckman et al., 2010). Other wording changes were also made, but do not significantly impact the diagnosis. The differences in wording can be seen in the following table, which contains the diagnostic criteria from both the DSM-IV-TR and DSM-5.

---

### DSM-IV-TR Diagnostic Criteria for Obsessive-Compulsive Disorder

A.  Either obsessions or compulsions:
    *Obsessions as defined by (1), (2), (3), and (4):*
    (1) recurrent and persistent thoughts, impulses, or images that are experienced, at some time during the disturbance, as intrusive and inappropriate and that cause marked anxiety or distress
    (2) the thoughts, impulses, or images are not simply excessive worries about real-life problems
    (3) the person attempts to ignore or suppress such thoughts, impulses, or images, or to neutralize them with some other thought or action

(4) the person recognizes that the obsessional thoughts, impulses, or images are a product of his or her own mind (not imposed from without as in thought insertion)

*Compulsions as defined by (1) and (2):*

(1) repetitive behaviors (e.g., hand washing, ordering, checking) or mental acts (e.g., praying, counting, repeating words silently) that the person feels driven to perform in response to an obsession, or according to rules that must be applied rigidly

(2) the behaviors or mental acts are aimed at preventing or reducing distress or preventing some dreaded event or situation; however, these behaviors or mental acts either are not connected in a realistic way with what they are designed to neutralize or prevent or are clearly excessive

B.  At some point during the course of the disorder, the person has recognized that the obsessions or compulsions are excessive or unreasonable. **Note:** This does not apply to children.

C.  The obsessions or compulsions cause marked distress, are time consuming (take more than 1 hour a day), or significantly interfere with the person's normal routine, occupational (or academic) functioning, or usual social activities or relationships.

D.  If another Axis I disorder is present, the content of the obsessions or compulsions is not restricted to it (e.g., preoccupation with food in the presence of an Eating Disorder; hair pulling in the presence of Trichotillomania; concern with appearance in the presence of Body Dysmorphic Disorder; preoccupation with drugs in the presence of a Substance Abuse Disorder; preoccupation with having a serious illness in the presence of Hypochondriasis; preoccupation with sexual urges or fantasies in the presence of a Paraphilia; or guilty ruminations in the presence of Major Depressive Disorder).

E.  The disturbance is not due to the direct physiological effects of a substance (e.g., a drug of abuse, a medication) or a general medical condition.

*Specify* if:

**With poor insight:** if, for most of the time during the current episode, the person does not recognize that the obsessions and compulsions are excessive or unreasonable

### *DSM-5 Diagnostic Criteria for Obsessive-Compulsive Disorder*

A.  Presence of obsessions, compulsions, or both:
    Obsessions are defined by (1) and (2):
    (1) Recurrent and persistent thoughts, urges, or images that are experienced, at some time during the disturbance, as intrusive and unwanted, and that in most individuals cause marked anxiety or distress.
    (2) The individual attempts to ignore or suppress such thoughts, urges, or images, or to neutralize them with some other thought or action (i.e., by performing a compulsion).
    Compulsions are defined by (1) and (2):
    (1) Repetitive behaviors (e.g., hand washing, ordering, checking) or mental acts (e.g., praying, counting, repeating words silently) that the individual feels driven to perform in response to an obsession or according to rules that must be applied rigidly.
    (2) The behaviors or mental acts are aimed at preventing or reducing anxiety or distress, or preventing some dreaded event or situation; however, these behaviors or mental acts are not connected in a realistic way with what they are designed to neutralize or prevent, or are clearly excessive.
    **Note:** Young children may not be able to articulate the aims of these behaviors or mental acts.

B.  The obsessions or compulsions are time-consuming (e.g., take more than 1 hour per day) or cause clinically significant distress or impairment in social, occupational, or other important areas of functioning.

C.  The obsessive-compulsive symptoms are not attributable to the physiological effects of a substance (e.g., a drug of abuse, a medication) or another medical condition.

D.  The disturbance is not better explained by the symptoms of another mental disorder (e.g., excessive worries, as in generalized anxiety disorder; preoccupation with appearance, as in body dysmorphic disorder; difficulty discarding or parting with possessions, as in hoarding disorder; hair pulling, as in trichotillomania [hair-pulling disorder]; skin picking, as in excoriation [skin-picking] disorder; stereotypies, as in stereotypic movement disorder; ritualized eating behavior, as in eating disorders; preoccupation with substances or gambling, as in substance-related and addictive disorders; preoccupation with having an illness, as in illness anxiety disorder; sexual urges or fantasies, as in paraphilic disorders;

impulses, as in disruptive, impulse-control, and conduct disorders; guilty ruminations, as in major depressive disorder; thought insertion or delusional preoccupations, as in schizophrenia spectrum and other psychotic disorders; or repetitive patterns of behavior, as in autism spectrum disorder).

*Specify* if:

**With good or fair insight:** The individual recognizes that obsessive-compulsive disorder beliefs are definitely or probably not true or that they may or may not be true.

**With poor insight:** The individual thinks obsessive-compulsive disorder beliefs are probably true.

**With absent insight/delusional beliefs:** The individual is completely convinced that obsessive-compulsive disorder beliefs are true.

*Specify* if:

**Tic-related:** The individual has a current or past history of a tic disorder.

---

*Classification of OCD in the ICD*

The next most popular diagnostic manual that clinicians use, both outside and inside the U.S., is the International Statistical Classification of Diseases and Related Health Problems (ICD), currently in its tenth revision. In the ICD-10, OCD is located in the Neurotic, Stress-related and Somatoform Disorders section, which is also where anxiety disorders are. Interestingly, OCD is actually separated from anxiety disorders and given its own subheading (World Health Organization, 2010), dissimilar to DSM-IV but consistent with its separation in DSM-5. However, they are closely grouped in the ICD-10 and it would be easy to miss this distinction. Another noticeable difference is in the definitions of obsessions and compulsions.

In ICD-10, obsessions are described as "ideas, images, or impulses that enter the patient's mind again and again in a stereotyped form. They are almost invariably distressing and the patient often tries, unsuccessfully, to resist them. They are, however, recognized as his or her own thoughts, even though they are involuntary and often repugnant (World Health Organization, 2010)." In DSM-5, obsessions are defined as "recurrent and persistent thoughts, urges, or images that are experienced as intrusive and unwanted" (American Psychiatric Association, 2013). In ICD-10, compulsions are described as "stereotyped behaviours that are repeated again and again. They are not inherently enjoyable, nor do they result in the completion of inherently useful tasks. Their function is to prevent some objectively unlikely event, often involving harm to or caused by the patient, which he or she fears might otherwise occur. Usually, this behaviour is recognized by the patient as pointless or ineffectual and repeated attempts are made to resist. Anxiety is almost invariably present. If compulsive acts are resisted the anxiety gets worse" (World Health Organization, 2010). In DSM-5, compulsions are defined as "repetitive behaviors or mental acts that an individual feels driven to perform in response to an obsession or according to rules that must be applied rigidly" (American Psychiatric Association, 2013).

Dissimilar to the ICD-10, the DSM-5 directly declares that there is an interactional relationship between obsessions and compulsions. That is, as presented in the DSM-5, obsessions are anxiety provoking and compulsions are performed to decrease stress and avoid an imagined unpleasant outcome (e.g., house burning down from leaving the stove on) (Leckman et al., 2010). Although the relief is typically brief in duration, the individual engages in one or more compulsions to alleviate their anxiety. The ICD-10 proclaims that "Underlying the overt behaviour is a fear, usually of danger either to or caused by the patient, and the ritual is an ineffectual or symbolic attempt to avert that danger" (World Health Organization, 2010)." This references obsessions but does not by name refer to obsessions, which contrasts the DSM-5. Unlike the DSM-IV-TR, the ICD-10 specifically notes that obsessions and compulsions are not enjoyable for the individual experiencing them (Leckman et al., 2010). The changes that came with the DSM-5 altered this disparity, however, and the DSM-5 mentions that obsessions are "intrusive and unwanted" (American Psychiatric Association, 2013).

## Common Types of Obsessions and Compulsions

Contrary to what some may think, the content and purpose of obsessions and compulsions (O/C) seems to differ little between clinical and non-clinical samples (Garcia-Soriano et al., 2011). Research has found that while compulsions are not as likely to be overt in non-clinical populations, people without OCD nonetheless engage in anxiety-reducing or anxiety-neutralizing behaviors (i.e., compulsions) when they have obsessive thoughts (Berman et al., 2010). Even the most commonly reported O/C, outlined below, are similar between those with and without OCD (Abramowitz et al., 2014).

Obsessions can be impulses (e.g., desire to loudly cuss during a funeral), wishes (e.g., wishing someone to die), images (e.g., imagining your house setting on fire because the oven was left on), or doubts (e.g., thinking that you forgot to lock a door) that repeatedly come to mind at a level beyond what would be considered typical worrying over genuine life problems (Challis, Pelling, & Lack, 2008). Most often, individuals with obsessions know that the intrusive thoughts are abnormal, which only increases their anxiety. Obsessions may focus on a variety of themes, including contamination (i.e., germs and sickness), aggression and violence (either towards others or self-harm), sexuality, orderliness, religiosity, and extreme uncertainty (e.g., fear of forgetting to lock the door or make sure the oven is off before leaving home).

## Most Common Obsessions Seen in OCD

| Type of Obsession | Examples |
| --- | --- |
| Contamination | Bodily fluids, disease, germs, dirt, chemicals, environmental contaminants |
| Religious Obsessions | Blasphemy or offending God, high concern about morality and what is right and wrong. |
| Superstitious ideas | Lucky numbers, colors, words |
| Perfectionism | Evenness and exactness, "needing" to know or remember, fear of forgetting or losing something |
| Harm | Fear of hurting others through carelessness, fear of being responsible for something terrible happening |
| Losing Control | Fear of acting on an impulse to harm self or others, fear or unpleasant mental images, fear of saying offending things to others |
| Unwanted Sexual Thoughts | Forbidden or "perverse" sexual thoughts, images, or impulses; obsessive thoughts about homosexuality; obsessions involving children or incest; obsessions about aggressive sexual behavior |

Compulsions, on the other hand, are repeated actions that are often performed as a means to reduce the anxiety and distress caused by an obsession (Challis, Pelling, & Lack, 2008). Obsessions almost always make persons with OCD highly anxious or distressed. Engaging in compulsions can serve to reduce the anxiety caused by obsessions, or sometimes to prevent the anxiety before it occurs; however, the anxiety reduction does not usually last for very long (for a more detailed explanation, see the following chapter on the etiology of OCD). While compulsions are volitional, it does not feel that way to people with OCD. Instead, they believe that something bad will happen if they do not engage in a compulsion (e.g., a loved one will die or they will catch a terrible disease). Compulsive behaviors may be performed from anywhere from a few times a day to several hundred times a day, depending on the severity of one's OCD (Abramowitz, Taylor, & McKay, 2009).

## Most Common Compulsions Seen in OCD

| Type of Compulsion | Examples |
|---|---|
| Checking | Making sure that you did not (or will not) harm yourself or others, or that you did not make a mistake, or that nothing "terrible" happened |
| Repeating | Repeating things in multiples or a certain number of times, certain body movements, rereading or rewriting |
| Washing / Cleaning | Washing hands excessively, excessive showering or bathing, cleaning outside the norm |
| Mental compulsions | Cancelling out bad thoughts with good ones, counting while walking or performing some task, prayer to prevent something terrible from happening |
| Hoarding | Collecting items due to compulsions |
| Ordering and Arranging | Putting things in "proper" order or until it "feels right" |

## Epidemiological Aspects of OCD

In the U.S., the lifetime prevalence rate of OCD is estimated at 2.3% in adults (Kessler et al., 2005) and around 1-2.3% in children and adolescents under 18 (Zohar, 1999). There are also a fairly substantial number of "sub-clinical" cases of OCD, around 5% of the population Ruscio et al., 2010), where symptoms are either not disturbing or not disruptive enough to meet full criteria and yet are still impairing to some degree. There is strong evidence that cultural differences do not play a prominent role in presence of OCD, with research showing few epidemiological differences across different countries (Fontenelle et al., 2004) and even between European and Asian populations (Matsunga, 2008). There are, however, cultural influences on symptom expression.

While OCD is equally present in males and females in adulthood, the disorder is heavily male in pediatric patients (Geller, 2006). There are some differences in comorbidity as well. Among men, hoarding symptoms are most often associated with GAD and tic disorders, but in women social anxiety, PTSD, body dysmorphic disorder, nail biting, and skin picking are more often observed (Kessler et al., 2005; Torres et al. 2006).

Presentation of OCD symptoms is generally the same in children and adults (Stewart et al., 2008). Unlike many adults, though, younger children will not be able to recognize that their obsessions and compulsions are both unnecessary (e.g., you don't really need to wash your hands) and extreme (e.g., washing hands for 15-20 seconds is fine, but 5 minutes in scalding water is too much) in nature. In young children, compulsions often occur without the patient being able to report their obsessions, while adolescents are often able to report multiple obsessions and compulsions. Children and adolescents are also more likely to include family members in their rituals and can be highly demanding of adherence to rituals and rules, leading to disruptive and oppositional behavior. As such, youth with OCD are generally more impaired than adults with the same type of symptoms (Piacentini et al., 2007).

Up to 75% of persons with OCD also present with comorbid disorders (Kessler et al., 2005). The most common in pediatric cases are ADHD, disruptive behavior disorders, major depression, and other anxiety disorders (Geller et al., 1996). In adults, the most prevalent comorbids are social anxiety, major depression, and alcohol abuse (Torres et al., 2006). Interestingly, the presence of comorbid diagnoses predict quality of life (QoL) more so than OCD severity itself in both children (Lack et al., 2009) and adults (Fontenelle et al., 2010). Different primary O/C are also associated with certain patterns of comorbidity, in both adults and youth (De Mathis et al., 2006). Primary symmetry/ordering symptoms are often seen with comorbid tics, bipolar disorder, obsessive-compulsive personality disorder, panic disorder, and agoraphobia, while those with contamination/cleaning symptoms are more likely to be diagnosed with an eating disorder. Those with hoarding cluster symptoms, on the other hand, are especially likely to be diagnosed with personality disorders, particularly Cluster C disorders.

## Psychological Assessment Measures for OCD

There are multiple measures available to help clinicians diagnose OCD symptomatology in adults and children. Some frequently used adult self-report measures are the Yale-Brown Obsessive Compulsive Scale (Y-BOCS), Padua Inventory-Revised (PI-R), and Obsessive Compulsive Inventory (OCI). Some commonly used self-report measures given to children are the Children's Yale-Brown Obsessive Compulsive Scale (CY-BOCS), and Children's Florida Obsessive Compulsive Inventory (C-FOCI) (see Storch, Benito, & Goodman, 2011 for a review). These measures inform clinicians about the level of OCD symptoms present and how much distress they cause a client on a daily basis. The aforementioned psychological assessments can help a clinician determine what type of treatment(s) would best serve a client and how often the client should receive therapy and/or medication.

## Impairment Issues Related to OCD

Most individuals with OCD experience both obsessions and compulsions (American Psychiatric Association, 2013). People with OCD (roughly 2-3% of the general population) usually spend a large amount of time (usually more than one hour) each day performing their ritualized behavior(s) and thinking obsessively (Challis, Pelling, & Lack, 2008). The obsessions and compulsions make even the easiest of daily chores or activities time-consuming and stressful. Individuals with OCD spend a great deal of time carrying out their compulsions. Specifically, obsessions and compulsions are considered clinically significant when they are performed for more than one hour each day (American Psychiatric Association, 2013).

Almost all adults and children with OCD report that their obsessions cause them significant distress and anxiety, as opposed to similar, intrusive thoughts in persons without OCD (Subramaniam et al., 2013). In terms of quality of life (QoL), persons with OCD report a pervasive decrease compared to controls. Youth show problematic peer relations, academic difficulties, and participate in fewer recreational activities than matched peers (Lack et al., 2009). Overall, there is a lower QoL in pediatric females than males, but in adults similar disruptions are reported. When compared to other anxiety disorders and unipolar mood disorders, a person with OCD is less likely to be married, more likely to be unemployed, and more likely to report impaired social and occupational functioning (Macy et al., 2013).

Daily, there are a number of problems that people with OCD face. One example is the avoidance of situations in which the objects of the obsessions are present. For example, a person may avoid using public restrooms or shaking hands with people because doing so will trigger their contamination obsession, which will lead to them having to do a cleansing compulsion. Some people will not leave their homes because that is the only way to avoid objects and situations that will trigger their obsessions. Frequent doctor visits may also occur because they fear that something is wrong with them physically, just like a hypochondriac would feel. Feelings of guilt can also be present, along with disrupted sleep patterns and extreme feelings of responsibility. Self-medication may also be present in adults, with alcohol and sedatives the most often abused substances (Fals-Stewart & Angarano, 1994).

# Conclusions

The current outlook on OCD is much more optimistic than it was in the past, when prognosis for OCD was bleak and understanding of it was poor (Franklin & Foa, 2008). Three decades ago, OCD was considered to be a permanent, untreatable mental disorder, as there were no effective medications or therapeutic methods for this disorder at that time. Over the last thirty years, our understanding of both basic aspects of OCD and treatment methods have progressed and OCD is now viewed as a treatable condition. A variety of empirically supported therapeutic methods and medication are available for individuals with OCD. With the proper treatment due to our increased understanding, people can learn to live with and reduce their OCD symptoms.

# References

Abramowitz, J. S., Fabricant, L. E., Taylor, S., Deacon, B. J., McKay, D., & Storch, E. A. (2014). The relevance of analogue studies for understanding obsessions and compulsions. *Clinical psychology review*, *34*(3), 206-217.

Abramowitz, J. S., Taylor, S., & McKay, D. (2009). Obsessive-compulsive disorder. *The Lancet*, *374*, 491-499.

American Psychiatric Association (2000). *Diagnostic and statistical manual of mental disorders* (4th ed., text revision).Washington DC: Author.

American Psychiatric Association. (2013). *Diagnostic and statistical manual of mental disorders* (5th ed.). Arlington, VA: American Psychiatric Publishing.

Berman, N. C., Abramowitz, J. S., Pardue, C. M., & Wheaton, M. G. (2010). The relationship between religion and thought –action fusion: Use of an in vivo paradigm. *Behaviour Research and Therapy*, *48*, 670–674

Boileau, B. (2003). A review of obsessive-compulsive disorder in children and adolescents. *Dialogues in Clinical Neuroscience*, *13, 401*-11.

Challis, C., Pelling, N., & Lack, C. W. (2008). The bio-psycho-social aspects and treatment of obsessive compulsive disorder: A primer for practitioners. *Australian Counseling Association Journal*, *8*(1), 3-13.

de Mathis, M.A., Diniz, J.B., do Rosário, M.C., Torres, A.R., Hoexter, M., Hasler, G., Miguel, E.C. (2006). What is the optimal way to subdivide obsessive-compulsive disorder? *CNS Spectrum*, *11(10)*, 762-8, 771-4, 776-9.

Falls-Stewart, W., & Angarano, K. (1994). Obsessive-Compulsive Disorder among patients entering substance abuse treatment: Prevalence and accuracy of diagnosis. *Journal of Nervous and Mental Disease*, *182*(12), 715-719.

Fontenelle I.S., Fontenelle, L.F., Borges, M.C., Prazeres, A.M., Rangé, B.P., Mendlowicz, M.V., Versiani M. (2010). Quality of life and symptom dimensions of patients with obsessive-compulsive disorder. *Psychiatry Research*, *179*(2), 198-203.

Fontenelle, L.F., Mendlowicz, M.V., Marques, C., & Versiani, M. (2004). Trans-cultural aspects of obsessive-compulsive disorder: a description of a Brazilian sample and a systematic review of international clinical studies. *Journal of Psychiatric Research, 38*, 403–411.

Franklin, M.E. &, Foa, E.B. (2008). Obsessive-compulsive disorder. In D. Barlow (Ed.), *Clinical Handbook of Psychological Disorders* (4th Edition). Guilford.

Garcia-Soriano, G., Belloch, A., Morillo, C., & Clark, D. A. (2011). Symptom dimensions in obsessive–compulsive disorder: From normal cognitive intrusions to clinical obsessions. *Journal of Anxiety Disorders, 25*, 474–482.

Geller, D. (2006). Obsessive-compulsive and spectrum disorders in children and adolescents. *Psychiatric Clinics of North America, 29*, 353–70.

Geller, D.A., Biederman, J., Griffin, S., et al (1996) Comorbidity of juvenile obsessive-compulsive disorder with disruptive behavior disorders. *Journal of the American Academy of Child & Adolescent Psychiatry, 3*, 1637–1646.

Greenberg, D. (1994). Cultural aspects of obsessive compulsive disorder. In E. Hollander (Ed.), *Current insights in obsessive compulsive disorder* (pp. 11–21). New York: Wiley.

Lack, C. W. (2013). *Anxiety disorders: An introduction.* United Kingdom: Onus Books.

Lack, C. W. (2012). Obsessive-compulsive disorder: Evidence-based treatments and future directions for research. *World Journal of Psychiatry, 2*(6), 86-90.

Lack, C. W., Storch, E. A., Keeley, M. L., Geffken, G. R., Ricketts, E. D., Murphy, T. K., & Goodman, W. K. (2009). Quality of life in children and adolescents with obsessive-compulsive disorder: Base rates, parent-child agreement, and clinical correlates. *Social Psychiatry and Psychiatric Epidemiology, 44*(11), 935-942.

Lack, C.W., Storch, E.A., & Murphy, T.K. (2006). More than just monsters under the bed: Assessing and treating pediatric OCD. *Psychiatric Times, 23*(3), 54-57.

Leckman, J. F., Denys, D., Simpson, H. B., Mataix-Cols, D., Hollander, E., Saxena, S., Miguel, E. C., Rauch, S. L., Goodman, W. K., Phillips, K. A., & Stein, D. J. (2010). Obsessive-compulsive disorder: A review of the diagnostic criteria and possible subtypes and dimensional specifiers for DSM-5. *Depression and Anxiety, 27*, 507-527.

Lemelson, R. (2003), Obsessive-Compulsive Disorder in Bali: The cultural shaping of a neuropsychiatric disorder. *Transcultural Psychiatry, 40*, 377-408.

Kessler R., Berglund, P., Demler, O., Jin, R., Walters, E. (2005). Lifetime prevalence and age-of-onset distributions of DSM-IV disorders in the National Comorbidity Survey Replication. *Archives of General Psychiatry, 62*, 593–602.

Krochmalik A, Menzies R. (2003). The classification and diagnosis of obsessive–compulsive disorder. In R. G. Menzies, & P. de Silva (Eds.), *Obsessive–*

*compulsive disorder: Theory, research, and treatment* (pp. 3–20). New York: Wiley.

Macy, A.S., Theo, J.N. Kaufmann, S.C., Chazzaoui, R.B., Pawlowski, P.A. et al. (2013). Quality of life in obsessive compulsive disorder. *CNS Spectrum, 18*(1), 21-33.

Matsunaga, H., Maebayashi, K., Hayashida, K., Okino, K., Matsui, T., Iketani, T., Kiriike, N., & Stein, D.J. (2008). Symptom structure in Japanese patients with Obsessive-Compulsive Disorder. *American Journal of Psychiatry, 165,* 251-253.

McCoy, C., Napier, D., Craig, L., & Lack, C. W. (2013) Controversies in pediatric obsessive-compulsive disorder. *Minerva Psichiatrica, 54*(2), 115-128.

Piacentini J, Peris TS, Bergman RL, Chang S, Jaffer M (2007). Functional impairment in childhood OCD: development and psychometrics properties of the child obsessive-compulsive impact scale-revised (COIS-R). *Journal of Clinical Child and Adolescent Psychology, 36,* 645–653.

Ruscio, A.M., Stein, D.J., Chiu, W.T., Kessler, R.C. (2010). The epidemiology of obsessive-compulsive disorder in the National Comorbidity Survey Replication. *Molecular Psychiatry, 15,* 53-63.

Salzman L, Thaler F. (1981). Obsessive-compulsive disorders: A review of the literature. *American Journal of Psychiaty, 138,* 286-296.

Stein, D. J., Fineberg, N. A., Bienvenu, O. J., Denys, D., Lochner, C., Nestadt, G., Leckman, J. F., Rauch, S. L., & Phillips, K. A. (2010). Should OCD be classified as an anxiety disorder in *DSM-5? Depression and Anxiety, 27,* 495-506.

Stewart SE, Rosario MC, Baer L, et al. (2008). Four-factor structure of obsessive-compulsive disorder symptoms in children, adolescents, and adults. *Journal of the American Academy of Child & Adolescent Psychiatry, 47,* 763–72.

Storch, E.A., Abramowitz, J., & Goodman, W.K. (2008). Where does obsessive-compulsive disorder belong in the DSM-V? *Depression and Anxiety, 25* (4), 336-347.

Storch, E. A., Benito, K., & Goodman, W. (2011). Assessment scales for obsessive-compulsive disorder. *Neuropsychiatry, 1*(3), 243-250.

Subramaniam, M., Soh, P., Vaingankar, J.A., Picco, L., & Chong, S.A. (2013). Quality of life in Obsessive-Compulsive Disorder: Impact of the Disorder and of Treatment. *CNS Drugs, 27* (5), 367-383.

Torres, A., Prince, M., Bebbington, P., et al. (2006). Obsessive-compulsive disorder: prevalence, comorbidity, impact, and help-seeking in the British National Psychiatric Comorbidity Survey of 2000. *The American Journal of Psychiatry, 163,* 1978–85.

World Health Organization (2010). *International statistical classification of diseases and related health problems tenth revision* (4th ed.).

Zohar, A.H. (1999). The epidemiology of obsessive-compulsive disorder in children and adolescents. *Child and Adolescent Psychiatric Clinics of North America, 8,* 445-460

# Chapter Two

# The Etiology of Obsessive-Compulsive Disorder

Caleb W. Lack, Alisa Huskey, David B. Weed,
Micah J. Highfill, & Lauren Craig

Obsessive-Compulsive Disorder (OCD) is defined as excessive or unreasonable obsessions or compulsions which cause marked distress in the individual experiencing them (American Psychiatric Association, 2013). Obsessions are recurrent or persistent thoughts, impulses or images that the person recognizes as internally generated and which are not just excessive worries about real-life problems that the person attempts to ignore or neutralize. Compulsions are repetitive behaviors or mental acts that are attempts to prevent or reduce distress as a response to an obsession but which are clearly excessive and usually not realistically connected to the event they should prevent.

The purpose of this chapter is to provide an overview of the current research on the causes and etiology of OCD. To do so, we will examine the state of the field from psychological, biological, and evolutionary perspectives, and attempt to synthesize the literature into a coherent picture of where we as a field are in our understanding of why 1-3% of the population qualifies for a diagnosis of OCD (Abramowitz, Taylor, & McKay, 2009). We will start by examining theories and research into psychological causes, move to examining biological causes, discuss evolutionary models, and finally examine how those can come together into a more comprehensive etiological model through an illustrative case study.

## Psychological Perspectives

Theories about the behaviors which are defined in modern times as obsessions and compulsions have been around for many centuries, from the religious explanations in the 17th and 18th centuries (e.g., demon or spirit possession), to theories of doubt and 'the doubting madness' in the 19th century, to multiple psychoanalytic explanations in the early 20th century (Himle et al., 2011; Goodman, 2006). Given the lack of empirical evidence to support such theories, they will not be reviewed here. Within the last century, theories about the cause(s)

25

of OCD have further expanded to include biological explanations (reviewed below) and evolutionary views (also reviewed below) of the mechanisms involved in the formation of obsessions and compulsions (Mineka, Zinbarg, 2006). Currently, heavily evidence-based theories of the psychological etiology of OCD have developed largely from the amount of empirical evidence showing the effectiveness of using cognitive-behavioral treatment for the disorder (Rector et al., 2001). Historically, these causes have been described under three separate iterations: behavioral, cognitive, and cognitive-behavioral.

*Behavioral*

Based on Mowrer's two-stage theory of fear and its maintenance, the behavioral theory for OCD states that individuals first learn anxiety or discomfort from associations between those feelings and an originally neutral stimulus (Mowrer, 1960). Through conditioning, the originally neutral stimulus becomes a conditioned anxiety stimulus to which the person goes on to develop avoidance and escape responses. These responses, through their effectiveness at reducing the original anxiety, are strengthened and maintained over time (Franklin, Foa, 2008). In other words, a neutral stimulus becomes a conditioned fear stimulus via classical conditioning processes, and this fear is then maintained via negative reinforcement.

To better illustrate this model, we offer the following case of "Mark." A young child is not initially worried, afraid, or concerned about seeing the symbol of an upside down cross (the neutral stimulus). At some point, after Mark drew this symbol, a parent yelled at him (unconditioned fear stimulus) because he was making a "blasphemous" or "evil" symbol. This previously neutral stimuli (the upside down cross) then comes to serve as a signal for something fearful occurring, causing it to become a conditioned fear stimulus. Mark, through religious education, has learned to pray and ask for forgiveness when he has acted in a "sinful" manner. The next time Mark saw or accidentally drew this (conditioned fear stimulus) symbol, he prayed for forgiveness, which alleviated his distress via negative reinforcement (removal of an aversive stimulus – in this case fear – that increases the chance of the behavior then reoccurring). Such fear and compulsive behavior then become more and more reinforced, causing typically observed OCD behaviors.

This cycle of conditioning and responses provides ample explanation for the formation of ritualistic behaviors associated with the compulsion aspect of OCD. However, it was insufficient to fully account for all aspects of the disorder, particularly the nature of obsessions, and this conceptual inefficiency, combined with the general movement away from neo-behaviorism in the 1970's, meant that a new explanation for OCD would arise.

*Cognitive*

Following the *zeitgeist* of the 1970's and the rise of cognitivism, researchers developed a new approach to the question of the psychological causes of OCD. Key in the early development of a cognitive theory of OCD was the idea that obsessions were formed from a basis of exaggerated concerns about normal events and an unusually high expectation of negative consequences from these otherwise normal events (Carr, 2008). Further developments of models along these lines lead to the theory that obsessions begin with a normal, intrusive thought, which interacts with a belief system held by the individual in such a way that it causes marked discomfort or anxiety. This anxiety is combined then with an enhanced sense of responsibility and self-blame (Salkovskis, 1985).

To illustrate this theory, we will use the same case from above. Everyone has intrusive thoughts pop into his/her head at some point, most of us on a daily basis. While most people will simply dismiss this intrusive thought and pay no attention to it, some people with a particular belief system do not. For example, Mark was raised in a fundamentalist Christian environment and believed that negative, intrusive thoughts are not naturally occurring, but instead put there by Satan. So, when the thought of "I should draw an upside-down cross on this Bible" pops into his head, Mark does not just dismiss it with a counter thought of "Huh, that's weird" but instead focuses on it, places special emphasis on it (e.g., "I had this thought so it must be something I really want to do."), and worries about the implications of the thought (e.g., "I'm going to hell because of this thought because I really am an evil person and a sinner."). This anxiety about the thoughts then results in the large amounts of distress and worry seen in persons with OCD in response to their obsessions.

While gaining support and explanation power throughout the following decades, cognitive explanations, much like behavioral explanations before them, failed to truly account for OCD as a whole. Still, it was the development of this theory which led to the next step in the theories of the psychological etiology of OCD.

*Cognitive-Behavioral*

The cognitive-behavioral theory of the development of OCD is, as its name implies, a combination of the behavioral and cognitive theories of OCD. It springs, like all such theories, from an understanding of the role that cognitions play in our behavior, and the subsequent impact behaviors have on cognitions. First widely elucidated by Bandura's social cognitive learning theory (Bandura, 1977), this bidirectional view of behavior and cognitions, both of which have an influence on emotions and each other, offers a much more complete framework for understanding the development and maintenance of OCD. This combination theory has, thus far, received the most empirical support of any psychological theory, both in terms of direct experimental evidence and through the use of the therapy practice which shares the same name, cognitive behavioral therapy (CBT).

The cognitive-behavioral model proposes that obsessions and compulsions arise from dysfunctional beliefs that one holds: the greater the strength of the beliefs, the greater the chance that a person will develop OCD. One of the major research findings to support this idea is that unwanted cognitive intrusions are experienced by most people, with similar contents to clinical obsessions, but are not believed and as such cause little to no distress. Conversely, in people with OCD, these intrusive thoughts can become obsessions if they are appraised as personally important, highly unacceptable or immoral, or posing a threat for which the individual is personally responsible. These types of appraisals will lead to high amounts of distress, which one then attempts to alleviate via compulsions. These compulsions result in anxiety reduction, but it is only temporary and actually reinforces the maladaptive beliefs that led to the negative appraisal in the first place, thus perpetuating the cycle of obsessions and compulsions, as seen in the case illustration below.

Mark was raised in a fundamentalist, evangelical religious household. Due to this upbringing, he developed a belief system that Satan could place thoughts into one's head in order to try and make them do sinful or evil things. One day, he was doodling on a sheet of paper and happened, by chance, to draw the symbol of an upside down lower-case "t." This did not mean anything to him (i.e., it was a neutral stimulus), until his mother came by, saw what he had drawn, tore the paper from him, and yelled at him about the blasphemous thing he had drawn. This response, appropriately, upset Mark (i.e., his mother's reaction was an unconditioned fearful stimulus) because he did want to a) disappoint his mother and b) go to hell for doing blasphemous activities. As a result of this incident, Mark now associates this particular symbol with a fearful response (i.e., it has become a conditioned fear stimulus). His mother then proceeds to tell him that he must pray for forgiveness, so that he will not go to hell. After praying for forgiveness, he feels much less distressed (i.e., this act was negatively reinforcing). Later, he has an intrusive, unwanted (but normal) thought about drawing an upside-down cross. This thought activates his belief system (i.e., "Satan is sending me this thought to deceive me and turn me from righteousness."), and makes him very emotionally distressed. Rather than naturally wait for this anxiety to dissipate, Mark instead uses the previously reinforced behavior of praying for forgiveness to decrease his anxiety (i.e., making it a compulsion), thus reinforcing the behavior further. Paradoxically, though, this continued behavior also reinforces his negative belief system, which in turn makes the intrusive, unwanted thoughts (i.e., obsessions) more likely to pop up again, at which point the compulsion will be repeated, ad infinitum.

CBT primarily focuses on the use of *exposure with response prevention* (ERP), which was first developed using Mowrer's theory of fear acquisition and maintenance, and follows the basic procedure of exposing the person to the conditioned cause of his/her fear and preventing him/her from responding with the normal pattern of behavior that both serves to reduce anxiety and at the same time maintains the fear (as in the example above; Mowrer, 1960). In combination with this technique, which addresses the behavioral side of OCD, cognitive therapy is used and focuses on discovering how the person with OCD interprets their obsessions and works towards re-evaluating those interpretation so that previous situations or stimuli which are viewed as high-anxiety situations can be changed to be viewed as a situation that does not provoke an unreasonable amount of anxiety (Rector et al., 2001). Treatment programs of persons with OCD utilizing a combination of ERP and cognitive therapy have been shown to be highly effective multiple times in the decades since the practice was first developed (see Franklin & Foa, 2008 for a detailed description of procedures and meta-analyses of the relevant research). While a large number of researchers, when writing about OCD and its origins, still preface any claims with a statement that the exact causes of OCD are unknown, the pool of evidence strongly supports a causal relationship between the above mentioned theories and the psychological roots of OCD.

## Biological Perspectives

While the psychological theories reviewed above have excellent explanatory power and have led to the development of highly effective treatments, they certainly do not completely explain why any one individual has OCD. For example, why would a particular segment of the population be, perhaps, more easily conditioned to turn a neutral stimulus into a conditioned stimulus? Why are some people more prone to pay that special attention to thoughts that we see in those with OCD? To help explain these types of questions, researchers have spent enormous effort in attempts to explore hereditary and other biological factors in the development and maintenance of OCD.

Much research has been undertaken in the past two decades to help decipher the underlying biological mechanisms behind OCD, but it is still an area plagued by controversy (McCoy et al., 2013). Despite this uncertainty, however, researchers have uncovered a great amount of knowledge pertaining to the genetics and neurobiology, as well as subtypical classification, of OCD. Family studies have revealed that there appears to be hereditary factors in OCD. Perhaps the most convincing evidence that genetic factors play a role in the transmission and expression of OC symptoms comes from twin studies (Rosario-Campos et al., 2005). Twin studies of OCD have a long history, beginning in 1929 (Van Grootheest et al., 2005) and are particularly beneficial when examining genetic contributions to the etiology of psychopathological phenomena (Taylor, 2011). While overall estimates of heritability of OC symptoms range from 45-65% (Hanna et al., 2005), twin studies of OCD suggest that monozygotic twins have the highest concordance rates between 80-87%, followed by dizygotic twins with concordance rates between 47-50% (Arnold et al., 2006). These rates are the highest of all of what have been traditionally described as the anxiety disorders (Meir, 2005). These types of studies, though, tell us little about specifically what genes are involved. For that, investigators need different approaches.

Although researchers have been attempting to localize specific genes contributing to OCD for some time, a common problem faced is that of replication failures (Taylor, 2011). Since OCD is not a homogenous disorder, the most systematic approach to gene discovery relies on segregation, linkage, and association studies of both twins and families (Grados, Walkup, Walford, 2003). Segregation analyses are often a preliminary step in genetic epidemiology and provide initial evidence that a specific gene has a significant effect on a particular trait. Although segregation analyses have been unable to establish the transmission model (Mercadante et al., 2004), they have predicted the existence of a major gene locus that goes beyond purely polygenic effects (Hanna et al., 2005).

Most candidate genes that have been studied are involved in the metabolism of central nervous system neurotransmitters (Grados, Walkup, Walford, 2003). The most studied genes in OCD include catechol-O-methyl-transferase (COMT), monoamine oxidase-A (MOA), dopamine transporter (DAT), dopamine receptors DRD1, DRD2, DRD3, DRD4, serotonin transporter SERT and g-HT2A and 5HT1B. (Hollander, Braun, Simeon, 2008) Of these, the most promising for OCD transmission and expression appear to ones in the serotonin systems (5HTTLPR and 5HT1B) and the glutamate systems (GRIN2B and SLC1A1; Hollander, Braun, & Simeon, 2008).

It is believed that the serotonin system likely facilitates the expression of symptoms in OCD, based on findings that SSRIs are effective in reducing OC symptoms (Stein, 2002). Additionally, data from pharmacological, genetic, and imaging studies indicate that the serotonin receptor 5-HT serves a role in OCD. Relatedly, genetic variants affecting glutamate neurotransmissions are implicated (Arnold et al., 2006). For example, researchers have identified the glutamate receptor ionotropic-N-methyl-D-aspartate-subunit 2B (GRIN2B) as a candidate gene, and the GABA type B receptor 1 may be a susceptibility factor in the disorder (Arnold et al., 2006). Additionally, the glutamate transporter SLC1A1, located on chromosomal region 9p24, codes for the excitatory amino acid carrier EAAC1, which has been shown to cause altered glutamatergic neurotransmission and is implicated in the pathogenesis of OCD. SLC1A1 is highly expressed within the cerebral cortex, striatum, and thalamus (Arnold et al., 2006). These brain

30

regions are connected to the cortico-striatal-thalamic circuit that is consistently implicated in the expression of OCD (see below for more details).

In a study conducted by Hemmings et. al, a large network of interconnected neurotransmitter and signaling pathways was investigated to determine whether different combinations of functional genetic variants mediated underlying traits of OCD (Hemmings et. al., 2008). The study looked at the role of particular variants to see if they significantly affected traits of OCD. They found that certain genotypes do increase the risk and severity of OCD in individuals. OCD is associated with a neurological disorder that appears during childhood, known as Tourette's syndrome (Rapoport, 1986). This finding led to the belief that there is a family association with tic disorders (Grados et al., 2001) and that OCD may have the same underlying genotype as tic disorders (Leonard et al., 1992; Grados et al., 2001).

To help examine these questions, researchers undertook two very large studies. In the fall of 2012, the results of these, the largest studies to date studying the possible genetic underpinnings of OCD and TS, were published in the journal *Molecular Psychiatry*. The OCD study (Stewart et al., 2012), for example, examined 1,465 persons with OCD and 5557 ancestry-matched controls. The TS study (Scharf et al., 1012) contained 1,285 clinical cases and 4964 ancestry-matched controls. Both, though, failed to find any single nucleotide polymorphisms (SNPs) that achieved a genome-wide threshold of significance. This finding points at the need for examining the genetics of OCD in a new way, perhaps by focusing on epigenetic expression rather than just genotypes.

Moving up from a molecular to a structural level, there has been a large amount of research on other biological aspects of OCD. For example, it is known that brain damage, including that caused by birth trauma, encephalitis, or head trauma, can result in development of OCD (Hollander, Braun, Simeon, 2008; Berthier, Kuliesevsky, Gironell, Haras, 1996). Damage to basal ganglia, cingulated gyrus, and the prefrontal cortex all appear to have a causal influence on development of OCD (Giedd, et al., 1995; Robinson et al., 1995). Damage to the basal ganglia possibly produces symptoms of OCD due to the increased size and inflammation in this area of the brain (Giedd et al., 2000). The presence of seizures, especially temporal lobe epilepsy, has also been associated with the childhood onset of OCD.

There appears to be increased activity in the caudate nucleus and the orbitofrontal cortex in individuals with OCD (Whiteside, Port, Abramowitz, & 2004; Saxena, Brody, Schwaltz, & Baxter, 1998; Guehl et al., 2008). The caudate nucleus receives information, along with the putamen, from the cerebral cortex. This information is then processed by the basal ganglia, which then goes through two pathways, the direct pathway and the indirect pathway, through the thalamus and back to the cortex. The direct pathway is excitatory whereas the indirect pathway is inhibitory. OCD may be the result of overactivity of the direct pathway. The orbitofrontal cortex can activate the two pathways resulting in an imbalance of the pathways that results in OCD behaviors (Saxena, Brody, Schwaltz, Baxter, 1998). The orbitofrontal cortex and basal ganglia receive input from serotonergic terminals (Lavoie, Parent, 1990; El Mansara, Blier, 1997). Many positron emission tomography (PET) studies of OCD have found an increased metabolism or blood flow in orbitofrontal and anterior cingulate cortex as well as the head of the caudate nucleus (Sanz, Molina, Calcedo, Martin-Loeches, Rubia, 2001). Functional magnetic resonance imaging (fMRI) studies provide significant correlation between orbitofrontal and anterior cingulated cortices and the mediation of OCD symptoms (Rotge et al., 2008). In a study by Jung et. al, fMRI was used to look at the perception of biological motion in individuals with OCD (Jung et al., 2009). Results indicated an increase in activity in the superior and middle temporal gyrus, which are associated with processing of biological motion. In a study conducted by Choi et. al, a volume reduction of the anterior part of the superior temporal gyrus, specifically the planum polare, was found to have significant relativity to the pathophysiology of OCD (Choi et al., 2006).

Let's return to the fictional case of Mark, as begun above, and examine what role biology may have played in his diagnosis of OCD. From a familial perspective, his parents have struggled with being overanxious, causing problems both at home and in the workplace. Mark in turn inherited an overall genetic predisposition towards displaying and experiencing anxiety. When activated, these genes impact the neurochemical transmission of specific neurotransmitters in his brain, primarily serotonin and glutamate, which in turn leads to disruptive patterns of activation across different areas of the brain. This patterning is most evident in those regions of the brain, such as the orbitofrontal cortex, responsible for two key problematic behaviors seen in OCD: repeated doubts and repetitive behaviors. In Mark, this biological over activation manifested behaviorally in repeatedly asking for forgiveness after having "blasphemous" thoughts or actions and questioning the validity of those who tell him that the obsessive thoughts are not accurate and congruent with reality.

## Evolutionary Perspectives

The above-reviewed components of and contributors to OCD, both psychological and biological, appear to have roots in normal functioning, suggesting that some level of evolutionary adaptability is involved (Fiske, Haslam, 1997; Leckman, Bloch, 2008). The most commonly observed obsession-compulsion combinations include contamination concerns and excessive cleaning, doubting, checking or praying, symmetry concerns, and organization or hoarding (Rasmussen, Eisen,

1992). Normal behavior, such as awareness of present and future threats in the environment, allow for planning and avoidance of such threats (Leckman, Mataix-Cols, Rosario-Campos, 2005). Intriguingly, OCD may be an exacerbated version of these normal, evolutionarily-adaptive avoidance behaviors. As seen above, genetic vulnerabilities and brain damage can cause deficits that lead to the development of OCD (Brune, 2006). But, it may be that, rather than just causing OCD, these neurological or genetic insults interfere with the normal development of adaptive regulators that inhibit fear and avoidance behaviors. In people who have pathology, one's response to "threats" enormously exceeds the actual threat involved, thus overwhelming an individual's daily cognitive and behavioral patterns as a result of a previously adaptive mechanism spinning out of control (Leckman, Bloch, 2008).

Describing OCD as an evolutionary adaption may seem counterintuitive, considering the mental and functional deficits the disorder can have on affected individuals; however, similar to many anxiety disorders, researchers suggest that components of OCD originate as adaptive survival traits and become dysregulated (Brune, 2006; Feygin, Swain, Leckman, 2006). There are four hallmarks that provide a framework for determining whether traits are adaptive. To be considered adaptive, a trait must a) have a lack of heritable variation, b) have evidence of good design, c) be evoked by appropriate triggers, and d) fitness must be reduced when it is absent (Nettle, 2003).

Adaptive traits are theorized to develop as a function of both ultimate and proximal origins. Proximal theories of OCD suggest that pathology develops when adaptive traits become dysfunctional due to genetic or biological deficits in the brain (Abed, De Pauw, 1999). This particular theory also supports the modular brain theory, suggesting that specific areas of the brain are associated with OCD features, and deficiency or damage in a specific part of the brain results in OCD. As previously indicated, damage to the basal ganglia can produce OCD symptomology (Carlson, 2010). The basal ganglia are theorized to play inhibitory roles in voluntary motor functions, and has involvement in procedural learning, particularly that of habitual behaviors (Brooks, Dunnett, 2013). Accordingly, damage may result in a lack of behavioral inhibition by decreasing executive functioning over habitual behavior. Unchecked repetitive behavior or mental activities fits the compulsive (behavioral) criteria for OCD.

Evolutionary perspectives argue that obsessions and compulsions develop as ultimate adaptions. The consistently high prevalence rates (1 to 3% prevalence rates within the general population; Leckman, Mataix-Cols, Rosario-Campos, 2005) of OCD across cultures (Fiske, Haslam, 1997) suggest that aspects of OCD have been selected for, and therefore continue to occur (Abed, De Pauw, 1999). One hypothesis contends that obsessions develop out of a naturally occurring inhibitory mechanism (Involuntary Risk Scenario Generating System; IRSGS) that cognitively produces virtual scenarios and outcomes, so that an individual can conceptualize consequences of risky behaviors without having to actually participate in the activities (Abed, De Pauw, 1999). In response, semi-voluntary harm avoidance practices are developed – compulsions. This neurobiological system is suggested to have been genetically preserved due to its ability to prevent potential harm in organisms that had an active IRSGS (Abed, De Pauw, 1999). Such a mechanism both provides evidence of a good design and could result in reduced fitness if absent, two hallmarks of an adaptive trait.

Researchers suggest an evolutionary perspective using mammal behavior as a model may aid in explaining the most common obsession-compulsion combinations as well as OCD prevalence across cultures (Evans, Leckman, 2006; Fiske, Haslam, 1997). Certain animal behaviors, such as hibernating and organizing and collecting food, are suggested to be the origins of obsessive compulsive behavior seen in humans (Brune, 2006). In a study reviewed by Evans and Leckman, "displaced" fixed action patterns (FAPs) were observed in a large number of species. FAPs are innate behavioral practices, contributive to species adaptability, triggered by particular external circumstances. Displacement occurs when behaviors are triggered out of context; that is, when the environment is not conducive to the performance of the behavior (Evans, Leckman, 2006). Grooming, feeding, cleaning, and nest building – components of typical FAPs – were the most commonly observed displacement behaviors in the animals studied (Dodman, 1998). The authors draw a comparison between displacement behaviors and aspects of OCD, suggesting both are reactions to a biological or environmental malfunction in normal adaptive behaviors. In fact, OCD-like behavior has been systematically observed in some animals (Stein, 2002). Incidentally, displacement behaviors closely resemble the most common subtypes of OCD (Rasmussen, Eisen, 1992). High prevalence rates across cultures and similarities between ritualistic animal behaviors and subtypes of OCD may be evidence for lack of heritable variation, another hallmark of adaptive traits.

Although providing explanations for the behavioral component of OCD, Brune argues that the animal behavior hypothesis does not account for the cognitive-obsessional component of in the disorder (Brune, 2006). He suggests that cognition and contemplation is the evolutionary catalyst that provided the potential for normal animal behavior – particularly, ritualistic/habitual behaviors – to develop into OCD symptomology (Brune, 2006). Specifically, the cognitive capacity to construct mental representations of potential future events, as with the IRSGS, provides the opportunity to exaggerate such events and respond accordingly.

Mental representations of potential future events require metacognition – a capability almost exclusively seen in humans. A large amount of brain growth has occurred in primates during relatively recent evolutionary history, particularly in the past 100,000 years. Specifically, the neocortex, thalamus, and limbic structures – areas of the brain associated with future planning and episodic memory – have increased most significantly in comparison to other parts of the brain. The anterior cingulate cortex, a part of the limbic system implicated in cognitive and emotional regulation, has increased in size significantly (Bush, Luu, Posner, 2000; Flinn, Geary, Ward, 2005). Evolutionary hypotheses suggest that these size increases, while energy expensive, were necessary, due to the increase in social activity among humans (Isler, Van Schaik, 2006). The ability to read others' emotions and intentions and imagine future events are very valuable traits, thus selecting for increased development in brain areas that are capable of such cognitions. Furthermore, Brune suggests that this metacognitive ability is the mechanism largely responsible for the obsessional aspects of OCD (Brune, 2006).

## A Comprehensive Etiological Model

As with most phenomena in the fields of psychology and psychiatry, trying to answer "Why do people develop OCD?" while only relying on one level of explanation (e.g., only biological, psychological, or evolutionary) falls short of providing a satisfying answer. Instead, attempting to understand OCD from a more comprehensive etiological model requires examining multiple levels of explanation as well as their potential interaction.

For example, considering normative and adaptive behaviors and what they might look like when disrupted from an evolutionary view can help to provide an understanding of the ultimate roots of the social construct that our species now calls OCD. In conjunction, considering the potential molecular, biochemical, and structural aspects of the brain related to OCD gives practitioners a more thorough understanding of a particular patient's overall vulnerability towards developing OCD, as well as some potential methods of intervention focusing on correcting biochemical abnormalities. Finally, the psychological underpinnings behind OCD, particularly the cognitive and behavioral aspects, provide both proximal explanatory power and excellent theory for developing interventions. While such interventions may not be directly addressing evolutionary history or changing one's genotype, they do appear to have a massive impact on the function of the brain itself (Saxena et al., 1998; Porto et al., 2009). The changes have been primarily observed in the in the pregenual anterior cingulate cortex and anterior middle cingulate cortex (O'Neill et al., 2013; O'Neill et al., 2012). That a particular therapeutic intervention can change cognitions, behaviors, and biological functioning just further reinforces the need to consider a multi-level explanation for the etiology of OCD. Returning, for one last time, to the fictional case study of Mark can help to show how these levels of explanation can be used together for very powerful explanatory power for why a particular individual experiences the debilitating effects of OCD.

Mark's distant ancestors, perhaps back 100 million years to the last common ancestors between birds and mammals, had evolutionary pressures upon them that helped to shape predispositions for certain types of ritualistic and habitual behaviors that aided survival. This coincides with the development of more sophisticated basal ganglia, an area of the brain highly implicated in these behaviors today. With the gradual development of the *Homo* genus (including *erectus, antecessor,* and *rhodesiensis*) and the rise of anatomically modern *Homo sapiens* 200,000 years ago, our species became increasingly cognitively sophisticated thanks to rapid brain growth, particularly in the neocortex, thalamus, and limbic areas. This sophistication exploded over the past 60,000 years or so, as humans developed new brain functions to increase survival chances in an increasingly social environment, including advanced communication and planning abilities. Concurrent to this brain development, humans began to develop the ability to conceptualize potential adverse outcomes of future actions, and such metacognitive functions were highly useful to the species as a whole. Unfortunately, due to a variety of insults, these adaptive functions (metacognition and ritualistic behaviors) can become hijacked and turn maladaptive, as will be illustrated below.

The changes in allele frequency that ultimately gave rise to these new adaptive brain structures and subsequent functional changes were passed from generation to generation, ultimately becoming very widespread among the population of *Homo sapiens* that eventually spread out from Africa in several waves over the past 60,000 years and, unlike morphological features such as skin and hair color, remained relatively intact as humans spread across the continents. Mark's ancestors carried these genes, as does he. In Mark, though, the adaptive functioning has been disrupted. Both of Mark's parents are highly anxious people, and so he subsequently inherited an overall genetic vulnerability to experiencing anxiety. In particular, a dysregulation of his serotonergic system has caused patterns of brain activation outside of those seen in most people. These disruptions have had effects across his entire brain, but the most problematic aspects have been seen in those brain areas mentioned above – the basal ganglia, thalamus, and the neocortex. This basal ganglia-thalamo-cortical circuit disruption means that Mark is more likely than most people to experience difficulties with excessive doubts and repetitive behaviors, but that he will also need some sort of activating events in his environment for these to become prominent and problematic. Unfortunately for Mark, his environment was rife with such opportunities.

36

In addition to being highly anxious, Mark's parents were also fundamentalist evangelical Christians. Due to this, Mark was exposed to beliefs that Satan could place thoughts into one's head in order to try and make them do sinful or evil things. One day, when he was young, Mark was doodling on a sheet of paper and happened, by chance, to draw the symbol of an upside down lower-case "t." This did not mean anything to him (i.e., it was a neutral stimulus), until his mother came by, saw what he had drawn, tore the paper from him and yelled at him about the "blasphemous" thing he had drawn. This response, appropriately, upset Mark (i.e., his mother's reaction was an unconditioned fearful stimulus) because he did not want to disappoint his mother and then go to hell for being blasphemous. Now, for most people, getting mildly upset would have been the end of the story and nothing further would have happened. But for Mark, as a result of his previously evolutionarily adaptive skills becoming hijacked by biological disruptions, he more readily associates this particular symbol with a fearful response. The prayers he is instructed to engage in by his mother as a result of his sinful behavior greatly alleviate his distress, reinforcing that he should pray when he encounters such blasphemous activity.

Later, Mark has an intrusive, unwanted (but normal) thought about drawing an upside-down cross. This cognition activates his belief system (i.e., "Satan is sending me this thought to deceive me and turn me from righteousness."), and makes him very emotionally distressed. Rather than naturally waiting for this anxiety to dissipate, Mark instead uses the previously reinforced behavior of praying for forgiveness to decrease his anxiety, thus reinforcing the behavior further and causing a compulsion. Unfortunately, this behavior only reinforces his negative belief system, which in turn makes the obsessions more likely to pop up again, at which point the compulsion will be repeated. In this way, a set of cognitive and behavioral adaptations that in most of the populations are useful become highly maladaptive, impacting both his biology and his psychosocial functioning.

## Conclusions

People, naturally, want to have simple and pat explanations for phenomena. Unfortunately, real life rarely cooperates with what we desire. As such, relying on only one level of explanation when trying to understand why we as a species have a vulnerability towards developing OCD (and other mental disorders), as well as why a particular individual may have such symptoms, can be a frustrating process. Instead, we as practitioners must embrace a multi-level explanation of mental disorders. Above, we have outlined a case for the consideration of a evo-bio-psychosocial model for the etiology of OCD that can help guide further etiological research taking into account an explanation that spans multiple levels of causes and factors that impact interactions between those levels.

# References

Abed RT, de Pauw KW. An evolutionary hypothesis for obsessive compulsive disorder: a psychological immune system? *Behav Neurol.* 1999; 11: 245-50.

Abramowitz JS, Taylor S, McKay D. Obsessive-compulsive disorder. *Lancet.* 2009; 374: 491-99.

American Psychiatric Association. *Diagnostic and Statistical Manual of Mental Disorders* (5th ed.). Washington, DC: American Psychiatric Association; 2013.

Arnold PD, Sicard T, Burroughs E, Richter MR, Kennedy JL. Glutamate transporter gene SLC1A1 associated with obsessive-compulsive disorder. *Arch Gen Psychiatry.* 2006; 63:769-76.

Bandura A. *Social learning theory.* Prentice Hall: Englewood Cliffs, NJ; 1977.

Berthier M, Kuliesevsky J, Gironell A, Heras JA. Obsessive-compulsive disorder associated with brain lesions: Clinical phenomenology, cognitive function, and anatomic correlates. *Neurology.* 1996; 47: 353-61.

Brooks SP, Dunnett SB. Animal models for studying cognitive processes and psychiatric disorders. *Brain Res Bul.* 2013; 92: 29-40.

Brune M. The evolutionary psychology of obsessive-compulsive disorder: the role of cognitive metarepresentation. *Perspec Biol Med.* 2006; 49(3): 317-29.

Bush G, Luu P, Posner MI. Cognitive and emotional influences in anterior cingulate cortex. *Trends Cogn Sci.* 2000; 4(6): 215-22.

Carlson NR. Anxiety disorders, autistic disorder, attention-deficit/hyperactivity disorder, and stress disorders: Obsessive-compulsive disorder. In: *Physiology of Behavior* (10th Ed.) New York, NY: Allyn & Bacon; 2010: 589-92.

Carr AT. Compulsive neurosis: A review of the literature. *Psychol Bul.* 1974; 81; 311-318.

Challis C, Pelling N, Lack CW. The biopsychosocial aspects of Obsessive-Compulsive Disorder: A primer for practitioners. *Couns Aust.* 2008; 6: 3-15.

Choi JS, Kim HS, Yoo SY, Ha TH, Chang JH, Kim YY, Shin YW, Kwon JS. Morphometric alterations of anterior superior temporal cortex in obsessive–compulsive disorder. *Depress Anxiety.* 2006; 23(5): 290-6. doi:10.1002/da.20171

Dodman NH. Veterinary models of obsessive-compulsive disorder. In: Jenike MA, Baer L, Minichiello WE, eds. *Obsessive-compulsive disorders: Practical management.* St. Louis, MO: Mosby; 1998: 318-34.

El Mansari M, Blier P. In vivo electrophysiological characterization of 5-HT receptors in the guinea pig head of a caudate nucleus and orbiotofrontal cortex. *Neuropharmacol.* 1997; 36: 577-88.

Evans DW, Leckman JF. Origins of obsessive-compulsive disorder: Developmental and evolutionary perspectives. In: Cicchetti D, Cohen D, eds. *Developmental Psychopathology* (2nd edition). NY: Wiley; 2006.

Feygin DL, Swain J E, Leckman JF. The normalcy of neurosis: Evolutionary origins of obsessive–compulsive disorder and related behaviors. *Prog Neuro Psychopharmacol Biol Psychiatry*. 2006; 30(5): 854-64.

Fiske AP, Haslam N. Is obsessive-compulsive disorder a pathology of the human disposition to perform socially meaningful rituals? Evidence of similar content. *J Nervous Ment Dis*. 1997; 185(4); 211-22.

Flinn MV, Geary DC, Ward CV. Ecological dominance, social competition, and coalitionary arms races: Why humans evolved extraordinary intelligence. *Evol Hum Behav*. 2005; 26: 10-46.

Franklin M, Foa E. Obsessive-compulsive disorder. In: Barlow DH, ed. *Clinical handbook of psychological disorders*. New York, NY: The Guilford Press; 2008: 164-215.

Giedd JN, Rapoport JL, Garvey, MA, Perlmutter S, Swedo SE. MRI assessment of children with obsessive-compulsive disorder on tics associated with streptococcal infection. *Amer J Psychiatry*. 2000; 157: 281-283.

Giedd JN, Rapoport JL, Kruesi, MJP, Parker C, Schapiro MB, Allen AJ, Leonard HL, Kaysen D, Dickstein DP, Marsh WL, et al. Sydenham's chorea: Magnetic resonance imaging of the basal ganglia. *Neurology*. 1995; 45: 2199-2202.

Goodman W. What causes Obsessive-Compulsive Disorder (OCD)?. *Psych Central*; 2006. Psych Central publication 000506.

Grados MA, Riddle MA, Samuels JF, Liang KY, Hoehn-Saric R, Bienvenu OJ, Walkup JT, Song D, Nestadt G. The familial phenotype of obsessive-compulsive disorder in relation to tic disorders: the Hopkins OCD family study. *Biol Psychiatry*. 2001; 50:559-65.

Grados MA, Walkup J, Walford S. Genetics of obsessive-compulsive disorders: new findings and challenges. *Brain Dev*. 2003; 25: 55-61.

Guehl D, Benazzouz A, Aouizerate B, Cuny E, Rotgé JY, Rougier A, Tignol J, Bioulac B, Burbaud P. Neuronal correlates of obsessions in the caudate nucleus. *Bio Psychiatry*. 2008; 63: 557-62.

Hanna GL, Fischer DJ, Chadha KR, Himle JA, Van Etten M. Familial and sporadic subtypes of early onset obsessive-compulsive disorder. *Biol Psychiatry*. 2005; 57:895-900.

Hemmings SJ, Kinnear CJ, Van Der Merwe L, Lochner C, Corfield VA, Moolman-Smook JC, Stein DJ. Investigating the role of the brain-derived neurotrophic factor (BDNF) val66met variant in obsessive-compulsive disorder (OCD). *World J Bio Psychiatry*. 2008; 9(2): 126-34. doi:10.1080/15622970701245003

Himle JA, Chatters LM, Taylor R, Nguyen A. The relationship between obsessive-compulsive disorder and religious faith: Clinical characteristics and implications for treatment. In: *Psychology of Religion and Spirituality*. 2011; doi:10.1037/a0023478

Hollander E, Braun A, Simeon D. Should OCD leave the anxiety disorders in DSM-V? The case for obsessive-compulsive-related disorders. *Depress and Anxiety*. 2008; 25: 317-29.

Isler K, van Schaik CP. Metabolic costs of brain size evolution. *Biology Lett*. 2006; 2(4): 557-60. doi:10.1098/rsbl.2006.0538. PMC 1834002. PMID 17148287.

Jung W, Gu B, Kang D, Park J, Yoo S, Choi C, *et al*. BOLD response during visual perception of biological motion in obsessive-compulsive disorder: An fMRI study using the dynamic point-light animation paradigm. *Euro Arch Psychiatry Clin Neurosci*. 2009; 259(1): 46-54. doi:10.1007/s00406-008-0833-8

Lavoie B, Parent A. Immunohistochemical study of the serotoninergic innervations of the basal ganglia in the squirrel monkey. *J Comp Neur*. 1990; 299: 1-16.

Leckman JF, Bloch MH. A developmental and evolutionary perspective on obsessive-compulsive disorder: Whence and whither compulsive hoarding? *Amer J Psychiatry*. 2008; 165(10): 1229-33.

Leckman JF, Mataix-Cols D, Rosario-Campos MC. A multidimensional model of obsessive-compulsive disorder. *Amer J Psychiatry*. 2005; 162(2): 228-38.

Leonard HL, Lenane MC, Swedo SE, Rettew DC, Gershon ES, Rapaport JL. Tics and Tourette's disorder: A 2- to 7- year follow-up of 54 obsessive compulsive children. *Amer J Psychiatry*. 1992; 149: 1244-51.

McCoy C, Napier D, Craig L, Lack CW. Controversies in pediatric obsessive-compulsive disorder. *Minerva Psichiatr*.2013; 54: 115-28.

Meir M. [internet] Obsessive compulsive disorder. [updated 2005 Nov 29; cited 2013 Feb 03]. Available from http://www1.appstate.edu~hillrw/OCD/etiology.htm

Mercadante MT, Rosario-Campos MC, Quarantini LC, Sato FP. The neurobiological bases of obsessive-compulsive disorder and Tourette syndrome. *J de Pediatria*. 2004; 80(2): S35-43.

Mineka S, Zinbarg R. A contemporary learning theory perspective on the etiology of anxiety disorders: It's not what you thought it was. *Amer Psychologist*, 2006; 61(1): 10-26. doi:10.1037/0003-066X.61.1.10

Mowrer OH. *Learning Theory and Behavior*. New York: Wiley; 1960.

Nettle D. Evolutionary origins of depression: a review and reformulation. *J Affect Dis*. 2003; 81: 91-102.

O'Neill J, Gorbis E, Feusner JD, Yip JC, Chang S, Maidment KM, Levitt JG, Salamon N, Ringman JM, Saxena S. Effects of intensive cognitive-behavioral therapy on cingulate neurochemistry in obsessive-compulsive disorder. *J Psychiatr Res*. 2013; 47(4):494-504. doi: 10.1016/j.jpsychires.2012.11.010.

O'Neill J, Piacentini JC, Chang S, Levitt JG, Rozenman M, Bergman L, Salamon N, Alger JR, McCracken JT. MRSI correlates of cognitive-behavioral therapy in pediatric obsessive-compulsive disorder. *Prog Neuropsychopharmacol Biol Psychiatry.* 2012; 10;36(1):161-8. doi: 10.1016/j.pnpbp.2011.09.007.

Porto PR, Oliveira L, Mari J, Volchan E, Figueira I, Ventura P. Does cognitive behavioral therapy change the brain? A systematic review of neuroimaging in anxiety disorders. *J Neuropsychiatry Clin Neurosci.* 2009; 21: 114-125.

Rapoport JL. Childhood obsessive compulsive disorder. *J Child Psychology Psychiatry.* 1986; 27(3): 289-95. doi:10.1111/j.1469-7610.1986.tb01833.x

Rasmussen SA, Eisen JL. The epidemiology and clinical features of obsessive compulsive disorder. *Psychiatric Clin N Amer.* 1992; 15(4):743-758

Rector NA, Bartha C, Kitchen K, Katzman M, Richter M. *Obsessive compulsive disorder: An information guide.* Canada: Centre for Addiction and Mental Health; 2001.

Robinson D, Wu H, Munne RA, Ashtari M, Alvir JJ, Lerner G, *et al.* Reduced caudate nucleus volume in obsessive-compulsive disorder. *Arch Gen Psychiatry.* 1995; 52: 393-98.

Rosario-Campos M, Leckman JF, Curi M, Quatrano S, Katsovitch L, Miguel EC, *et al.* A family study of early-onset obsessive-compulsive disorder. *Am J Med Gen.* 2005; 136B:92-7.

Rotge JY, Guehl D, Dilharreguy B, Cuny E, Tignol J, Bioulac B, *et al.* Provocation of obsessive--compulsive symptoms: a quantitative voxel-based meta-analysis of functional neuroimaging studies. *J Psychiatry Neurosci.* 2008; 33(5): 405-12.

Salkovskis PM. Obsessional compulsive problems: A cognitive-behavioral analysis. *Beh Res Ther.* 1985; 23: 571-83.

Sanz M, Molina V, Calcedo A, Martin-Loeches M, Rubia FJ. The Wisconsin Card Sorting Test and the assessment of frontal function in obsessive-compulsive patients: An event-related potential study. *Cog Neuropsychiatry.* 2001; 6(2), 109-29. doi:10.1080/13546800042000089

Saxena S, Brody AL, Schwaltz JM, Baxter LR. Neuroimaging and frontal-subcortical circuitry in obsessive-compulsive disorder. *Brit J Psychiatry.* 1998; 35: 26-37.

Saxena S, Gorbis E, O'Neill J, Baker SK, Mandelkern MA, Maidment KM, *et al.* Rapid effects of brief intensive cognitive-behavioral therapy on brain glucose metabolism in obsessive-compulsive disorder. *Mol Psychiatry.* 2009;14(2):197-205. doi: 10.1038/sj.mp.4002134.

Scharf JM, Yu D, Mathews CA, Neale BM, Stewart SE, Fagerness JA, Evans P et al. Genome-wide association study of Tourette's syndrome. *Mol Psychiatry.* 2012 [Epub ahead of print].

Stewart SE, Yu D, Scharf JM, Neale BM, Fagerness JA, Mathews CA et al. Genome-wide association study of obsessive-compulsive disorder. *Mol Psychiatry*.2012 [Epub ahead of print].

Stein DJ. Obsessive compulsive disorder. *Lancet*. 2002; 360: 397-405.

Taylor S. Etiology of obsessions and compulsions: a meta-analysis and narrative review of twin studies. *Clin Psychiatry Rev*. 2011; 31: 1361-72.

Van Grootheest DS, Cath DC, Beekman AT, Boomsma DI. Twin studies on obsessive-compulsive disorder: a review. *Twin Res Hum Genet*. 2005; 8(5):450-8.

Whiteside SP, Port JD, Abramowitz JS. A meta-analysis of functional Neuroimaging in obsessive-compulsive disorder. *Psychiatry Res: Neuroimag*. 2004; 132: 69-79.

# Chapter Three

# Obsessive-Compulsive Disorder Symptom Dimensions: Etiology, Phenomenology, and Clinical Implications

Jennifer M. Park, Natasha L. Burke, & Adam B. Lewin

The *Diagnostic and Statistical Manual of Mental Disorders – Fifth Edition* (*DSM-5*; APA, 2013) categorizes obsessive-compulsive disorder (OCD) as a single nosological disorder that encompasses the various symptom presentations. Core features of OCD include *obsessions* (intrusive or anxiety-provoking thoughts) and *compulsions* (rituals or repetitive behaviors that serve to decrease or prevent anxiety) (Lewin, Park, & Storch, 2013). Despite these requisite hallmarks of OCD, there is considerable heterogeneity in symptom presentation, which can vary widely across individuals. The possible connection between OCD symptom variation and phenomenology has sparked considerable research interest. For example, does a specific phenotype of OCD present with differential clinical impairment, course of disorder, and treatment outcome? Accordingly, the following review provides an overview of the extant literature on the symptom dimensions of OCD with regard to treatment, neurobiology, genetics, clinical characteristics, and comorbidity. Please note that, in the OCD literature, symptom dimensions are clusters of symptoms, thoughts, and behaviors posited to overlap and be functionally related (e.g., contamination and cleaning).

## Categorization of OCD Symptom Dimensions

*Methodologies of categorization.* Obsessive-compulsive symptom dimensions are generally conceptualized and measured by either a categorical or dimensional approach (Leckman, Rauch, & Mataix-Cols, 2007). In the categorical approach, a symptom dimension is viewed as either present or absent. In the dimensional approach, consideration is given to the magnitude of the symptoms. That is, the dimensions are considered to be on a continuous scale. Within the dimensional approach, the symptoms in a given dimension are added together and the sum represents the magnitude of severity.

The dimensional approach to quantifying OCD symptom dimensions accounts for the presence of overlapping symptom dimensions in individuals and allows patients to "fit" into multiple categories (Mataix-Cols, Rosario-Campos, & Leckman, 2005). Given the heterogeneous symptom presentation of OCD, the ability to allow for qualification in multiple categories provided by the dimensional approach is useful. For example, the dimensional approach allows for possible overlapping OCD symptom dimensions in patients (e.g., an individual with primarily aggressive/checking symptoms also presents with some contamination/washing symptoms). Nevertheless, there are caveats to using the dimensional approach. First, simply summing the symptoms may misrepresent presenting severity, as more symptoms automatically imply greater severity; however, several mild symptoms in a given category may be less impairing than one extremely severe symptom in that same category. Second, to appropriately compare dimensions, investigators must control for the number of symptoms in each category to ensure that dimensions with fewer symptoms are appropriately compared to dimensions with more symptoms. Overall, both the categorical and dimensional approaches have merit. The dimensional approach allows for more flexibility, with certain stated limitations, while the categorical approach is clear and straightforward. Additionally, studies differ in how the symptom dimensions are reported, with some studies identifying the dimension that is of primary concern, while other studies do not.

Original conceptualizations of symptom dimensions were rationally-based on clinical accounts (Summerfeldt, Richter, Antony, & Swinson, 1999). For example, thoughts or behaviors with similar presentations or putatively-related domains were grouped together (e.g., "washers" versus "checkers"; Horesh, Dolberg, Kirschenbaum-Aviner, & Kotler, 1997; Khanna & Mukherjee, 1992). However, within the past two decades, researchers have begun to empirically-derive symptom dimensions using statistical techniques that determine common covariance structures such as item- and category-level exploratory and confirmatory factor analyses, cluster analyses, and latent class modeling.

Symptom dimensions have primarily been assessed via factor or cluster analysis of the Yale-Brown Obsessive Compulsive Scale (Y-BOCS; Goodman, et al., 1989) checklist, a semi-structured interview for adults that assesses the presence of common obsessions and compulsions. While initial studies identified a three-factor model with pure obsessions, contamination/cleaning, and symmetry/hoarding factors based off the Y-BOCS symptom checklist (Baer, 1994; Hantouche & Lancrenon, 1996), later factor analytic studies identified a four or five factor structure (e.g., Leckman, et al., 1997; Summerfeldt, et al., 1999; see Table 1). Indeed, subsequent confirmatory factor analyses found that the four-factor solution (consisting of obsessions and checking, cleanliness/washing, hoarding, symmetry/ordering; Leckman, et al., 1997) was the only model with adequate fit when compared to models with one-factor (i.e., OCD as a homogeneous, single dimension), two-factors (i.e., obsessions and compulsions), and the previously identified three-factors (Summerfeldt et al., 1999).

A meta-analytic study that investigated symptom dimensions in over 5,000 adults and children with OCD found support for four factors on the Y-BOCS (Goodman, et al., 1989) and Children's Yale-Brown Obsessive-Compulsive Scale (CY-BOCS; Scahill, et al., 1997): contamination/cleaning, symmetry/ordering, hoarding, and forbidden thoughts (Bloch, Landeros-Weisenberger, Rosario, Pittenger, & Leckman, 2008). The latter factor consisted of aggressive, sexual, religious, somatic, and harm obsessions along with checking compulsions. This four-factor model of OCD symptom dimensions was supported as the best fit for a study of OCD patients across the lifespan (Stewart, et al., 2008).

Table 1

*Examples of 3-, 4-, and 5-Factor Structures within Adult Populations*

| No. of Factors | Authors (Year) | Factors |
|---|---|---|
| 3 | Baer (1994) | 1. Pure obsessions |
| | | 2. Contamination/cleaning |
| | | 3. Symmetry/hoarding |
| 4 | Leckman et al. (1997) | 1. Obsessions and checking |
| | | 2. Cleanliness/washing |
| | | 3. Hoarding |
| | | 4. Symmetry/ordering |
| 5 | Pinto et al. (2008) | 1. Harm obsessions/checking compulsions |
| | | 2. Aggressive/sexual/religious obsessions |
| | | 3. Contamination/cleaning |
| | | 4. Hoarding |
| | | 5. Symmetry/ordering |

Further support for similar symptom dimension structures between children and adults was demonstrated in a study where a four-factor model (contamination/cleaning, symmetry/ordering, pure obsessional, and hoarding/checking) accounted for 55% of the total variance in a sample of children and adolescents with OCD (Mataix-Cols, Nakatani, Micali, & Heyman, 2008). Of note, checking compulsions loaded on to the same factor as hoarding, which is inconsistent with the adult literature and the findings from Stewart et al. (2008). Overall, however, most symptom dimensions were found to overlap for both children and adults (Mataix-Cols, et al., 2008). In addition, both prospective studies and retrospective patient reports provide evidence for the stability of OCD dimensions over time (Mataix-Cols, Rauch, et al., 2002; Pinto, Mancebo, Eisen, Pagano, & Rasmussen, 2006; Rufer, Grothusen, Mass, Peter, & Hand, 2005). Perhaps not surprisingly then, the greatest predictor of current OCD symptoms was endorsement of the same symptoms in the past (Mataix-Cols, Rauch, et al., 2002). Longitudinal studies are needed, however, to fully ascertain the stability of symptom dimensions across the lifespan (Mataix-Cols, et al., 2008). One longitudinal study that followed 76 children with OCD over 2-7 years found that no symptoms remained the same (Rettew, Swedo, Leonard, Lenane, & Rapoport, 1992). Although not tested in that study, it is likely that changes occurred within rather than between symptom dimensions, given subsequent studies.

*Miscellaneous Obsessive or Compulsive Symptoms.* Miscellaneous symptoms, which include superstitious obsessions, fears of losing things, compulsive need to ask, tell, or confess or ritualistic staring or blinking, are often neglected in discussions about OCD dimensions. While adults and children commonly endorse miscellaneous symptoms, these symptoms have often been omitted from factor analytic studies because the symptoms do not fit within the standard symptom categories listed on the Y-BOCS (or CY-BOCS) checklists, either because studies were not sufficiently powered for item-level analysis, or simply due to convention (Storch, et al., 2007).

## Symptom dimensions as predictors of treatment

Understanding how differential OCD symptom presentation relates to treatment responsiveness has been a focus of numerous studies (Abramowitz, Franklin, Schwartz, & Furr, 2003; Alonso, et al., 2001; Mataix-Cols, Rauch, Manzo, Jenike, & Baer, 1999; Saxena, et al., 2002). Although cognitive-behavioral therapy (CBT) and serotonin reuptake inhibitors (SRIs) are considered efficacious treatments for OCD (Franklin & Foa, 2011; Geller & March, 2012; Lewin & Piacentini, 2009; Lewin, Wu, McGuire, & Storch, 2014), several studies have shown symptom dimension type moderates treatment outcome (e.g., Abramowitz, et al., 2003; Alonso, et al., 2001; Mataix-Cols, et al., 1999; Saxena, et al., 2002). The majority of these studies utilized the categorical approach to examine the associations between OCD dimensions and treatment outcome (Abramowitz et al., 2003; Alonso et al., 2001; Saxena et al., 2002). Sexual/religious obsessions predicted poorer long-term treatment outcome in 60 adult patients with OCD with prolonged SRI pharmacotherapy who had completed behavioral therapy (Alonso, et al., 2001). In a 15-week CBT trial with 132 adults with OCD, those classified as hoarders had greater post-treatment OCD severity relative to the other symptom dimensions (Abramowitz et al., 2003). Similarly, in a 6-week multimodal treatment approach (i.e., intensive CBT, medication and psychosocial counseling), hoarders responded to treatment more poorly than those who were not hoarders (Saxena et al., 2002).

There are also some studies that utilized the dimensional approach to quantify symptom dimensions in the context of examining treatment outcome (Mataix-Cols, Marks, Greist, Kobak, & Baer, 2002; Mataix-Cols, et al., 1999; Rufer, Fricke, Moritz, Kloss, & Hand, 2006; Storch et al., 2008). For 153 adult patients with OCD, increased hoarding symptoms significantly predicted premature treatment termination and trended towards poorer treatment outcome relative to those with less hoarding symptoms (Mataix-Cols, Marks, et al., 2002). Similar results were found in an inpatient sample of 104 adults with OCD; after 9 weeks of intensive CBT and auxiliary group counseling, those with a greater magnitude of hoarding symptoms were less likely to respond to treatment than those without hoarding symptoms (Rufer, et al., 2006). Mataix-Cols and colleagues (1999) retrospectively examined differential treatment outcome in 354 adult outpatients with OCD from various randomized, controlled SRI treatment trials (clomipramine, fluvoxamine, fluoxetine, sertraline, and paroxetine). Within this sample, higher extent of hoarding symptoms significantly predicted poorer SRI treatment outcome (Mataix-Cols, et al., 1999). Higher scores on sexual/religious obsessions also significantly predicted worse post-treatment outcome compared to those with lower scores on this symptom dimension.

Few studies have examined the relationship between OCD dimensions and treatment outcome amongst youth. However, in line with the adult literature, a naturalistic study of children with OCD revealed that those with hoarding symptoms had poorer treatment response to SRIs ($N = 7$, 14.3% response) when compared to children with symmetry obsessions and ordering, counting, and repeating compulsions ($N = 30$, 76.7% response), aggressive, sexual, religious, and somatic obsessions and checking compulsions ($N = 21$, 57.1% response), and contamination obsessions and cleanliness and washing compulsions ($N = 23$, 78.3% response; Masi, et al., 2005). Storch and colleagues (2008) found that after 14 sessions of weekly or intensive CBT ($N = 92$, ages 7-19 years), youth with aggressive/checking symptoms showed a trend towards greater improvements in treatment response relative to those who endorsed only non-aggressive/checking symptoms. Importantly, the limited number of studies precludes any definitive conclusions on treatment response by symptom dimension in the pediatric population.

From the studies that have investigated differential treatment outcome by OCD symptom dimension in adults, findings suggest that hoarding is associated with poorer response rates relative to the other symptom dimensions (Abramowitz, et al., 2003). This finding may be due to specific traits associated with hoarding that may hinder the therapeutic process, such as poor insight, low compliance, personality disorder symptoms, and cognitive impairments (e.g., poor executive functioning skills; Frost, Steketee, Williams, & Warren, 2000; Grisham, Brown, Savage, Steketee, & Barlow, 2007; Lawrence, et al., 2006; Mataix-Cols, Marks, et al., 2002; Steketee & Frost, 2003). Indeed, increasing research suggests that compulsive hoarding may be a distinct syndrome from OCD, as evidenced by differing phenomenological traits and treatment response rates (e.g., Pertusa et al., 2008). Accordingly, in the most recent edition of the *DSM-5* (APA, 2013), hoarding disorder was added as a new diagnosis under the broader category of obsessive-compulsive and related disorders. Further, most of the extant findings stem from secondary analyses with various methodological limitations and thus should be interpreted cautiously – i.e., associations between symptom dimensions and differences in treatment outcomes should not be considered definitive.

## Neural correlates

Proposed etiological models for the development of OCD were derived from functional and structural neuroimaging studies, which implicated abnormalities within the frontalstriatothalamic circuit in the pathogenesis of OCD (Greisberg & McKay, 2003; Rosenberg & Keshavan, 1998; Saxena, Brody, Schwartz, & Baxter, 1998). As the preponderance of these neuroimaging studies did not account for the heterogeneous symptom manifestations of OCD, there are relatively few studies regarding the neurobiological correlates of specific symptom dimensions. One functional magnetic resonance imaging (fMRI) study examined neural responses of 8 washers and 8 healthy controls when shown disgust-inducing pictures. Relative to the healthy controls, washers had significantly increased activation in the right insula (Shapira, et al., 2003), an area implicated in disgust perception and response (Royet, Plailly, Delon-Martin, Kareken, & Segebarth, 2003; Small, et al., 2003; Zald & Pardo, 2000). Similarly, in another fMRI study, neural responses between OCD patients with primarily washing and checking symptoms were compared (Phillips, et al., 2000). When shown washer-relevant disgust-inducing photos, washers demonstrated increased activations in the visual regions (areas associated with perception of fearful/aversive stimuli; Taylor, Liberzon, & Koeppe, 2000) and the anterior insula, while checkers showed increased activations in the thalamus and frontalstriatal regions.

Marked differences have also been found between individuals with compulsive hoarding in contrast to those presenting with other OCD symptom dimensions. Saxena and colleagues (2004) utilized positron emission tomography (PET) to examine cerebral glucose metabolism in 12 subjects with hoarding, 33 patients with other OCD symptoms (but no hoarding), and 17 healthy controls. Relative to patients with OCD but without hoarding, those with hoarding demonstrated significantly decreased glucose metabolism in the dorsal anterior cingulate gyrus, an area implicated in motivation, decision-making, and executive control (Awh & Gehring, 1999; Devinsky, Morrell, & Vogt, 1995; Krawczyk, 2002).

Utilizing the dimensional approach to examine neural activations within the same patients, Mataix-Cols (et al. 2004) implemented a symptom-provocation paradigm where 16 patients with OCD having mixed symptoms were administered fMRI scans as they viewed pictures of and imagined experiences with hoarding, washing and checking. Compared to controls, patients with OCD experienced (a) increased activation in the left precentral gyrus and right orbitofrontal cortex during the hoarding condition, (b) increased activation in the thalamus, dorsal cortical areas, and the putamen/globus pallidus during the checking condition, and (c) greater activation in the bilateral ventromedial prefrontal regions and right caudate nucleus during the washing condition. Additionally, subjective levels of anxiety were also correlated with differing OCD symptom dimensions as well as different patterns of neural activation in patients with OCD. From these findings, the study's authors suggested that the varying OCD symptom dimensions were mediated by the distinct, but partially overlapping neural systems.

Within structural imaging studies, the findings for studies examining mixed OCD groups have been largely inconsistent, with some suggesting volume reduction and enlargement amongst OCD patients where others reports no differences between patient and control groups (e.g., Aylward et al., 1996; Rosenberg et al., 1997; Scarone et al., 1992). From these studies only a few have analyzed structural differences by symptom dimension (Pujol et al., 2004; van den Heuvel et al., 2009). Pujol and colleagues (2004) found reduced gray matter in the right amygdala of 30 patients with OCD and "prominent" aggressive/checking symptoms, relative to patients with OCD without these symptoms. Utilizing the dimensional approach to further examine neuro-structural differences by OCD symptom dimensions, Van den Heuvel and colleagues (2009) administered whole-brain voxel-based morphometry (VBM) to 50 OCD patients. The researchers found that increased contamination/washing symptoms were associated with decreased volumes in the dorsal caudate nucleus, while increased harm/checking symptoms were associated with decreased gray and white matter volumes in the anterior temporal lobes. Finally, symmetry/ordering symptoms were negatively correlated with global gray and white matter volume.

Studies regarding the neurobiology of OCD symptom dimensions in children and adolescents are scant. In a functional imaging study, Gilbert et al. (2009) utilized the dimensional approach to examine the neural correlates of OCD symptom dimensions in 18 children and adolescents. A similar symptom provocation paradigm used in adults (Mataix-Cols et al., 2004) was utilized in this study; the symptom provocation images used in this study were associated with contamination/washing and symmetry/ordering (rather than contamination/washing, aggression/checking and hoarding). The symmetry/ordering condition was associated with decreased activation in the insula and thalamus, while the contamination/washing condition was associated with reduced activation in the thalamus, dorsolateral prefrontal cortex, putamen and insular and ventral prefrontal regions.

These findings suggest possible neuroendophenotypic differences within the frontalstriatothalamic circuits among different OCD symptom dimensions. Still, while neuroimaging studies have provided important information regarding possible neural correlates of the varying OCD symptom dimensions, inconsistent results have highlighted the need for further investigation into these areas. The majority of these studies were marked by small sample sizes, which limit statistical power and prohibit extensive examination of neurobiological correlates of specific OCD dimensions. Differences in methodology (e.g., categorizing symptom dimensions, neuroimaging techniques, outcome measures) also may have contributed to the inconsistent findings. Although these studies contribute to the existing knowledge base, without comparisons to larger control populations it is unclear how these findings differ from normal variants.

## Neuropsychological correlates

As neurobiological studies provide evidence of brain activation anomalies within patients with OCD, these findings have been further reflected through neuropsychological studies, which have shown strong associations between OCD and cognitive and executive functioning deficits (e.g., Abbruzzese, Ferri, & Scarone, 1995; Christensen, Kim, Dysken, & Hoover, 1992; Lawrence et al., 2006; Nedeljkovic et al., 2009; Tallis, Pratt, & Jamani, 1999). However, only a handful of studies have examined the relationship between neuropsychological functioning and OCD symptom dimensions. Increased deficits in distinct executive functioning areas, such as decision-making, reaction time, and impulsivity have been consistently associated with the hoarding dimension (Grisham, et al., 2007; Hartl, et al., 2004; Lawrence, et al., 2006). Conversely, findings regarding other OCD symptom dimensions have produced inconsistent results, with some studies linking deficits with inhibition and set-shifting with the symmetry/ordering dimensions, while other studies suggesting no relationship between symptom dimensions and executive functioning deficits (Abbruzzese, et al., 1995; Hashimoto, et al., 2011; Lawrence, et al., 2006; Omori, et al., 2007).

Previous studies investigating working memory performance and OCD symptom dimensions have primarily focused on checkers when compared to noncheckers (Nakao, et al., 2009; Nedeljkovic, et al., 2009; Tallis, et al., 1999). While several studies have noted a significant relationship between checking symptoms and increased deficits in spatial working memory, relative to other symptom dimensions (Nakao, et al., 2009; Nedeljkovic, et al., 2009), others found that checking severity was not related to any observed memory deficits (Tallis, et al., 1999). When utilizing the dimensional approach to examine 63 OCD patients, increased contamination/cleaning symptoms were associated with better performance on memory and inhibition tasks, while those with increased symmetry/ordering symptoms demonstrated worse performance on memory tasks (Hashimoto, et al., 2011).

While results have been inconsistent, overall, the research suggests that specific OCD symptom dimensions are likely associated with differences in neuropsychological performance. Discrepancies in findings in the aforementioned studies may be due to a number of variables, including different methodological approaches (categorical vs. dimensional) utilized to examine the symptom dimensions, variations in neuropsychological batteries administered, and/or differing study aims.

## Genetics

Twin and family studies have suggested that the presentation of OCD symptom dimensions may be partly familial (Alsobrook, Leckman, Goodman, Rasmussen, & Pauls, 1999; Leckman et al., 2003). For example, in 418 families with OCD, the OCD Collaborative Genetics Study found strong correlations between sibling pairs with religious/aggressive obsessions (Hasler, et al., 2007). Within the same sample, distinct familial associations were found for individuals with hoarding as well. Hoarding symptoms were highly correlated in sibling pairs (Samuels, Bienvenu, et al., 2007). Additionally, hoarding symptoms were present in 12% of first-degree relatives of patients with hoarding (as opposed to 3% in non-hoarders). Within a study of 128 families, obsessions/checking and symmetry/ordering symptom dimensions were found to have strong sibling associations within those patients with comorbid Tourette's syndrome (Leckman et al., 2003). Alsobrook et al. (2003) found that within families with OCD, those with higher scores on the obsessions/checking and symmetry/ordering factors were more likely to have a relative with OCD than those who scored lower in those domains.

Studies have also sought genetic markers for OCD symptom dimensions (Cavallini, Di Bella, Siliprandi, Malchiodi, & Bellodi, 2002; Zhang, Leckman, Tsai, Kidd, & Rosaio-Campos, 2002). The OCD Collaborative Genetics Study linked compulsive hoarding with a marker on the chromosome 14q in families with OCD; the link was strengthened when the data was re-examined to include only families with multiple compulsive hoarders (Hasler, et al., 2007; Samuels,

Bienvenu et al., 2007; Samuels, Shugart et al., 2007). In a separate study, genome scans were utilized in sibling pairs with Tourette Disorder to identify significant allele sharing on chromosomes 4q, 5q, and 17q for the hoarding phenotype (Zhang, et al., 2002). Associations between specific markers on the 17q chromosome and the repeating/counting symptom dimension have also been identified (Cavallini et al., 2002). Despite impressive pilot findings in the aforementioned studies, replication is essential to extrapolate any conclusive findings.

## Clinical Characteristics

There has been conflicting data as to whether age of OCD onset is related to symptom dimensions. Some found that those with early-onset OCD were more likely to report aggressive and religious obsessions and repeating and miscellaneous compulsions than those with late-onset OCD (Pinto, et al., 2006). Nakatani et al. (2011) found higher rates of ordering/repeating compulsions in youth with OCD onset prior to age 10 years (in contrast to you ages 10-18 years old). Others have not found any statistically significant differences between early and late-onset OCD groups in terms of symptom dimensions (Rosario-Campos, et al., 2001). One possible reason for the conflicting findings is the heterogeneous definition of early-onset OCD across the literature. While some consider early-onset to be OCD symptom presentation before puberty (Kalra & Swedo, 2009), others consider early-onset to occur at or prior to a specific age, e.g., 10 years; (Carter, Pollock, Suvak, & Pauls, 2004; Rosario-Campos, et al., 2001), 15 years (Hemmings, et al., 2004), or even 18 years (Pinto, et al., 2006). Given this, demarcation of early vs. late-onset age may account for inconsistent findings examining variations between age of OCD onset and symptom dimensions.

Gender has been investigated in relation to symptom dimensions. Generally, sexual and religious symptoms tend to manifest more in men and contamination and cleaning symptoms tend to manifest more in women (e.g., Bogetto, Venturello, Albert, Maina, & Ravizza, 1999; Lochner, et al., 2004; Sobin, et al., 1999; Stein, Andersen, & Overo, 2007; Torresan, et al., 2013). Results for the symmetry-ordering and hoarding dimensions are less consistent, with some finding no evidence of gender differences (Bogetto, et al., 1999; Torresan, et al., 2013; Tukel, Polat, Genc, Bozkurt, & Atli, 2004; Wheaton, Timpano, Lasalle-Ricci, & Murphy, 2008) and others finding a higher frequency among men (Hantouche & Lancrenon, 1996; Leckman, et al., 1997; Samuels, et al., 2002). Results are also equivocal for the severity of symptom dimensions by gender. Whereas some have found women to display more severe symptomology across dimensions (Fischer, Himle, & Hanna, 1996; Torresan, et al., 2013), others have not (Bogetto et al., 1999; Tukel et al., 2004; Labad et al., 2008).

52

Symptom dimensions are also associated with differing levels of insight. Studies have consistently reported poorer insight in those with hoarding symptoms relative to those with non-hoarding OCD symptoms (Frost, Steketee, & Williams, 2000; Kim, Steketee, & Frost, 2001; Samuels, Shugart, et al., 2007; Tolin, Fitch, Frost, & Steketee, 2010). For example, in a survey of 558 family members of patients with hoarding, more than half described the family member with hoarding as lacking insight or being delusional about their hoarding symptoms (Tolin, et al., 2010). Outside of hoarding, poor insight has also been associated with the contamination dimension, while those with aggressive obsessions were described as having good insight (Cherian, et al., 2012). As poor insight is associated with greater impairment (Lewin, Caporino, Murphy, Geffken, & Storch, 2010) as well as attenuated treatment response, symptom dimension and level of insight should be examined further.

## Comorbidities

Co-occuring Axis I disorders are common in patients with OCD (LaSalle et al., 2004; Pinto et al., 2006). Aggressive, sexual, religious, and somatic obsessions and checking compulsions are associated with anxiety and depressive disorders, whereas contamination obsessions and cleaning compulsions are more commonly associated with eating disorders (Hasler, et al., 2005; Lewin, Menzel & Strober, 2013). Symmetry obsessions and compulsions related to repeating, counting, and arranging are also associated with comorbid diagnoses of bipolar disorders, panic disorders, and agoraphobia. In addition, tic comorbidity is associated with obsessions related to symmetry, aggression, and religion, as well as compulsions related to cleaning, ordering and arranging, repeating, and hoarding (Jaisoorya, Reddy, Srinath, & Thennarasu, 2008). Frequency of symmetry, ordering, and arranging is also higher for those with Tourette syndrome (Kano, et al., 2010). Amongst children and adolescents with comorbid autism spectrum disorder, there are decreased rates of checking, washing, and repeating compulsions (Lewin, Wood, Gunderson, Murphy, & Storch, 2011).

Notably, no associations between the hoarding dimension and other Axis I psychiatric disorders have been identified (Hasler, et al., 2005). This is in contrast to findings that suggest that, when analyzed by gender, hoarding is associated with body dysmorphic disorder, post-traumatic stress disorder, social phobia, and body-focused repetitive behaviors for women, and generalized anxiety disorder and tic disorders for men (Wheaton, et al., 2008). Studies have linked the hoarding dimension with various Axis II personality disorders in adults (Frost, Steketee, Williams, et al., 2000; Mataix-Cols, Baer, Rauch, & Jenike, 2000). In comparison to other dimensions, hoarding was associated with the presence of *any* Axis II diagnosis and was correlated most highly with Cluster C disorders (Mataix-Cols, et al., 2000). Hoarding is also associated with sub-clinical personality disorder symptoms, especially dependent personality characteristics (Frost, Steketee, Williams, et al., 2000). The association with dependent personality characteristics is consistent with research suggesting that individuals with hoarding have difficulty making decisions and working alone (Frost & Gross, 1993; Frost, Steketee, Williams, et al., 2000).

## Conclusions

Obsessive-compulsive disorder has a heterogeneous symptom presentation where the phenomenology of the disorder can vary substantially among individuals. Although previous research did not account for the heterogeneity of the disorder and examined OCD as a single entity, current research has started to conceptualize OCD as a disorder composed of several symptom dimensions. Approaches to the conceptualization of OCD symptom dimensions vary, however, limiting cross study comparisons. In addition, replication is minimal and many findings are based on secondary or tertiary data analyses rather than well-controlled prospective studies. Nevertheless, within the context of these methodological limitations, some interesting albeit preliminary findings have emerged. Fairly consistently, research has identified hoarding as a distinctive dimension with respect to clinical characteristics, biomarkers, and treatment outcome, which led to its recent classification as a distinct syndrome in the *DSM-5*. At present, connecting OCD symptom dimensions to underlying neurosubstrates, disease trajectory, and treatment recommendations remains an area for further examination prior to forming any definitive conclusions.

## References

Abbruzzese, M., Ferri, S., & Scarone, S. (1995). Wisconsin Card Sorting Test performance in obsessive-compulsive disorder: no evidence for involvement of dorsolateral prefrontal cortex. *Psychiatry Res, 58*(1), 37-43.

Abramowitz, J. S., Franklin, M. E., Schwartz, S. A., & Furr, J. M. (2003). Symptom presentation and outcome of cognitive-behavioral therapy for obsessive-compulsive disorder. *J.Consult Clin.Psychol., 71*(6), 1049-1057.

Alonso, P., Menchon, J. M., Pifarre, J., Mataix-Cols, D., Torres, L., Salgado, P., et al. (2001). Long-term follow-up and predictors of clinical outcome in obsessive-compulsive patients treated with serotonin reuptake inhibitors and behavioral therapy. *J Clin Psychiatry, 62*(7), 535-540.

Alsobrook, J. P., Leckman, J. F., Goodman, W. K., Rasmussen, S. A., & Pauls, D. (1999). Segregation analysis of obsessive-compulsive disorder using symptom-based factor scores. *American Journal of Medical Genetics, 88*, 669-675.

American Psychiatric Association. (2013). *Diagnostic and statistical manual of mental disorders: DSM-5 (5th Edition)*. Washington, DC: American Psychiatric Association.

Awh, E., & Gehring, W. J. (1999). The anterior cingulate cortex lends a hand in response selection. *Nat Neurosci, 2*(10), 853-854. doi: 10.1038/13145

Aylward, E. H., Harris, G. J., Hoehn-Saric, R., Barta, P. E., Machlin, S. R., & Pearlson, G. D. (1996). Normal caudate nucleus in obsessive-compulsive disorder assessed by quantitative neuroimaging. *Arch Gen Psychiatry, 53*(7), 577-584.

Baer, L. (1994). Factor analysis of symptom subtypes of obsessive compulsive disorder and their relation to personality and tic disorders. *J Clin Psychiatry, 55 Suppl*, 18-23.

Bloch, M. H., Landeros-Weisenberger, A., Rosario, M. C., Pittenger, C., & Leckman, J. F. (2008). Meta-analysis of the symptom structure of obsessive-compulsive disorder. *Am J Psychiatry, 165*(12), 1532-1542. doi: 10.1176/appi.ajp.2008.08020320

Bogetto, F., Venturello, S., Albert, U., Maina, G., & Ravizza, L. (1999). Gender-related clinical differences in obsessive-compulsive disorder. *Eur Psychiatry, 14*(8), 434-441.

Carter, A. S., Pollock, R. A., Suvak, M. K., & Pauls, D. L. (2004). Anxiety and major depression comorbidity in a family study of obsessive-compulsive disorder. *Depress Anxiety, 20*(4), 165-174. doi: 10.1002/da.20042

Cavallini, M. C., Di Bella, D., Siliprandi, F., Malchiodi, F., & Bellodi, L. (2002). Exploratory factor analysis of obsessive-compulsive patients and association with 5-HTTLPR polymorphism. *Am J Med Genet, 114*(3), 347-353. doi: 10.1002/ajmg.1700 [pii]

Cherian, A. V., Narayanaswamy, J. C., Srinivasaraju, R., Viswanath, B., Math, S. B., Kandavel, T., et al. (2012). Does insight have specific correlation with symptom dimensions in OCD? *J Affect Disord, 138*(3), 352-359. doi: 10.1016/j.jad.2012.01.017

Christensen, K. J., Kim, S. W., Dysken, M. W., & Hoover, K. M. (1992). Neuropsychological performance in obsessive-compulsive disorder. *Biol Psychiatry, 31*(1), 4-18.

Devinsky, O., Morrell, M. J., & Vogt, B. A. (1995). Contributions of anterior cingulate cortex to behaviour. *Brain, 118 ( Pt 1)*, 279-306.

Fischer, D. J., Himle, J. A., & Hanna, G. L. (1996). Age and gender effects on obsessive-compulsive symptoms in children and adults. [Research Support, U.S. Gov't, P.H.S.]. *Depress Anxiety, 4*(5), 237-239. doi: 10.1002/(SICI)1520-6394(1996)4:5<237::AID-DA5>3.0.CO;2-A

Franklin, M. E., & Foa, E. B. (2011). Treatment of obsessive compulsive disorder. [Review]. *Annu Rev Clin Psychol, 7*, 229-243. doi: 10.1146/annurev-clinpsy-032210-104533

Frost, R. O., & Gross, R. C. (1993). The hoarding of possessions. *Behav Res Ther, 31*(4), 367-381.

Frost, R. O., Steketee, G., & Williams, L. (2000). Hoarding: A community health problem. *Health Soc Care Community, 8*(4), 229-234.

Frost, R. O., Steketee, G., Williams, L. F., & Warren, R. (2000). Mood, personality disorder symptoms and disability in obsessive compulsive hoarders: a comparison with clinical and nonclinical controls. *Behav Res Ther, 38*(11), 1071-1081.

Geller, D. A., & March, J. (2012). Practice parameter for the assessment and treatment of children and adolescents with obsessive compulsive disorder. *J Am Acad Child Adolesc Psychiatry, 51*(1), 98-113. doi: 10.1016/j.jaac.2011.09.019

Goodman, W. K., Price, L. H., Rasmussen, S. A., Mazure, C., Fleischmann, R. L., Hill, C. L., et al. (1989). The Yale-Brown Obsessive Compulsive Scale. I. Development, use, and reliability. *Arch.Gen.Psychiatry, 46*(11), 1006-1011.

Greisberg, S., & McKay, D. (2003). Neuropsychology of obsessive-compulsive disorder: A review and treatment implications. *Clinical Psychology Review, 23*(1), 95-117. doi: S0272735802002325 [pii]

Grisham, J. R., Brown, T. A., Savage, C. R., Steketee, G., & Barlow, D. H. (2007). Neuropsychological impairment associated with compulsive hoarding. *Behav Res Ther, 45*(7), 1471-1483. doi: 10.1016/j.brat.2006.12.008

Hantouche, E. G., & Lancrenon, S. (1996). Modern typology of symptoms and obsessive-compulsive syndromes: Results of a large French study of 615 patients. *Encephale, 22 Spec No 1*, 9-21.

Hartl, T. L., Frost, R. O., Allen, G. J., Deckersbach, T., Steketee, G., Duffany, S. R., et al. (2004). Actual and perceived memory deficits in individuals with compulsive hoarding. *Depress Anxiety, 20*(2), 59-69. doi: 10.1002/da.20010

Hashimoto, N., Nakaaki, S., Omori, I. M., Fujioi, J., Noguchi, Y., Murata, Y., et al. (2011). Distinct neuropsychological profiles of three major symptom dimensions in obsessive-compulsive disorder. *Psychiatry Res, 187*(1-2), 166-173. doi: 10.1016/j.psychres.2010.08.001

Hasler, G., LaSalle-Ricci, V. H., Ronquillo, J. G., Crawley, S. A., Cochran, L. W., Kazuba, D., et al. (2005). Obsessive-compulsive disorder symptom dimensions show specific relationships to psychiatric comorbidity. *Psychiatry Res, 135*(2), 121-132. doi: 10.1016/j.psychres.2005.03.003

Hasler, G., Pinto, A., Greenberg, B. D., Samuels, J., Fyer, A. J., Pauls, D., et al. (2007). Familiality of factor analysis-derived YBOCS dimensions in OCD-affected sibling pairs from the OCD Collaborative Genetics Study. *Biol Psychiatry, 61*(5), 617-625.

Hemmings, S. M., Kinnear, C. J., Lochner, C., Niehaus, D. J., Knowles, J. A., Moolman-Smook, J. C., et al. (2004). Early- versus late-onset obsessive-compulsive disorder: investigating genetic and clinical correlates.

[Research Support, Non-U.S. Gov't]. *Psychiatry Res, 128*(2), 175-182. doi: 10.1016/j.psychres.2004.05.007

Horesh, N., Dolberg, O. T., Kirschenbaum-Aviner, N., & Kotler, M. (1997). Personality differences between obsessive-compulsive disorder subtypes: Washers versus checkers. *Psychiatry Res, 71*(3), 197-200.

Jaisoorya, T. S., Reddy, Y. C., Srinath, S., & Thennarasu, K. (2008). Obsessive-compulsive disorder with and without tic disorder: a comparative study from India. [Comparative Study]. *CNS Spectr, 13*(8), 705-711.

Kalra, S. K., & Swedo, S. E. (2009). Children with obsessive-compulsive disorder: are they just "little adults"? [Review]. *J Clin Invest, 119*(4), 737-746. doi: 10.1172/JCI37563

Kano, Y., Kono, T., Shishikura, K., Konno, C., Kuwabara, H., Ohta, M., et al. (2010). Obsessive-compulsive symptom dimensions in Japanese tourette syndrome subjects. *CNS Spectr, 15*(5), 296-303.

Khanna, S., & Mukherjee, D. (1992). Checkers and washers: Valid subtypes of obsessive compulsive disorder. *Psychopathology, 25*(5), 283-288.

Kim, H. J., Steketee, G., & Frost, R. O. (2001). Hoarding by elderly people. *Health Soc Work, 26*(3), 176-184.

Krawczyk, D. C. (2002). Contributions of the prefrontal cortex to the neural basis of human decision making. [Review]. *Neurosci Biobehav Rev, 26*(6), 631-664.

Labad, J., Menchon, J. M., Alonso, P., Segalas, C., Jimenez, S., Jaurrieta, N., Leckman, J. F., & Vallejo, J. (2008). Gender differences in obsessive-compulsive symptom dimensions, *Depression and Anxiety, 25*, 832-838.

LaSalle, V. H., Cromer, K. R., Nelson, K. N., Kazuba, D., Justement, L., & Murphy, D. L. (2004). Diagnostic interview assessed neuropsychiatric disorder comorbidity in 334 individuals with obsessive-compulsive disorder. *Depress Anxiety, 19*(3), 163-173. doi: 10.1002/da.20009

Lawrence, N. S., Wooderson, S., Mataix-Cols, D., David, R., Speckens, A., & Phillips, M. L. (2006). Decision making and set shifting impairments are associated with distinct symptom dimensions in obsessive-compulsive disorder. *Neuropsychology, 20*(4), 409-419. doi: 10.1037/0894-4105.20.4.409

Leckman, J. F., Grice, D. E., Boardman, J., Zhang, H., Vitale, A., Bondi, C., et al. (1997). Symptoms of obsessive-compulsive disorder. [Research Support, U.S. Gov't, P.H.S.]. *Am J Psychiatry, 154*(7), 911-917.

Leckman, J. F., Pauls, D. L., Zhang, H., Rosario-Campos, M. C., Katsovich, L., Kidd, K. K., et al. (2003). Obsessive-compulsive symptom dimensions in affected sibling pairs diagnosed with Gilles de la Tourette syndrome. *Am J Med Genet B Neuropsychiatr Genet, 116B*(1), 60-68. doi: 10.1002/ajmg.b.10001

Leckman, J. F., Rauch, S. L., & Mataix-Cols, D. (2007). Symptom dimensions in obsessive-compulsive disorder: implications for the DSM-5. *CNS Spectr, 12*(5), 376-387, 400.

Lewin, A. B., Caporino, N., Murphy, T. K., Geffken, G. R., & Storch, E. A. (2010). Understudied clinical dimensions in pediatric obsessive compulsive disorder. *Child Psychiatry Hum Dev, 41*(6), 675-691. doi: 10.1007/s10578-010-0196-z

Lewin, A.B., Menzel, J. & Strober M. (2013). Assessment and treatment of comorbid anorexia nervosa and obsessive compulsive disorder. In E.A. Storch & D. McKay (eds.) *Handbook of Treating Variants and Complications in Anxiety Disorders.* New York, NY: Springer, 337-348.

Lewin, A. B., Park, J. M., & Storch, E. A. (2013). Obsessive Compulsive Disorder in Children and Adolescents. In R. A. Vasa and A. K. Roy (eds.) *Pediatric Anxiety Disorders – A clinical guide.* New York, NY: Humana Press, 157-175.

Lewin, A. B., & Piacentini, J. (2009). Obsessive-compulsive disorder in children. In B. Sadock & V. Sadock (Eds.), *Kaplan and Sadock's Comprehensive Textbook of Psychiatry, 9th ed.* (Vol. 2, pp. 3671-3678). Philadelphia: Lippincott Williams and Wilkins.

Lewin, A. B., Wood, J. J., Gunderson, S., Murphy, T. K., & Storch, E. A. (2011). Obsessive compulsive symptoms in youth with high functioning autism specrum disorders. *Journal of Developmental and Physical Disabilities, 23*, 543-553.

Lochner, C., Hemmings, S. M., Kinnear, C. J., Moolman-Smook, J. C., Corfield, V. A., Knowles, J. A., et al. (2004). Gender in obsessive-compulsive disorder: Clinical and genetic findings. *Eur Neuropsychopharmacol, 14*(2), 105-113. doi: 10.1016/S0924-977X(03)00063-4

Masi, G., Millepiedi, S., Mucci, M., Bertini, N., Milantoni, L., & Arcangeli, F. (2005). A naturalistic study of referred children and adolescents with obsessive-compulsive disorder. *J Am Acad Child Adolesc Psychiatry, 44*(7), 673-681. doi: 10.1097/01.chi.0000161648.82775.ee

Mataix-Cols, D., Baer, L., Rauch, S. L., & Jenike, M. A. (2000). Relation of factor-analyzed symptom dimensions of obsessive-compulsive disorder to personality disorders. [Research Support, Non-U.S. Gov't]. *Acta Psychiatr Scand, 102*(3), 199-202.

Mataix-Cols, D., Frost, R. O., Pertusa, A., Clark, L. A., Saxena, S., Leckman, J. F., et al. (2010). Hoarding disorder: a new diagnosis for DSM-5? *Depress Anxiety, 27*(6), 556-572. doi: 10.1002/da.20693

Mataix-Cols, D., Marks, I. M., Greist, J. H., Kobak, K. A., & Baer, L. (2002). Obsessive-compulsive symptom dimensions as predictors of compliance with and response to behaviour therapy: results from a controlled trial. *Psychother Psychosom, 71*(5), 255-262. doi: pps71255

Mataix-Cols, D., Nakatani, E., Micali, N., & Heyman, I. (2008). Structure of obsessive-compulsive symptoms in pediatric OCD. *J Am Acad Child Adolesc Psychiatry, 47*(7), 773-778. doi: 10.1097/CHI.0b013e31816b73c0

Mataix-Cols, D., Rauch, S. L., Baer, L., Eisen, J. L., Shera, D. M., Goodman, W. K., et al. (2002). Symptom stability in adult obsessive-compulsive disorder: data from a naturalistic two-year follow-up study. *Am J Psychiatry, 159*(2), 263-268.

Mataix-Cols, D., Rauch, S. L., Manzo, P. A., Jenike, M. A., & Baer, L. (1999). Use of factor-analyzed symptom dimensions to predict outcome with serotonin reuptake inhibitors and placebo in the treatment of obsessive-compulsive disorder. *Am J Psychiatry, 156*(9), 1409-1416.

Mataix-Cols, D., Rosario-Campos, M. C., & Leckman, J. F. (2005). A multidimensional model of obsessive-compulsive disorder. *Am J Psychiatry, 162*(2), 228-238. doi: 10.1176/appi.ajp.162.2.228

Nakao, T., Nakagawa, A., Nakatani, E., Nabeyama, M., Sanematsu, H., Yoshiura, T., et al. (2009). Working memory dysfunction in obsessive-compulsive disorder: a neuropsychological and functional MRI study. *J Psychiatr Res, 43*(8), 784-791. doi: 10.1016/j.jpsychires.2008.10.013

Nakatani, E., Krebs, G., Micali, N., Turner, C., Heyman, I., & Mataix-Cols, D. (2011). Children with very early onset obsessivecompulsive disorder: clinical features and treatment outcome. *Journal of Child Psychology and Psychiatry, 52(12)*, 1261-1268.

Nedeljkovic, M., Kyrios, M., Moulding, R., Doron, G., Wainwright, K., Pantelis, C., et al. (2009). Differences in neuropsychological performance between subtypes of obsessive-compulsive disorder. *Aust N Z J Psychiatry, 43*(3), 216-226. doi: 10.1080/00048670802653273

Omori, I. M., Murata, Y., Yamanishi, T., Nakaaki, S., Akechi, T., Mikuni, M., et al. (2007). The differential impact of executive attention dysfunction on episodic memory in obsessive-compulsive disorder patients with checking symptoms vs. those with washing symptoms. *J Psychiatr Res, 41*(9), 776-784. doi: 10.1016/j.jpsychires.2006.05.005

Phillips, M. L., Marks, I. M., Senior, C., Lythgoe, D., O'Dwyer, A. M., Meehan, O., et al. (2000). A differential neural response in obsessive-compulsive disorder patients with washing compared with checking symptoms to disgust. *Psychol Med, 30*(5), 1037-1050.

Pinto, A., Mancebo, M. C., Eisen, J. L., Pagano, M. E., & Rasmussen, S. A. (2006). The Brown Longitudinal Obsessive Compulsive Study: Clinical features and symptoms of the sample at intake. *J Clin Psychiatry, 67*(5), 703-711.

Pujol, J., Soriano-Mas, C., Alonso, P., Cardoner, N., Menchon, J. M., Deus, J., et al. (2004). Mapping structural brain alterations in obsessive-compulsive disorder. *Arch Gen Psychiatry, 61*(7), 720-730. doi: 10.1001/archpsyc.61.7.720

Rettew, D. C., Swedo, S. E., Leonard, H. L., Lenane, M. C., & Rapoport, J. L. (1992). Obsessions and compulsions across time in 79 children and adolescents with obsessive-compulsive disorder. *J Am Acad Child Adolesc Psychiatry, 31*(6), 1050-1056. doi: 10.1097/00004583-199211000-00009

Rosario-Campos, M. C., Leckman, J. F., Mercadante, M. T., Shavitt, R. G., Prado, H. S., Sada, P., et al. (2001). Adults with early-onset obsessive-compulsive disorder. *Am J Psychiatry, 158*(11), 1899-1903.

Rosenberg, D. R., & Keshavan, M. S. (1998). Toward a neurodevelopmental model of of obsessive--compulsive disorder. *Biol Psychiatry, 43*(9), 623-640.

Rosenberg, D. R., Keshavan, M. S., O'Hearn, K. M., Dick, E. L., Bagwell, W. W., Seymour, A. B., et al. (1997). Frontostriatal measurement in treatment-naive children with obsessive-compulsive disorder. *Arch Gen Psychiatry, 54*(9), 824-830.

Royet, J. P., Plailly, J., Delon-Martin, C., Kareken, D. A., & Segebarth, C. (2003). fMRI of emotional responses to odors: influence of hedonic valence and judgment, handedness, and gender. *Neuroimage, 20*(2), 713-728. doi: 10.1016/S1053-8119(03)00388-4

Rufer, M., Fricke, S., Moritz, S., Kloss, M., & Hand, I. (2006). Symptom dimensions in obsessive-compulsive disorder: Prediction of cognitive-behavior therapy outcome. *Acta Psychiatr Scand, 113*(5), 440-446. doi: 10.1111/j.1600-0447.2005.00682.x

Rufer, M., Grothusen, A., Mass, R., Peter, H., & Hand, I. (2005). Temporal stability of symptom dimensions in adult patients with obsessive-compulsive disorder. *J Affect Disord, 88*(1), 99-102. doi: 10.1016/j.jad.2005.06.003

Samuels, J. F., Bienvenu, O. J., 3rd, Pinto, A., Fyer, A. J., McCracken, J. T., Rauch, S. L., et al. (2007). Hoarding in obsessive-compulsive disorder: results from the OCD Collaborative Genetics Study. *Behav Res Ther, 45*(4), 673-686. doi: S0005-7967(06)00118-5

Samuels, J. F., Bienvenu, O. J., Riddle, M. A., Cullen, B. A., Grados, M. A., Liang, K. Y., et al. (2002). Hoarding in obsessive compulsive disorder: Results from a case-control study. *Behav Res Ther, 40*(5), 517-528.

Samuels, J. F., Shugart, Y. Y., Grados, M. A., Willour, V. L., Bienvenu, O. J., Greenberg, B. D., et al. (2007). Significant linkage to compulsive hoarding on chromosome 14 in families with obsessive-compulsive disorder: results from the OCD Collaborative Genetics Study. *Am J Psychiatry, 164*(3), 493-499.

Saxena, S., Brody, A. L., Schwartz, J. M., & Baxter, L. R. (1998). Neuroimaging and frontal-subcortical circuitry in obsessive-compulsive disorder. *Br J Psychiatry Suppl*(35), 26-37.

Saxena, S., Maidment, K. M., Vapnik, T., Golden, G., Rishwain, T., Rosen, R. M., et al. (2002). Obsessive-compulsive hoarding: symptom severity and response to multimodal treatment. *J Clin Psychiatry, 63*(1), 21-27.

Scahill, L., Riddle, M. A., McSwiggin-Hardin, M., Ort, S. I., King, R. A., Goodman, W. K., et al. (1997). Children's Yale-Brown Obsessive Compulsive Scale: reliability and validity. *J.Am.Acad.Child Adolesc.Psychiatry, 36*(6), 844-852.

Scarone, S., Colombo, C., Livian, S., Abbruzzese, M., Ronchi, P., Locatelli, M., et al. (1992). Increased right caudate nucleus size in obsessive-compulsive disorder: detection with magnetic resonance imaging. [Comparative Study]. *Psychiatry Res, 45*(2), 115-121.

Shapira, N. A., Liu, Y., He, A. G., Bradley, M. M., Lessig, M. C., James, G. A., et al. (2003). Brain activation by disgust-inducing pictures in obsessive-compulsive disorder. *Biol Psychiatry, 54*(7), 751-756.

Small, D. M., Gregory, M. D., Mak, Y. E., Gitelman, D., Mesulam, M. M., & Parrish, T. (2003). Dissociation of neural representation of intensity and affective valuation in human gustation. *Neuron, 39*(4), 701-711.

Sobin, C., Blundell, M., Weiller, F., Gavigan, C., Haiman, C., & Karayiorgou, M. (1999). Phenotypic characteristics of obsessive-compulsive disorder ascertained in adulthood. *J Psychiatr Res, 33*(3), 265-273.

Stein, D. J., Andersen, E. W., & Overo, K. F. (2007). Response of symptom dimensions in obsessive-compulsive disorder to treatment with citalopram or placebo. *Rev Bras Psiquiatr, 29*(4), 303-307.

Steketee, G., & Frost, R. (2003). Compulsive hoarding: current status of the research. *Clin Psychol Rev, 23*(7), 905-927.

Stewart, S. E., Rosario, M. C., Baer, L., Carter, A. S., Brown, T. A., Scharf, J. M., et al. (2008). Four-factor structure of obsessive-compulsive disorder symptoms in children, adolescents, and adults. *J Am Acad Child Adolesc Psychiatry, 47*(7), 763-772. doi: 10.1097/CHI.0b013e318172ef1e

Storch, E. A., Lack, C., Merlo, L. J., Marien, W. E., Geffken, G. R., Grabill, K., et al. (2007). Associations between miscellaneous symptoms and symptom dimensions: an examination of pediatric obsessive-compulsive disorder. *Behav Res Ther, 45*(11), 2593-2603. doi: 10.1016/j.brat.2007.06.001

Storch, E. A., Merlo, L. J., Larson, M. J., Bloss, C. S., Geffken, G. R., Jacob, M. L., et al. (2008). Symptom dimensions and cognitive-behavioural therapy outcome for pediatric obsessive-compulsive disorder. *Acta Psychiatr Scand, 117*(1), 67-75. doi: 10.1111/j.1600-0447.2007.01113.x

Summerfeldt, L. J., Richter, M. A., Antony, M. M., & Swinson, R. P. (1999). Symptom structure in obsessive-compulsive disorder: A confirmatory factor-analytic study. [Research Support, Non-U.S. Gov't]. *Behav Res Ther, 37*(4), 297-311.

Tallis, F., Pratt, P., & Jamani, N. (1999). Obsessive compulsive disorder, checking, and non-verbal memory: a neuropsychological investigation. *Behav Res Ther, 37*(2), 161-166.

Taylor, S. F., Liberzon, I., & Koeppe, R. A. (2000). The effect of graded aversive stimuli on limbic and visual activation. *Neuropsychologia, 38*(10), 1415-1425.

Tolin, D. F., Fitch, K. E., Frost, R., & Steketee, G. (2010). Family informants' perceptions of insight in compulsive hoarding. *Cogn Ther Res, 34*, 69-81.

Torresan, R. C., Ramos-Cerqueira, A. T., Shavitt, R. G., do Rosario, M. C., de Mathis, M. A., Miguel, E. C., et al. (2013). Symptom dimensions, clinical course and comorbidity in men and women with obsessive-compulsive disorder. *Psychiatry Res.* doi: 10.1016/j.psychres.2012.12.006

Tukel, R., Polat, A., Genc, A., Bozkurt, O., & Atli, H. (2004). Gender-related differences among Turkish patients with obsessive-compulsive disorder. *Compr Psychiatry, 45*(5), 362-366. doi: 10.1016/j.comppsych.2004.06.006

van den Heuvel, O. A., Remijnse, P. L., Mataix-Cols, D., Vrenken, H., Groenewegen, H. J., Uylings, H. B., et al. (2009). The major symptom dimensions of obsessive-compulsive disorder are mediated by partially distinct neural systems. *Brain, 132*(Pt 4), 853-868. doi: 10.1093/brain/awn267

Wheaton, M., Timpano, K. R., Lasalle-Ricci, V. H., & Murphy, D. (2008). Characterizing the hoarding phenotype in individuals with OCD: associations with comorbidity, severity and gender. *J Anxiety Disord, 22*(2), 243-252. doi: 10.1016/j.janxdis.2007.01.015

Zald, D. H., & Pardo, J. V. (2000). Functional neuroimaging of the olfactory system in humans. *Int J Psychophysiol, 36*(2), 165-181.

Zhang, H., Leckman, J. F., Tsai, C. P., Kidd, K. K., & Rosaio-Campos, M. C. (2002). Genome wide scan of hoarding in sibling pairs both diagnosed with Gilles de la Tourette syndrome. *American Jouranl of Human Genetics, 70*, 896-904.

# Chapter Four

# Cultural Manifestations of Obsessive-Compulsive Disorder

Monnica T. Williams & Ashleigh Steever

Obsessive-compulsive disorder (OCD) is a severe anxiety disorder involving distressing obsessions and repetitive compulsions. Obsessions are intrusive, unwanted thoughts, images, or impulses that increase anxiety, whereas compulsions are repetitive behaviors or mental acts used to decrease anxiety. OCD is highly disabling, with nearly two-thirds of those afflicted reporting severe role impairment (Ruscio, Stein, Chiu, & Kessler, 2010).

In the United States, the National Comorbidity Survey Replication (NCS-R) showed that approximately 1.6% of the population met criteria for OCD at some point in their lives (Kessler, Berglund, et al., 2005), with 1% of the sample meeting criteria within the last year (Kessler, Chiu, Demler, Merikangas, & Walters, 2005). The prevalence of OCD appears to be roughly consistent across ethnic groups in the US. For example, a recent epidemiological study of African and Caribbean Americans showed an OCD lifetime prevalence of 1.6% (Himle, et al., 2008). Epidemiologic studies conducted in other countries find similar rates cross-nationally (Weismann et al., 1994), as presented in Figure 1. The rates range from 0.3% in Brazil to 2.7% in Hungary. Based on the current world population (US Census Bureau, 2011), it can be estimated that 112 million people worldwide are afflicted with OCD during their lifetime.

Although many with OCD worry about cleanliness, symmetry, arranging, and perfectionism, OCD is a complex disorder that can manifest itself in a variety of symptom dimensions, including unacceptable thoughts, ruminations about morality, and hoarding (e.g., Bloch et al, 2008; Williams et al., 2011). It is important that cultural differences be taken into account when conducting psychopathology research, as culture can have profound effects on the manifestation of psychopathology, particularly in a disorder as multi-faceted as OCD. Culture can be defined as a set of attitudes, behaviors, and symbols shared

63

by a large group of people that is usually communicated generationally (Shiraev & Levy, 2010).

The aim of the current study is to present a survey of the cross-cultural manifestation of OCD worldwide, based on a systematic review of the psychological literature. Critical summaries and analyses were taken of featured texts and compiled to illustrate differences and similarities in symptom presentation cross-culturally. We include an examination of differences found based on factors such as ethnicity, nationality, and religion. In the United States, OCD tends to be regarded by laypeople as a quirky disorder that results in excessive cleaning, checking, and arranging. Preconceived notions about this disorder may affect the symptom profiles of treatment-seeking samples (Sussman, 2003). Therefore, we present findings from epidemiological studies whenever possible, followed by findings from large national multi-site studies and meta-analyses. When such studies are not available for a given population, findings are presented from single site studies.

## OCD in European Americans & Western Cultures

An investigation of OCD in the US by the National Comorbidity Survey Replication (NCS-R; Ruscio et al., 2010), found a wide range of symptoms, illustrated in Table 1. This was an epidemiological sample that was assessed for psychopathology using a computer-guided structured interview. It should be noted, however, that the symptom categories used in the NCS-R were not empirically derived; rather, they represent symptoms commonly reported by individuals diagnosed with OCD. These findings are subject to a number of study limitations, including a small sample size (N=73), problems with the computerized data collection procedures, and the lack of a clear categorical distinction between obsessive and compulsive symptoms.

Additional information about symptom profiles can be garnered from clinical samples. Symptom distributions obtained from the DSM-IV Field Trial of OCD, a large treatment-seeking sample (N=431; Foa, Kozak, Goodman, Hollander, Jenike, & Rasmussen, 1995) differed from NCS-R findings. For example, the data from the NCS-R shows that 62.3% reported Hoarding as a symptom while in the DSM-IV Field Trial sample this symptom was only reported by 4.8% of the participants. This same trend is seen again with the symptom of Checking, with only 28.2% of the sample reporting it versus 79.3% in the NCS-R sample. Moreover, the symptom of Ordering was only reported by 5.7% of the DSM-IV Field Trial participants, while in the NCS-R data set it was ten times as prevalent at 57%.

Table 1
*Distribution of OCD Symptoms in the NCS-R*

| | *% of OCD Cases Reporting each Symptom* |
|---|---|
| Checking | 79.3 |
| Hoarding | 62.3 |
| Ordering | 57.0 |
| Moral | 43.0 |
| Sexual/religious | 30.2 |
| Contamination | 25.7 |
| Harming | 24.2 |
| Illness | 14.3 |
| Other | 19.0 |

*Note. Totals exceed 100% given that each participant was allowed to choose multiple obsessions and compulsions.*

These differences are partially accounted for by differences in study methodology and category classification. The DSM-IV Field Trial reported percentages based on the total number of primary symptoms reported by participants. Additionally, Ruscio et al. drew from a community-derived sample whereas Foa et al. utilized clinical samples. Thus, caution must be taken when generalizing from one study to the other, given that the treatment-seeking individuals in the Foa et al. study may not be representative of the OCD population as a whole. Secondly, methodology differed with regard to diagnostic procedures. Ruscio and colleagues utilized the World Health Organization's Composite International Diagnostic Interview (CIDI 3.0; Kessler & Üsütun, 2004), intended to be administered by lay-persons, whereas Foa and colleagues used the OCD section of the Structured Clinical Interview for DSM-III-R (SCID; First, Spitzer, Gibbon, & Williams, 1997) and an expanded version of the Yale-Brown Obsessive Compulsive Symptom Checklist (YBOCS-SC; Goodman et al., 1989), which is administered by clinicians experienced with OCD.

Most studies of symptom dimensions in US samples utilize the YBOCS-SC, as it includes a comprehensive list of obsessions and compulsions that represent the majority of OC symptoms observed clinically in Western samples (Goodman et al., 1989). Since its development, there have been several attempts to establish an empirically-based classification system that corresponds to the symptoms listed within it. Baer (1994) was the first to conduct a principal components analysis (PCA) of the 13 major Y-BOCS-SC symptom categories. Three factors were identified: Symmetry/Hoarding, Contamination/Cleaning, and Pure Obsessions.

Pure Obsessions corresponded to individuals with religious, aggressive, and/or sexual obsessions, for whom no compulsions were identified. In a meta-analysis of 21 clinical studies involving 5,124 participants, Bloch, Landeros-Weisenberger, Rosario, Pittenge, and Leckman (2008) found few differences with respect to symptom dimensions cross-culturally, especially among the three quarters of the studies (76%) from Western nations. Still, while most of those studies found a four-factor model, more recent studies that have included other types of compulsions, such as mental compulsions and reassurance, tend to find five specific dimensions: Contamination/Cleaning, Hoarding, Symmetry/Ordering, Taboo Thoughts/Mental Compulsions, and Doubt/Checking (e.g., Abramowitz et al., 2003; Pinto et al., 2007; Williams et al., 2011).

In Western cultures, it is widely believed that OCD is a mental disorder caused by biological factors (Coles & Coleman, 2010). Washing, checking, and symmetry related dimensions are more quickly recognized as OCD symptoms than aggressive, religious or sexual symptoms. It also appears that the taboo obsessions are less well-accepted, which could lead to delays in treatment seeking or hiding symptoms due to increased fears of stigma and shame (Simonds & Thorpe, 2003). Thus it is possible that this symptom presentation is underrepresented in the treatment-seeking population. Alternately, it could be that people with these symptoms may be more motivated to seek treatment due to the high-levels of distress caused by such thoughts (*e.g.*, Williams, Wetterneck, Tellawi, & Duque, in press). More work is needed to determine the impact of these issues on help-seeking.

## OCD in African Americans

Until recently, not much was known about African Americans with OCD, as US ethnic minorities have been underrepresented in many types of OCD studies, including the factor analytic studies included in meta-analyses such as those described above (Williams, Powers, Yun, & Foa, 2010). Hatch, Friedman, and Paradis (1996) were among the first to report their observations about OCD in African Americans in a naturalistic study of treatment-seeking adults in an urban clinic. The authors noted differences in treatment-seeking patterns, as only 2% of Black patients out of their entire clientele were diagnosed with OCD. This could be attributed to a lack of treatment-seeking in African Americans, who instead tended to obtain help from informal social networks such as members of the clergy. It is also possible that OCD may be misdiagnosed in African Americans, especially in cases where the obsessional content is unusual. African Americans tend to be over diagnosed with psychotic disorders compared to European Americans and are more likely to hospitalized, even after controlling for severity of illness and SES (Snowden, Hastings, & Alvidrez, 2009; Whaley & Hall, 2009).

Thus, unusual symptoms may be considered symptoms of psychosis rather than OCD (i.e., Ninan & Shelton, 1993).

New insights into African American health have been uncovered through a series of investigations sponsored by the Program for Research on Black Americans. The National Survey of American Life (NSAL; Heeringa et al., 2004) is the most in-depth study of mental health disorders in African Americans and other U.S. racial and ethnic minorities ever completed. The study primarily drew from three nationally representative adult samples, including African Americans (N=3,570), Blacks of Caribbean descent (N=1,623), and Non-Hispanic Whites (N=1,006). In examining OCD specifically in this group, Himle et al. (2008) found that 1.6% met diagnostic criteria for the disorder. OCD is highly associated with overall mental health impairment, and the majority of the participants also met the criteria for at least one other lifetime psychiatric disorder, with 93.2% of African Americans and 95.6% of Caribbean Blacks also experiencing symptoms for major depressive disorder, social phobia, and generalized anxiety disorder, among others. This is not unexpected given that diagnoses of OCD have often been found to overlap with other psychological disorders (Ruscio et al., 2010; Saleem & Mahmood, 2009).

Williams, Proetto, Casiano, and Franklin (2012) conducted the largest study of clinically diagnosed African Americans with OCD to date (N=75). In studying the characteristics of the sample, six discrete symptom dimensions were identified, which included Contamination/Washing, Hoarding, Sexual/Reassurance, Aggression/Mental Compulsions, Symmetry/Perfectionism, and Doubt/Checking. Factors identified were similar to those of previous studies in primarily White samples, however African Americans with OCD reported contamination symptoms at double the rate of European Americans, and were twice as likely to report excessive concerns about animals. These findings were compared to symptom data from the NSAL study, which also noted increased contamination concerns (Williams, Elstein, Buckner, Abelson, & Himle, 2012). The study found cultural differences with respect to cleanliness and animal concerns, which is consistent with findings among non-clinical samples (Williams, Abramowitz, & Olatuni, 2012; Williams & Turkheimer, 2007). A higher level of obsessions and compulsions linked to cleanliness may be culturally relevant as African Americans historically experienced segregation, where it was thought that European Americans would be contaminated through close contact or sharing items (i.e., drinking fountains, swimming pools, etc.) Additionally, Williams et al. found that participants with a lower SES reported greater concern with contamination, which is consistent with the hypothesis that lower incomes could be associated with more exposure to contaminants, resulting in greater contamination concerns and cleaning behaviors in this cultural group (Williams & Turkheimer, 2007; Williams, Abramowitz, & Olatunji, 2011).

## OCD in Western Christian Samples

Abramowitz, Deacon, Woods, and Tolin (2004) conducted a study of undergraduates to better understand the relationship between Protestant religiosity and an assortment of OCD symptoms, such as washing, checking, and the importance of controlling one's thoughts. The participants were given self-report questionnaires to determine their degree of religiosity and the prevalence of OCD symptoms. The resulting feedback divided the students into three groups of varying religiosity (from atheist/agnostic to highly religious). Students reporting high levels of religiosity reported more obsessional symptoms than the moderately religious and atheist/agnostic subgroups (Abramowitz et al., 2004). The highly religious participants also reported greater levels of certain cognitions like the importance of their thoughts as well as the need to control them relative to the reports of the other participants. The authors referenced the Book of Matthew in the Bible with respect to the Sermon on the Mount, in which Jesus Christ makes the assertion that the thought of committing a sinful act is equal to having already done it. This could help explain the importance placed on thought control for the highly religious participants.

In a similar study by Sica, Novara, and Sanavio (2002), the aim was to understand the role of religion in OCD phenomenology. A community sample of Italian participants ascribing to the Catholic faith was surveyed for degree of religiosity and prevalence of certain OCD cognitions and obsessions. Those participants who reported a high or medium degree of religiosity also reported high levels of obsessions like the importance of thought control compared to those reporting low levels of religiosity. The authors cited Catholic precepts such as the equality of thoughts and behaviors, as well as Catholic teaching about purity and perfectionism as the reason for these findings. In sum, the findings indicate differences with respect to the importance of thought control and the idea that thoughts and actions are interchangeable.

## OCD in Jewish Communities

Scrupulosity is a form of OCD in which individual obsessions are focused on moral or religious issues like sin and divine retribution (Huppert, Siev, & Kushner, 2007). As Judaism is a religion oriented around traditions and customarily focuses on rituals and laws that are fundamental to Jewish life, many Jewish OCD sufferers experience scrupulosity and will rely upon rabbinical help with their symptoms. Huppert et al. (2007) found that in treating Jewish patients who suffer from scrupulosity, there may be difficulties in distinguishing between religious rituals and compulsive behaviors. What is normally a religious ritual, if found in the extreme and outside of the religious context, could be scrupulosity rather than simply increased religious devotion.

Rosmarin, Pirutinsky, and Siev (2010) conducted a community study that examined attitudes towards OCD symptoms in Orthodox and non-Orthodox Jews in the US. Participants were given descriptions of either religious (scrupulosity) or non-religious OCD symptoms. When confronted with the religious themes in the descriptions (such as excessive prayer, repeated crossings, and sky-gazing toward God) the Orthodox participants more often recognized the scrupulosity as OCD and recommend psychological treatment than did the non-Orthodox participants. This was in direct opposition to the hypothesis set forth in the study, which was that Orthodox Jews, because of the value they place on careful adherence to religious laws, would be less likely to recognize scrupulosity than the Non-Orthodox Jews and less likely to recommend some form of treatment. One reason could have been that the Orthodox participants had a more stringent awareness of normal religious practices due to a more "strict adherence to religious law" and were thereby able to identify scrupulosity more easily. Conversely, the non-Orthodox participants may have been less likely to identify scrupulosity as OCD or recommend psychological evaluation due to not wanting to offend other religious individuals or "disrespecting bona fide religious standards" (Rosmarin et al., 2010).

## OCD in Middle Eastern Islamic Cultures

Several studies about the cultural components of OCD and its symptom expression have been conducted in Middle Eastern countries where there is a high Islamic population. In the first study of its kind to originate in Saudi Arabia, Mahghoub and Abdel-Hafeiz (1991) found strong religious themes in the OCD symptomatology of a conservative Muslim clinical sample. The most often reported symptoms were obsessions with prayers and washing (50%), contamination (41%), and faith (34%). Obsessions with prayers and washings could have stemmed from religious practices that included praying and washing oneself systematically in a practice called Al-woodo, as the body must be clean before prayers can be made. The authors cite the frequency of these actions, and the need for their proper execution as being possibly causative of repeating, washing, and checking compulsions that were noted at 50%, 37%, and 31%, respectively in the sample.

A study by Okasha, Saad, Khalil, and Dawla (1994) reported the content of obsessions in a clinical Egyptian sample to be most often religious in nature, with 60% reporting obsessions with religious themes. To explain this, the researchers cited the tendency of the participants to feel the need to ward off evil spirits through various religious rituals and repeated sayings. This could account for the high frequency of religious obsessions as well as repeating compulsions, which were reported by 67.7% of the participants. The majority of participants in this study were rated on the Y-BOCS as having moderate to severe symptom presentation, which is said to indicate an especially high tolerance in Egyptian patients for psychiatric morbidity. The study also found that in most cases the mental health professional is a last resort for help, with the participants instead seeking help in an informal social network of native healers, friends, elderly family members, and religious people and then a general practitioner (Okasha et al., 1994). These same types of help-seeking attitudes have been observed in the African American treatment-seeking community (Hatch et al., 1996) and suggest a preference for culturally and religiously relevant assistance with issues concerning psychological disorders including OCD.

In a similar non-clinical study by Yorulmaz and Işık (2011), the results were much the same. The majority of the participants, who were of Turkish descent, reported high levels of obsessions related to fear of contamination and cleanliness. The dominant religion in Turkey is Islam, which the researchers described as "ritualistic and rule-based," and as such the participants were subject to certain rigid beliefs about purity and cleanliness. The authors in particular described an aspect of Islam known as "waswas," which is religious doubt, and how this concept could affect the content of the obsessions reported.

Participants in the study also experienced what is known as Thought-Action Fusion (TAF). Also noted in Western cultures (Abramowitz et al., 2004), this symptom highlights the importance of thoughts and the need to control them. This could be explained by the prevalence of "superficial similarities" between certain beliefs in Islam and characteristics of OCD. In Yorulmaz and Işık (2011), although all of the participants reported an Islamic affiliation, the differences found in symptom presentation here are culturally significant because they exist between participants of reportedly equivalent ethnic descent. The participants who had lived in Turkey since birth reported higher levels of symptom expression, particularly with respect to contamination/cleaning, when compared to Bulgarian-born Turkish participants, and Turkish remigrants. The authors cite the possibility of the rigorous Islamic institution in Turkey as being explanatory of the higher levels of symptomatology for those participants who were born and raised there.

Ghassenzadeh, Mojtabai, Khamseh, Ebrahimkhani, Issazadegan and Saif-Nobakht (2002), found the most commonly reported symptoms in their Iranian sample to be obsessive doubts and indecisiveness, as well as a washing compulsion. There were also marked differences in reported symptoms between males and females, with males reporting blasphemous thoughts and compulsions concerning orderliness and females reporting greater concerns with impurity and contamination as well as obsessive thoughts centered on personal impurity and washing compulsions. The authors noted that 70% of the female participants were housewives. This could possibly influence the content of obsessions as cleaning would be a part of daily chores associated with housework. The authors also note the strong cultural affiliation to religion in Iran and the spiritual symbolism of cleanliness and cleaning behaviors as a way to prepare oneself for daily prayers.

Al-Salaim and Loewenthal (2011) also found religious themes in the symptoms of a sample of 15 young women suffering with OCD in Saudi Arabia. There were trends in help-seeking behavior, with all of the participants reporting first seeking assistance from a religious leader in the community. This was described as either a man with a long beard or a woman who covers her face, and was accompanied with the use of religious rhetoric (e.g., quoting the Qura'an or teachings of the prophet Muhammad). This was preferable, as a religious professional was considered less likely to manipulate or harm a patient. One of the causes of OCD as reported by some of the participants was an "evil eye," which is described as being caused by a person admiring one of his or her own possessions. The authors also found that religious symptoms were reported in the sample as being more disturbing than other OCD symptoms, and in some instances were the reason for seeking help with the disorder.

In Bahrain, where the state religion is Islam, Shooka, Al-Haddad, and Raees (1998) found religious themes in both obsessions and compulsions in a clinical sample, with religious content in 40% of the symptoms. Obsessional thoughts, the most commonly reported form of obsession (68%), were followed by an obsession with images (26%) and doubt (12%). Content of obsessions also reflected obsessions with dirt/contamination and sexual themes, at 38% and 32%, respectively. Shook et al. also found a disproportionate male to female ratio in the sample with women making up 74% of participants as well as higher levels of reported severity of symptoms in females. The authors believed this could have influenced the help-seeking behaviors of the women in the study as women would have sought help for more severe symptoms. There were also higher levels of the obsession with cleaning and washing in the women, a trend we have seen in other cultures (Labad et al., 2008; Jaisoorya, et al., 2009); it is also worth noting that 81% of the female sample worked in the home, similar to Ghassenzadeh et al. (2002).

Saleem and Mahmood (2009) found the most frequently reported compulsion in a clinical sample of participants from Pakistan, a country where the dominant religion is also Islam, to be hand-washing. This compulsion was reported by 97% of participants, and 82% experienced a fear of germs. This is, again, a compulsion related to cleanliness and purity. The researchers discussed an aspect of Islamic culture called "Napak," which is a feeling of contamination that includes religious connotations of being unclean or unholy. Two-thirds (67%) of the participants in this study added Napak to the questionnaire as an item within the broader category of Contamination. When a Muslim is in the state of Napak, he is unable to take part in religious rituals until he has cleaned himself systematically in an action is called ablution.

An emphasis on cleanliness, purity, and religion appears to be normative in cultures with Islamic religious backgrounds. It is important to note, however, that when the actions surrounding such beliefs are committed in excess, and the beliefs become obsessions, they can then become culturally significant aspects of OCD symptomatology.

## OCD in India

Studies in India have reported typical OCD obsessions to include contamination, aggression, symmetry, sexual, religious, and pathological doubt. Girishchandra and Khanna (2001) found that the most commonly reported symptoms in a clinical sample of 202 Indian participants were doubts about having performed daily activities (64.9%) and contamination concerns about dirt and germs (50%). In a comprehensive review of the Indian literature, Reddy, Jaideep, Khanna, and Srinath (2005) also observed that contamination concerns and pathological doubt were highly prevalent. Reddy et al. found the lifetime prevalence rate of OCD to be approximately 0.6% in India. This is relatively low compared to the lifetime prevalence rate in other countries (Figure 1). Girishchandra and Sumant (2001) also noted a disproportionate number of males in the study compared to females at a ratio of over two to one.

Jaisoorya, Reddy, Srinath, and Thennarasu (2009) found differences in in their clinical study with regard to symptom presentation between men and women of an Indian sample. Male participants had a tendency to report sexual and symmetry obsessions coupled with checking and bizarre compulsions, while symptoms surrounding dirt, contamination, and cleaning were reported more often by females, a finding similar to Western samples (e.g., Labad et al., 2008). The authors commented that women were more often subjected to unclean conditions and as such could be more concerned with contamination than males. In Western samples, it has been suggested that biological make-up and brain chemistry, specifically greater numbers of steroid hormone receptors the female brain may be causing a sexual dimorphism (physical difference), which could possibly explain the higher level of cleaning and contamination concerns (Labad et al., 2008). The authors also mentioned that environmental differences could mediate the differences found, such as females being socialized to do a greater share of the domestic work such as housecleaning.

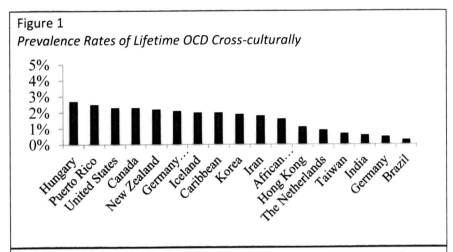

Figure 1
*Prevalence Rates of Lifetime OCD Cross-culturally*

*Figure presents the lifetime prevalence rates of OCD as reported cross-culturally (Fontenelle et al.,2006; Himle et al., 2008; Ruscio et al., 2010; Reddy et al., 2005).*

The majority of participants in the study by Jaisoorya et al. were men, a phenomenon also noted in Girishchandra and Sumant (2001). Historically, in Western samples, there has been no difference in help-seeking between men and women with OCD (Goodwin et al., 2002; Torres et al., 2007). In the Indian sample, the authors commented that this was possibly due to differences in male versus female societal status, and greater access to medical care as a result.

In a study by Chowdhury, Mukherjee, Ghosh, and Chowdhury (2003) the authors found an association between a culture bound disorder termed "puppy pregnancy" and OCD. Cases uncovered in rural West Bengal India describe fears of being pregnant with a canine embryo after having been bitten, and symptoms are comparable to those found in OCD, unusual content notwithstanding. Puppy pregnancy includes a fear of internal contamination (from the puppy fetus), disability (impotence due to damage to internal sexual organs), and death. One case reported a symptom reminiscent of checking after having observed a dog licking milk cans and being bitten by the same dog. Thereafter, the subject was fearful that he was being chased by a dog, and would check all milk cans, sure that they had been licked by a dog. The authors also noted obsessive thoughts involving fear of dog bites and avoidance.

In general, however, research to date has found few differences in symptom dimensions in India from those found in studies conducted in Western societies. One notable exception is Bloch et al. (2008), who noted some differences in symptom presentation for Indian participants when compared to studies of White and Non-White clinical samples. In Indian studies, the five-factor model of symptoms included one described as a need to touch, tap, and rub, which could possibly be associated with cultural traditions involving touching (*i.e.*, touching the feet of elders as a sign of respect).

## OCD in Indonesia

In Bali, which is primarily Hindu, Lemelson (2003) conducted a study of 19 patients suffering from OCD to understand the degree to which Balinese culture affected the illness experience. The most common obsession was a need-to-know obsession, which was literally the necessity of knowing the identities of passers-by. Lemelson also found obsessions surrounding themes of magic, witchcraft, and spirits, which are all religious themes entwined in the Balinese culture. These findings are different from those seen in Western studies where typical symptoms include concerns about contamination, hoarding, and checking (e.g., Foa et al., 1995).

As a caveat, it is important to note that other than in Bali, where the practiced religion is Hindu with emphases on magic, witchcraft, and ancestor worship, the main religious affiliation of Indonesia is Islam. Therefore the phenomenology of OCD in other parts of Indonesia may be more similar to findings in Islamic cultures.

## OCD in Hispanic and South American Samples

To date there have been few studies conducted that address OCD with respect to Hispanic and South American populations. Studies that have compared prevalence rates of OCD between Latino and European American populations in the US have yielded inconsistent findings. For instance, one study demonstrated no significant differences in prevalence rates between European Americans and Mexicans (Karno et al., 1989), while another found significant differences between European Americans and Puerto Ricans (Weissman et al., 1994). Studies of OCD in Latin America note a lifetime prevalence rate of 1.4% in Mexico City, 1.2% in Chile and 3.2% in Puerto Rico (Canino et al., 1987; Caraveo-Anduaga & Bermudez, 2004; Vicente, 2006).

Although there have been few studies of symptom dimensions in Hispanic Americans, one study did note greater contamination concerns in a non-clinical sample (Williams et al., 2005). In a clinical study conducted in Costa Rica, participants reported lower levels of symptom severity, including lower levels of functional impairment and lesser amounts of perceived distress, when compared to their US counterparts in the same study (Chavira, Garrido, Bagnarello, Azzam, Reus, & Mathews, 2008). The study cited a number of culturally relevant reasons for the differences, including a possible lack of psychosocial stressors in the Costa Rican sample, as the participants were from a primarily agrarian region of the country. In addition, the lower levels of perceived stress were found to possibly reflect the ability of the participants to "accommodate" their symptoms. For example, one participant reported avoiding driving due to the fear of harming others and this was easily avoided due to the ease of access in Costa Rican society (Chavira, et al., 2008).

A study conducted on a clinical sample in Rio de Janeiro outlined differences with respect to content of obsessions, as the most commonly reported obsessions included the theme of aggression, (69.7%), followed by contamination (53.5%) (Fontenelle, Mendlowicz, Marques, & Versiani, 2004). This is important because in many other cultures issues of contamination seem to overshadow others in the spectrum with respect to the OCD symptom manifestation (i.e. Matsunaga et al., 2008). The authors discussed possible reasons for the findings of their study, and cited the climbing rates of mortality and morbidity resulting from violent causes, and that the population has likely prioritized of avoiding violence. It is important to note, however, that this study is from a single site and reflects the surrounding and, in the case of Brazil, the metropolitan culture of the participants.

In a clinical study in Mexico by Nicolini, Orozco, Giuffra, Páez, Mejía, Sánchez de Carmona, Sidenberg, and de la Fuente (1997), contamination obsessions were reported by 58% of the clinical sample, making it the most common. Sexual and aggressive obsessions followed, at 31% and 13%, respectively. The proportion of men to women in the study was uneven with only approximately 37% of the sample being men. The authors, citing an earlier study, considered a cultural phenomenon in which Mexican men have the tendency to deny having a mental illness. An interesting, but marginally reported obsession, was one concerned with "treasuring," reported by 3% of the sample. Treasuring is described as keeping things (i.e., the hair from a hairbrush), and can be understood to be similar to hoarding. For an excellent review of OCD in Hispanic populations, see Wetterneck et al. (2012).

## OCD in East Asia

Matsunaga et al. (2008) noted the most common obsessions in a clinical Japanese sample as fear of contamination (48%) followed by obsessions with symmetry or exactness (42%) and aggression (36%). The most common compulsive symptoms reported were checking and washing at 47%, followed by repeating rituals at 31%. The authors' focus was more psychobiological than cultural, and the authors described "transcultural stability" in the symptom presentation of OCD. However, the researchers only compared their results with Western studies rather than results from other cultures.

The lifetime prevalence rate for OCD in Taiwan is 0.7% (Figure 1). In the first study of its kind from Taiwan, Juang and Liu (2001) found in a group of 200 outpatient Taiwanese participants the most commonly reported obsessions to be fears of contamination, pathological doubt, and a need for symmetry, at 37%, 34%, and 19%, respectively. The most commonly reported compulsions consisted of checking, washing, and orderliness/precision.

Kim, Lee, and Kim (2005) determined symptom dimensions, based on a factor analysis of the Y-BOCS-SC checklist in a clinical genetic study of Koreans with OCD. The study outlined the factors as hoarding/repeating, contamination/cleaning, aggressive/sexual, and religious/somatic. The latter two dimensions were described as "pure obsessional" due to a lack of identified corresponding compulsions. Most Western studies group these two in to a single component termed unacceptable/taboo thoughts (Bloch et al, 2008). The study also grouped the hoarding obsession together with repeating and counting compulsions, a combination not seen in a majority of Western samples. Moreover, unlike the Western samples in Bloch et al. (2008), the Korean sample did not include in any dimension an obsession with symmetry, which is also at odds with other studies originating in Asia that have shown symmetry obsessions to be among those most highly reported (Matsunaga et al., 2008; Li, Marques, Hinton, Wang, & Xiao 2009).

In the first such study to originate in mainland China, Li et al. (2009) assessed 139 patients with OCD. The study sought to determine if the five symptom dimensions documented in other studies (unacceptable/taboo thoughts, symmetry/ordering, contamination/cleaning, and hoarding) were applicable in this particular culture. The most common symptoms reported were obsessions with symmetry and contamination at 67.6% and 43.2%, respectively, followed by aggression at 31.7%. Li et al. cited a cultural propensity towards harmonious interpersonal relationships due to the presence of Confucianism and its precepts in China as a possible explanation for fewer reports of aggression when compared to other cultures. The authors also noted a disproportionate ratio of males to females in the demographics of the study (almost 2:1). It was unclear whether this could have possibly been mediated by cultural norms regarding help-seeking behavior in women as the authors noted that the males of the sample seemed more willing to participate than their female counterparts. This same trend has been observed in a number of Indian samples as well (Jaisoorya et al., 2009; Girishchandra & Sumant, 2001).

In Eastern cultures such as China and Japan there is a cultural emphasis on conformity, collectivism, and harmony (Li et al., 2009). An emphasis on symmetry may reflect these tenets to some degree, and cultural norms involving conformity are instilled from an early age in some Asian cultures. Nonetheless, there are some important differences in symptoms between Chinese and Japanese with OCD, as reported by Liu, Cui, and Fang (2008). After studying two groups of patients hospitalized with OCD, the authors concluded that aggressive and contamination obsessions were more common in Japanese than Chinese OCD sufferers, while religious and symmetry/exactness obsessions are more common among Chinese patients. Likewise, Japanese OCD patients were more likely to have cleaning/washing and ordering/arranging compulsions, while Chinese counterparts were more likely to have checking compulsions. Perhaps these differences are reflective of the greater emphasis on symmetry in Chinese culture than Japanese culture (Li et al., 2009; Kim et al., 2005).

## Discussion

Through this review we have described differences in OCD symptomatology that appear to be associated with culture. Obsessional content often stems from that which is culturally relevant, resulting in a profound effect on symptomatology that cannot be ignored.

*Religious Differences*

In Christian samples the most often reported symptoms were obsessions with contamination and thought control. There was also an emphasis on perfectionism in the Catholic subgroup. As discussed earlier, the presence of religious ritual in the symptomatology of OCD is generally a manifestation of that ritual in excess of cultural norms. In the Jewish subgroup, the content of obsessions was also of a religious nature (Huppert et al., 2007), and involved themes of morality and divine retribution. There were differences in symptom recognition and thus help-seeking behaviors between Ultra-Orthodox Jews and their less observant counterparts. In Middle Eastern cultures we see high Islamic affiliation and symptom dimensions that reflect this (e.g., Okasha et al., 1994). The content of obsessions in the Islamic subgroup was centered on purity and religious themes (e.g., Okasha et al., 1994; Abramowitz et al., 2004). The obsession with physical cleanliness in the symptomatology of highly religious cultures could be a manifestation of the emphasis on spiritual purity within the society. OCD in Near Eastern countries tends to also reflect religious beliefs, as well as familial and societal values (e.g., kissing the feet of respected elders) that are an integral part of the culture. Jaisoorya et al. (2009) cited a possible link between Hinduism, the dominant religion in India, and the prevalence of obsessions with cleaning and contamination found in multiple other studies (Girishchandra & Sumant, 2011; Reddy et al., 2005).

*Regional Differences*

Western studies have shown symptom dimensions that are generally centered around a four or five factor model, with an emphasis on contamination/cleaning, hoarding, symmetry/ordering, taboo thoughts/mental compulsions, and doubt/checking (Abramowitz et al., 2003; Blotch et al., 2008). There is, however, a dearth of literature concerning differences in symptom dimensions among ethnic minorities, such as African Americans (Williams et al., 2010). In Hispanic and Latin American groups, themes of contamination and aggression were prominent. Indian samples emphasized themes concerning contamination and pathological doubt, as well as differences in the symptom dimensions reported by men and women. In East Asian groups, there were greater concerns with contamination and symmetry. Cultural differences were noted between Japan and China, with china reporting greater needs for symmetry, and Japan reporting greater obsessions with contamination and aggression (Liu et al. 2008). In general, there seem to be thematic elements that cluster in certain regions and religious groups across the world.

*Similarities in Symptoms*

Most of the studies presented here exhibit some type of cross-cultural similarity in addition to noted differences. Almost all of the presented studies and surrounding cultures include contamination fears as a primary dimension (e.g., Nicolini et al., 1997; Okasha et al., 1994; Reddy et al., 2005). Fear of contamination manifests as hand washing compulsions, prevalent in many cultures (Buckner et al., 2011; Okasha et al., 1994; Kim et al., 2005; Jaisoorya et al., 2009). Each of the 21 studies included in the meta-analysis performed by Bloch et al. (2008) contained a symptom factor that included hoarding compulsions and obsessions, although hoarding was not emphasized in any studies cross-culturally. Each of these symptoms was also found to in the NCS-R, thus it is not surprising that some authors cite a "transcultural stability" in the symptomatology of the disorder (Matsunaga et al., 2008). Matsunaga et al. suggest biology as a determining factor in the expression of specific OCD symptoms, and highlight similarities across cultures. The presence of symptom dimensions such as contamination fears and hoarding that are salient features in multiple cultural contexts supports this hypothesis. Additionally, Kim et al. (2005) found differences between the two genotypic groups with respect to religious/somatic obsessions, which provide additional evidence for a biological basis for symptom dimensions.

*Limitations*

It should be noted that the findings herein are limited by the available literature. In some cases the studies presented are single-site studies and limited in sample size.

Furthermore, many of the studies presented are limited based upon use of the Y-BOCS-SC in determining symptom dimensions. The individual items that comprise the measure were selected based on clinical observations in Western cultures. Furthermore, the *a priori* structure of the Y-BOCS-SC measure causes it to rely upon fixed categories of symptoms instead of individual symptoms as they are presented. Thus the Y-BOCS-SC could potentially restrict recognition of cross-cultural differences in symptomatology.

*Future Directions*

The importance of cultural context in the diagnosis and treatment of OCD is undeniable. Limited extant literature has restricted this study to some measure, and more research is needed to determine the extent to which culture and beliefs can magnify, diminish, or change the symptom presentation and experience of OCD for those diagnosed. There is also a dearth of research in certain regions and cultures that should be addressed. For example, there is no literature available from an African sample except the highly Muslim Egyptian region and White South Africa (e.g., Stein et al., 2008), as well as a lack of literature pertaining to differences in the symptom presentation of Hispanic Americans. The implications herein are important for diagnosis and the development of empirically supported treatments for individuals of different cultural backgrounds as well as for determining the applicability of contemporary literature to diverse cultural groups.

*Acknowledgements: The authors would like to thank Beth Mugno, M.A., and Carolina Santillán, Ph.D. for assistance with the literature review.*

## References

Abramowitz, J. S., Deacon, B. J., Woods, C. M., & Tolin, D. F. (2004). Association between protestant religiosity and obsessive-compulsive symptoms and cognitions. *Depression and Anxiety*, 20(2), 70-76. doi:10.1002/da.20021

Bloch M.H., Landeros-Weisenberger, A., Rosario, M.C., Pittenge, C., & Leckman, J.F. (2008). Meta-analysis of the symptom structure of obsessive-compulsive disorder. *American Journal of Psychiatry*, *165*, 1532–1542. doi:10.1176/appi.ajp.2008.08020320

Chavira, D. A., Garrido, H., Bagnarello, M., Azzam, A., Reus, V. I., & Mathews, C. A. (2008). A comparative study of obsessive-compulsive disorder in Costa Rica and the United States. *Depression and Anxiety*, 25(7), 609-619. doi:10.1002/da.20357

Coles, M. E. & Coleman, S.L. (2010). Barriers to treatment seeking for anxiety disorders: initial data on the role of mental health literacy. *Depression and Anxiety*, *27*, 63–71. doi:10.1002/da.20620

Foa, E. B., Kozak, M. J., Goodman, W. K., Hollander, E., Jenike, M. A., & Rasmussen, S. A. (1995). DSM-IV field trial: Obsessive-compulsive disorder. *American Journal of Psychiatry, 152*(1), 90–96.

Fontenelle, L. F., Mendlowicz, M. V., Marques, C., & Versiani, M. (2004). Transcultural aspects of obsessive-compulsive disorder: A description of a Brazilian sample and a systematic review of international clinical studies. *Journal of Psychiatric Research*, 38(4), 403-411. doi:10.1016/j.jpsychires.2003.12.004

Ghassencadeh, Moitabia, Khamseh, Ebrahimkhani, Issazadegan, & Saif-Nobakht. (2002) Symptoms of obsessive-compulsive disorder in a sample of Iranian patients. *International Journal of Social Psychiatry*, 48(1), 20-28. doi:10.1177/002076402128783055

Girischandra, B.G., & Sumant, K. (2001). Phenomenology of obsessive-compulsive disorder: a factor analytic approach. *Indian Journal of Psychiatry, 43*(4), 306-316.

Hatch, M. L., Friedman, S., & Paradis, C. M. (1996). Behavioral treatment of obsessive-compulsive disorder in African Americans. *Cognitive and Behavioral Practice, 3*(2), 303-315. doi:10.1016/S1077-7229(96)80020-4

Himle, J. A., Muroff, J. R., Taylor, R. J., Baser, R. E., Abelson, J. M., Hanna, G. L., ...Jackson, J.S. (2008). Obsessive-compulsive disorder among African Americans and blacks of Caribbean descent: Results from the national survey of American life. *Depression and Anxiety, 25,* 993–1005. doi:10.1002/da.20434

Jaisoorya, T. S., Reddy, Y., Srinath, S. S., & Thennarasu, K. K. (2009). Sex differences in Indian patients with obsessive-compulsive disorder. *Comprehensive Psychiatry, 50*(1), 70-75. doi:10.1016/j.comppsych.2008.05.003

Karadağ, F., Oğuzhanoğlu, N., Özdel, O., Ateşci, F. Ç., & Amuk, T. (2006). OCD Symptoms in a Sample of Turkish Patients: A Phenomenological Picture. *Depression and Anxiety,* 23(3), 145-152. doi:10.1002/da.20148

Kessler, R. C., Berglund, P., Demler, O., Jin, R., Merikangas, K. R., & Walters, E. E. (2005). Lifetime prevalence and age-of-onset distributions of DSM-IV disorders in the National Comorbidity Survey Replication. *Archives of General Psychiatry, 62*(6), 593–602. doi:10.1001/archpsyc.62.6.593

Kessler, R. C., Chiu, W. T., Demler, O., Merikangas, K. R., & Walters, E. E. (2005).Prevalence, severity, and comorbidity of 12-month DSM-IV disorders in the National Comorbidity Survey Replication. *Archives of General Psychiatry, 62*(6), 617–627. doi:10.1001/archpsyc.62.6.617

Kessler, R. C., & Üsütun, T. B. (2004). The World Mental Health (WMH) Survey initiative version of the World Health Organization (WHO) Composite International Diagnostic Interview (CIDI). *International Journal of Methods in Psychiatric Research, 13,* 93-121. doi:10.1002/mpr.168

Kim, S. J., Lee, H. S., & Kim, C. H. (2005). Obsessive-compulsive disorder, factor analyzed symptom dimensions and serotonin transporter polymorphism. *Neuropsychobiology, 52*, 176–182. doi:10.1159/000088860

Labad, J., Mencho, J., Alonso, P., Segalas, C., Jimenez, S., Jaurrieta, N., & ... Vallejo, J. (2008). Gender differences in obsessive-compulsive symptom dimensions. *Depression and Anxiety, 25*(10), 832-838. doi:10.1002/da.20332

Lemelson, R. (2003). Obsessive-compulsive disorder in Bali: The cultural shaping of a neuropsychiatric disorder. Transcultural Psychiatry, 40(3), 377-408. doi:10.1177/13634615030403004

Li, Y., Marques, L., Hinton D.E., Wang, Y., & Xiao, Z. (2009). Symptom dimensions in Chinese patients with obsessive-compulsive disorder. *CNS Neuroscience and Therapeutics*, 15(3), 276-282. doi:10.1111/j.1755-5949.2009.00099.x

Nicolini, H., Benilde, O., Giuffra, L., Paez, F., Mejia, J., Sanchez de Carmona, M., Sidenberg, D., & Ramon de la Fuente, J. (1997). Age of onset, gender and severity in obsessive-compulsive disorder: a study on a Mexican population. *Salud Mental, 20*(3), 1-4.

Ninan, P. T. & Shelton, S. (1993). Managing psychotic symptoms when the diagnosis is unclear. *Hosp Community Psychiatry*, 44, 107–8.

Okasha, A. A., Saad, A. A., Khalil, A. H., & Dawla, A. (1994). Phenomenology of obsessive-compulsive disorder: A transcultural study. *Comprehensive Psychiatry, 35*(3), 191-197. doi:10.1016/0010-440X(94)90191-0

Reddy, Y. C.,Janardhan, Jaideep, T.,Khanna, S, & Srinath, S. (2005). Obsessive-Compulsive Disorder Research in India: A Review. In *Obsessive compulsive disorder research*. (pp. 93-120). ix, 284 pp. Ling, B. E [Ed]. Hauppauge, NY, US: Nova Biomedical Books; US.

Rosmarin, D. H., Pirutinsky, S., & Siev, J. (2010). Recognition of scrupulosity and non-religious OCD by Orthodox and non-Orthodox Jews. *Journal of Social and Clinical Psychology, 29*(8), 930-944. doi:10.1521/jscp.2010.29.8.930

Saleem, S., & Mahmood, Z. (2009). OCD in a cultural context: A phenomenological approach. *Pakistan Journal of Psychological Research, 24*(1-2), 27-42.

Simonds, L.M., & Thorpe, S.J. (2003). Attitudes toward obsessive-compulsive disorders: An experimental investigation. *Social Psychiatry and Psychiatric Epidemiology, 38*, 331–336.

Shiraev, E.B. & Levy, D.A. (2010). *Cross-Cultural Psychology: Critical Thinking and Contemporary Applications*, 4th Edition. Pearson.

Shooka, A. A., Al-Haddad, M. K., & Raees, A. A. (1998). OCD in Bahrain: A phenomenological profile. *International Journal of Social Psychiatry, 44*(2), 147-154. doi:10.1177/002076409804400207

Sica, C., Novara, C., & Sanavio, E. (2002). Religiousness and obsessive-compulsive cognitions and symptoms in an Italian population. *Behaviour Research and Therapy, 40*(7), 813-823. doi:10.1016/S0005-7967(01)00120-6

Snowden, L.R., Hastings, J.F., Alvidrez, J. (2009). Overrepresentation of Black Americans in Psychiatric Inpatient Care. *Psychiatr Serv, 60*(6), 779-785.

Stein, D.J., Carey, P.D., Lochner, C., Seedat, S., Fineberg, N., Andersen, E.W. (2008). Escitalopram in obsessive-compulsive disorder: response of symptom dimensions to pharmacotherapy. *CNS Spectrums, 13*(6), 492-8.

Sussman, N. (2003). Obsessive-Compulsive Disorder: A Commonly Missed Diagnosis in *Primary Care, Primary Psychiatry, 10*(12), 14.

U.S. Census Bureau. (2011). Population Clock. Retrieved from http://www.census.gov/population/popclockworld.html.

Weissman, M. M., Bland, R. C., Canino, G. J., Greenwald, S., Hwu, H. G., Chung … Yeh, E. K. (1994). The cross national epidemiology of obsessive compulsive disorder: The Cross National Collaborative Group. *Journal of Clinical Psychiatry, 55*(3 Suppl.), 5–10.

Wetterneck, C., Little, T., Rinehart, K., Cervantes, M. E., Hyde, E., & Williams, M. T. (2012). Latinos with Obsessive-Compulsive Disorder: Mental Healthcare Utilization and Inclusion in Clinical Trials, *Journal of Obsessive-Compulsive & Related Disorders, 1*(2), 85-97.

Whaley, A. L., & Hall, B. N. (2009). Effects of cultural themes in psychotic symptoms on the diagnosis of schizophrenia in African Americans. *Mental Health, Religion & Culture, 12*(5), 457-471. doi:10.1080/13674670902758273

Williams, M. T., Abramowitz, J. S., & Olatunji, B. O. (2012).The Relationship between Contamination Cognitions, Anxiety, and Disgust in Two Ethnic Groups. *Journal of Behavior Therapy and Experimental Psychiatry*, 43, 632-637. doi: 10.1016/j.jbtep.2011.09.003

Williams, M.T., Elstein, J., Buckner, E., Abelson, J., Himle, J. (2012). Symptom Dimensions in Two Samples of African Americans with Obsessive-Compulsive Disorder, *Journal of Obsessive-Compulsive & Related Disorders*, 1(3), 145-*152*. doi: 10.1016/j.jocrd.2012.03.004

Williams, M. T., Farris, S. G., Turkheimer, E., Pinto, A., Ozanick, K., Franklin, M. E., Simpson, H. B., Liebowitz, M., & Foa, E. B. (2011). The Myth of the Pure Obsessional Type in Obsessive-Compulsive Disorder, *Depression & Anxiety, 28*(6), 495–500.

Williams, M., Powers, M., Yun, Y. G., & Foa, E. B. (2010). Minority representation in clinical trials for obsessive-compulsive disorder. *Journal of Anxiety Disorders, 24*, 171-177.

Williams, M. T., Proetto, D., Casiano, D., & Franklin, M. E. (2012). Recruitment of a Hidden Population: African Americans with Obsessive-Compulsive Disorder, *Contemporary Clinical Trials, 33*(1), 67-75. doi:10.1016/j.cct.2011.09.001

Williams, M. T., & Turkheimer, E. (2007) Identification and explanation of racial differences on contamination measures. *Behavior Research and Therapy, 45*(12), 3041-3050. doi:10.1016/j.brat.2007.08.013

Williams, M.T., Turkheimer, E, Magee, E., & Guterbock, T. (2008). The effects of race and racial priming on self-report of contamination anxiety. *Personality and Individual Differences, 44*(3), 744-755. doi:10.1016/j.paid.2007.10.009

Williams, M. T., Wetterneck, C., Tellawi, G., & Duque, G. (in press). Domains of Distress Among People with Sexual Orientation Obsessions. *Archives of Sexual Behavior.* doi: 10.1007/s10508-014-0421-0

# Chapter Five

# A Review of Cognitive-Behavioral Therapy for Obsessive-Compulsive Disorder

Robert R. Selles, Michael L. Sulkowski, & Eric A. Storch

Obsessive-compulsive disorder (OCD) affects approximately 1-2% of individuals in the United States (Kessler et al., 2005; Zohar, 1999), with many others experiencing subclinical obsessive-compulsive symptoms (Douglass et al., 1995). The disorder is characterized by anxiety provoking, time-consuming, and impairing intrusive thoughts (i.e., obsessions) and anxiety/distress-reducing compulsions (American Psychiatric Association, 2000). If untreated, the course of OCD often is chronic and unremitting after symptom presentation; therefore, early and aggressive OCD treatment is warranted (Eisen et al., 2006).

Two treatment approaches for OCD are empirically validated: cognitive behavioral therapy (CBT) with exposure and response prevention (E/RP)[1] and pharmacotherapy involving the use of serotonin reuptake inhibitors (SRIs). Although SRI monotherapy has demonstrated efficacy in randomized placebo controlled trials, CBT has emerged as the first line treatment for OCD due to superior treatment gains relative to SRIs, greater long-term symptom relief, and a lower risk for untoward treatment effects (Abramowitz, Whiteside, & Deacon, 2005; Eddy, Dutra, Bradley, & Westen, 2004; Mancuso, Faro, Joshi, & Geller, 2010). Furthermore, CBT's benefits may extend to comorbid conditions (e.g., depression) and is associated with overall improvements in quality of life (Diefenbach, Abramowitz, Norberg & Tolin, 2007; Rector, Cassin, & Richter, 2009; Storch et al., 2008a).

---

[1] Use of "CBT" automatically implies the combined use of exposure and response prevention in the remainder of the manuscript.

\-

## Cognitive-Behavioral Therapy: An Integrative Treatment Approach

The Task Force on Promotion and Dissemination of Psychological Procedures (1995) awarded CBT "well established" status for treating OCD given its efficacy in randomized controlled trials suggesting that up to 85% of individuals are treatment responders and approximately 50% experience disorder remission (Foa et al., 2005; Franklin et al., 2011; POTS, 2004; Simpson, Huppert, Petkova, Foa, & Liebowitz, 2006). In addition, recent meta-analytic studies illustrate the efficacy of CBT for treating both children and adults (Eddy et al., 2004; Stewart & Chambless, 2009; Watson, & Rees, 2008) and highlight strong effect sizes (*ES>* .80; Eddy et al., 2004).

Cognitive-behavioral therapy is based on behavioral conditioning principles and cognitive mediation theory (Foa, & Kozak, 1985; Salkovskis, 1985). Behaviorally, a previously neutral stimulus becomes associated with a conditioned response (e.g., fear, disgust), which contributes to obsessive thoughts about and active avoidance/ritualized behavior when confronted by the newly conditioned stimulus. The conditioned emotional/fear reaction is further reinforced through the performance of anxiety-reductive rituals and/or pathological avoidance of anxiety-provoking stimuli. Compulsions gradually become more time-consuming/interfering as individuals with OCD become increasingly reliant on rituals to cope with obsessional anxiety. Because compulsions prevent individuals from naturally habituating to anxiety and only provide temporary relief, the performance of these behaviors can trap patients in a cycle that develops, amplifies, and sustains the presence of obsessive thinking and associated ritualizing.

With the goal of interrupting this cycle, CBT aims to break the association between obsessive thinking and the need to perform anxiety-reductive compulsions. Patients are systematically (i.e., moving from 'easier' to more difficult anxiety triggers) exposed to anxiety-provoking situations without ritualizing, which allows them to habituate to anxiety naturally. Through repeated exposure to progressively more challenging stimuli, the association between the neutral stimuli and the fear response is weakened. Additionally, CBT aims to inoculate individuals to intrusive or obsessive thoughts by encouraging them to challenge these thoughts through cognitive restructuring and placing patients in situations in which feared outcomes do not occur in the absence of rituals.

*Treatment Structure and Course*

Regardless of patient age or type of treatment protocol (e.g., individual, group-based), CBT for OCD most commonly includes the following components:

psychoeducation, development of an exposure hierarchy, behavioral exposures with response prevention, cognitive exercises and relapse prevention. Of these components, exposure and response prevention in particular appears to be associated with robust treatment outcomes (Deacon & Abramowitz, 2004; Rosa-Alcázar, Sánchez-Meca, Gómez-Conesa, & Marín-Martínez, 2008). Psychoeducation generally is provided at treatment outset and includes teaching patients about the nature of OCD and the ways in which it is maintained, as well as the expected process of therapy. Specifically, patients are educated about how OCD is a neurobiological disorder that is caused by a combination of biological and environmental factors. Additionally, patients should be taught about the efficacy of CBT and how the treatment involves behavioral exposures and cognitive restructuring. While providing psychoeducation, the therapist may also address expectations for treatment compliance and homework completion to reduce attrition and disabuse patients of inaccurate notions they may have.

Following psychoeducation, the patient and therapist develop a customized fear hierarchy. With the help of a therapist, the patient creates a list of situations or stimuli that are associated with varying levels of distress and then ranks/orders these situations/stimuli using subjective units of distress (SUDs; e.g., the subjective intensity of distress experienced by an individual in a certain situation) on an E/RP hierarchy. Some items may have the same basic stimulus (e.g., germs/contamination) yet involve significantly different levels of contact with that stimulus from imaginal (e.g., thinking about touching a toilet, scripts of feared triggers) to *in vivo* (e.g., being near a toilet, touching a toilet).

The patient and therapist collaborate to begin behavioral exposures after developing the exposure hierarchy. Exposure and response prevention involves exposing patients to anxiety-provoking situations/stimuli while encouraging them to resist performing compulsions. Patients are exposed to mildly anxiety provoking stimuli or situations early in treatment to eschew flooding, which can overwhelm a patient's capacity to resist performing anxiety-reducing compulsions. As treatment progresses, progressively more difficult items on the exposure hierarchy are attempted to allow the patient to habituate to anxiety without performing compulsions. Additionally, as an integral part of CBT, patients are provided with homework and between-session exposure tasks to reinforce their progress in session. As a general rule of thumb, homework exposures should be comparable to exposures performed in session and should recapitulate progress made in therapy.

Some CBT practitioners emphasize the use of cognitive therapy techniques for treating OCD such as identifying and challenging maladaptive thoughts, although E/RP remains the mainstay for CBT (for review see Wilhelm & Steketee, 2006). With this treatment approach, the therapist helps the patient critically examine and

87

evaluate their thoughts through techniques such as Socratic questioning, identifying cognitive errors, using thought records, the downward arrow technique, listing advantages and disadvantages, and the double standard technique (Wilhelm et al., 2009). However, caution may be warranted at times when using cognitive therapy for treating OCD to ensure that cognitive interventions do not become ritualized behaviors and increase rather than decrease obsessive-compulsive symptomology (van Oppen & Arntz, 1994). For example, Wilhelm and Steketee (2006) describe a phenomenon in which cognitive restructuring can become a new mental ritual and caution therapists to ensure that patients respond to intrusive thoughts directly instead of challenging their interpretations of these thoughts.

Relapse prevention is completed at the end of treatment and functions to terminate treatment while encouraging patient success beyond treatment completion. Most commonly, relapse prevention is a collaborative process between the therapist and patient that involves brainstorming future situations in which obsessions may arise/return and developing plans to deal with this anxiety. Relapse prevention allows the therapist to evaluate patient understanding of treatment concepts, encourage generalization of treatment gains, and prepare patients for possible future increases in anxiety while increasing the likelihood of treatment maintenance (Hiss, Foa, & Kozak, 1994).

*CBT for Pediatric OCD*

In contrast to adults, insight is not a prerequisite for children to be diagnosed with OCD (APA, 2000). Children may lack insight into their obsessive-compulsive symptoms or not view them as a problem, even if they cause functional impairment. However, obsessive-compulsive symptoms are influenced by patient insight and have a bi-directional impact with family dynamics/functioning (March, 1995). For example, families that contain an individual with OCD are more likely to show high levels of accommodation or behaviors conducted by the family that assist in the completion of rituals (e.g. removal of feared stimuli, reassurance provision). Considering how this dynamic influences and is influenced by obsessive-compulsive symptoms, CBT for children with OCD should heavily include patient's primary caregivers (Storch et al., 2007).

Modeling CBT for parents and caregivers and coaching them through using exposures for homework practice can expedite treatment as well as empower caregivers to help their children after treatment termination. Additionally, including caregivers in treatment allows the therapist to address and improve family factors that may have contributed to the child's development or maintenance of OCD. For example, patients with relatives who express antagonistic or accommodating attitudes toward OCD demonstrate poorer response to treatment and an increased likelihood of relapse (Renshaw, Steketee, & Chambless, 2005). Further, the presence of poor social or familial functioning and patient-rated negative household interactions has been predictive of poor treatment gains (Steketee & Van Noppen, 2003).

Eliminating problematic family dynamics and teaching parents how to support their child's treatment can help create an environment that fosters long-term improvement and maintenance of treatment gains (O'Leary, Barrett, & Fjermestad, 2009). Specific strategies for connecting family members to treatment may include providing targeted psychoeducation to family members to decrease OCD ritual accommodation, employing cooperative family members as treatment assistants, and providing support for family members dealing with frustrating patient behaviors (Steketee & Van Noppen, 2003). Ultimately, because of the strong influence parents exert on children's behavior, the treatment of pediatric OCD should be contextualized within the family system.

Other considerations for treating pediatric OCD involve using developmentally appropriate language during treatment, using analogies and play scenarios to facilitate exposure tasks, encouraging children to engage in "behavioral experiments," and consulting or collaborating with members involved in a child's educational programming (e.g., teachers or school psychologists; Piacentini, March, & Franklin, 2006). Through working with members of school communities, therapists can decrease the likelihood of symptom accommodation in the school environment while increasing the number of individuals who can support a child's healthy psychosocial functioning and emotional well-being (Sulkowski, Wingfield, Jones, & Coulter, 2011). Furthermore, a predominately school-based CBT intervention approach may be warranted in the absence of trained community providers (Sloman, Gallant, & Storch, 2007). On balance, however, many barriers to treatment exist in school settings (e.g., difficulty incorporating family members, confidentiality, duration of treatment sessions) and there are a limited number of trained CBT practitioners who work in school settings. Therefore, it is important to consult with members of school communities to assess their level of expertise in CBT for OCD and how they can best support a child who is receiving treatment.

The aforementioned CBT strategies for pediatric OCD have applications for different populations of youth including pre-school aged children (Freeman et al., 2008; Ginsburg, Burstein, Becker, & Drake, 2011), school-aged children, and adolescents (Barrett, Healy-Farrell, & March, 2004; Storch et al., 2007). In addition to the expected treatment gains, these models have been associated with reductions in family accommodation and OCD-related impairment (Storch et al., 2007).

*Intensive CBT*

Most CBT treatment protocols include between 12-16 weekly sessions; however, intensive CBT condenses a standardized treatment approach into a 3-4 week period through increasing the frequency and duration of sessions (Pence, Storch, & Geffken, 2010). Weekly CBT may not be realistic for patients who cannot find providers in their area. In contrast, the condensed session format of intensive CBT reduces logistical burdens associated with traveling to receive treatment, which may be appeal to individuals and families who do not have local access to providers (Storch et al., 2007). Further, intensive CBT may allow for more rapid symptom reduction, which may increase patient motivation and make this treatment approach better suited for patients with significant functional impairment (Storch et al., 2007). Independent of their differences, intensive and weekly CBT are associated with similar declines in obsessive-compulsive symptoms at post-treatment (Foa et al., 2005; Storch et al., 2007; Storch et al., 2008b; Storch et al., 2010).

*Group-Based CBT*

In addition to intensive CBT, group-based CBT is an alternative approach to delivering CBT for OCD. Group-based CBT typically includes one therapist and five or fewer participants, thus allowing a number of participants to receive treatment concomitantly (Himle, Van Etten, & Fischer, 2003). In addition to potentially reaching more individuals, group-based CBT has other advantages. The treatment requires a therapist to spend less time on each patient and may lower overall treatment costs (Himle et al., 2003; Jónsson, Hougaard, & Bennedsen, 2011). Further, group-based CBT may help normalize obsessive-compulsive symptoms for participants, provide members with peer and social support, and motivate some members due to group contingencies (e.g., competition, fear of loafing; Himle et al., 2003). Conversely, group-based CBT also has specific disadvantages compared to individually delivered CBT. Patients may disclose less during group sessions and the task of providing individual attention to each patient may prove difficult, especially in groups with a problematic or domineering patient (Himle et al., 2003). Further, due to the diverse presentation of obsessive-compulsive symptoms, group-based CBT may be less personalized and more generally focused (Himle et al., 2003). As a result, exposure and cognitive exercises may not directly pertain to all group members. Group-based CBT has demonstrated comparable efficacy to individually administered CBT in both adult and pediatric populations, although it must be cautioned that fewer methodologically rigorous trials have been published (Barrett et al., 2004; Jónsson & Hougaard, 2009; Jónsson et al., 2011).

*Alternative Dissemination*

While group and intensive cognitive-behavioral therapy are two ways of addressing the current shortage of trained CBT practitioners, developing forms of administration include bibliotherapy, self-help with minimal therapist contact, computer guided therapy, and web-camera administered CBT (Andersson et al., 2012; Fritzler, Hecker, & Losee, 1997; Greist et al., 2002; Storch et al., 2011; Tolin, Maltby, Diefenbach, Hannan, &Worhunsky, 2004). Stepped care, in which patients are first given a low-intensity and low-cost treatment followed by a more intense and costly intervention if they do not respond to the first intervention displays promise as an emerging treatment approach. In a recent investigation, Tolin, Diefenbach, and Gilliam (2011) provided adult OCD patients ($N = 30$) patients with 6 weeks of low-intensity counseling with E/RP bibliotherapy followed by 17 sessions of therapist-driven CBT if they did not respond to the first intervention. Results indicated that two treatments were equally efficacious as 67% of stepped care completers and 50% of therapist-driven CBT completers experienced clinically significant symptom reductions at post-treatment. Overall, however, the aforementioned disseminations are fairly novel and await rigorous empirical validation. Therefore, therapist administered CBT remains the first-line treatment for OCD.

## Factors Affecting Treatment Response and CBT Augmentation

Despite the well-established efficacy of CBT for treating OCD, many patients still display impairing symptoms after treatment (de Haan, 2006). Furthermore, some people refuse to participate in CBT or prematurely dropout of treatment for a variety of reasons (Keeley, Storch, Merlo, & Geffken, 2008). Although wide variability exists in OCD symptom presentation and severity, many treatment avoidant and refractory patients share similar characteristics that can compromise and attenuate their treatment response.

In a recent review, McKay, Storch, Nelson, Morales, and Moretz (2009) identified several treatment-interfering factors for pediatric OCD including the presence of comorbid conditions, scrupulosity and overvalued ideation, low cognitive functioning, stimulus-environment and stimulus-outcome relations, and biological factors. Additionally, Pence, Sulkowski, Jordan, and Storch (2010) discuss difficult scenarios that may emerge during CBT treatment for OCD such as incidental exposures (i.e., when a patient accidentally is exposed to a highly distressing stressor during exposure therapy), when patients fail to habituate to anxiety, misjudge the intensity of exposures, perform mental/covert rituals that interfere with treatment, and display unusually high levels of anxiety sensitivity. Below, we discuss such common treatment-interfering factors as well as ways to address these and improve treatment outcomes.

*Comorbid Conditions*

The presence of other psychiatric disorders or conditions along with OCD can exacerbate symptoms and negatively impact patient's psychosocial functioning. Thus, disorder comboridity can exert a deleterious effect on patients and complicate CBT. Disruptive behavior disorders (e.g., oppositional defiant disorder, conduct disorder, attention deficit/hyperactivity disorder) and certain types of mood disorders are associated with attenuated CBT response rates in youth with OCD (Abramowitz, Franklin, Street, Kozak, & Foa, 2000; Storch et al., 2008c). However, other comorbid conditions do not appear to impact children's treatment response and mixed findings exist regarding others. For example, the presence of a comorbid anxiety disorder (e.g., generalized anxiety disorder, social phobia, panic disorder) did not negatively affect children's response to CBT for pediatric OCD (Storch et al., 2010). Similarly, the presence of comorbid tics (e.g., Tourette's disorder) did not affect the efficacy of CBT in a recent trial (March et al., 2007). In one study, major depression was a poor prognostic indicator for CBT response in children with OCD (e.g., Storch et al., 2008c), but previous investigations and subsequent studies did not establish this relationship (Foa, Kozak, Steketee, & McCarthy, 1992; Storch et al., 2010).

Although the task of disentangling anxiety-driven or reactive behaviors from oppositional/defiant ones can be difficult, the unique needs of children with comorbid OCD and disruptive behavior disorders can be addressed through flexibly employing a combination of behavioral and CBT interventions (Ale & Krackow, 2012). A case study by Lehmkuhl et al. (2009) provides preliminary support for the use of behavior management training prior to using CBT to treat a child with OCD and disruptive behavior disorder symptoms. This intervention approach involved providing psychoeducation to the patient's mother (primary caregiver) on OCD, CBT, and disruptive behavior as well as coaching in the delivery of positive attention and planned ignoring, strategies to deliver effective commands, and the effective implementation of a token economy. Following four behavior management training sessions, 11 sessions of exposure-based CBT were delivered to treat the patient's obsessive-compulsive symptoms. Additionally, this part of the treatment involved psychoeducation and modeling to reduce maladaptive accommodation of the child's anxiety symptoms and regular meetings with the patient's mother to reinforce various components learned during behavior management training. Overall, this combined treatment approach was effective as the patient displayed significant reductions in both disruptive behavior and OCD symptoms.

In adults, severe depression in patients with OCD is associated with lower CBT response rates compared to non-depressed or patients with mild depression (Abramowitz & Foa, 2000; Abramowitz et al., 2000; Steketee, Chambless, Tran,

2001). Additionally, GAD has been found to predict treatment dropout in adult OCD patients (Steketee et al., 2001), while the presence of PTSD symptoms also may increase treatment dropout and attenuate response rates (Gershuny, Baer, Jenike, Minichiello, & Wilhelm, 2002). Lastly, adult patients with comorbid personality disorders have been reported to respond poorly to CBT (AuBuchon & Malatesta, 1994; Minichiello, Baer, & Jenike, 1987); however, other studies suggest that the presence of personality disorders do not negatively impact the influence of CBT on reducing OCD symptoms (Dreessen, Hoekstra, & Arntz, 1993; Fricke et al., 2006; Steketee et al., 2001). Fricke et al. (2006) suggest that identifying and addressing specific personality traits that can interfere with treatment (e.g., schizotypal traits; Minichiello et al., 1987) early in treatment is important, so CBT can be adapted to the unique needs of individual patients. For example, in lieu of spending a lot of time working on establishing a strong therapeutic relationship, a therapist could modify treatment for individuals with comorbid OCD and schizotypal traits to focus on how they may directly benefit from treatment.

*Poor Treatment Adherence*

Commitment and investment in CBT is associated with a positive treatment response (March, Franklin, Nelson, & Foa, 2001). However, experiencing extreme fear when thinking about confronting anxiety-provoking stimuli and situations can forestall some individuals from engaging in this process and experiencing positive outcomes that may result from participating in E/RP. This phenomenon is particularly evident when individuals experience secondary gains from their OCD symptoms such as feeling morally superior to others because of specific rituals that they perform (e.g., compulsive praying), sacrificing for (or engaging in) certain behaviors to protect others (e.g., checking door locks to lessen the possibility of home intrusion, robbery, or murder), and when caregivers purposefully or inadvertently reinforce the performance of certain rituals (e.g., compulsively checking homework for accuracy). Thus, these individuals may feel ambivalent about giving up their OCD symptoms and display low motivation for CBT, a change-based therapy approach.

Motivational interviewing (MI), a therapeutic approach with roots in humanistic psychology that has been popularized by Miller and Rollnick (2002), aims to resolve ambivalence between patients' current behavior and their goals. Although not necessarily the central focus of this approach, MI can enhance individual's motivation for change or willingness to engage in therapy through illustrating the discrepancy between his or her ideal or desired life and current behavior. In one study, Maltby and Tolin (2005) provided four MI sessions prior to conducting CBT to engage adult patients who had previously refused exposure-based CBT to engage in treatment. Most (86%) of patients who received MI agreed to attempt E/RP and these patients also displayed greater reductions in OCD symptoms at post-treatment compared to patients in a waitlist condition. However, more recent studies do not support the adjunctive benefit of adding MI to CBT for adults with OCD as measured in patient adherence to exposure tasks (Simpson, Zuckoff, Page, Franklin, & Foa, 2008; Simpson et al., 2010). As suggested by Simpson et al. (2010) the appropriate dosing and spacing of MI sessions may have an important impact on the effectiveness of a combined MI and CBT treatment approach. For example, a study by Merlo et al. (2010) involved providing MI prior to key or particularly challenging exposure sessions whereas the previous studies (e.g., Simpson et al., 2008; Simpson et al., 2010) involved providing MI at the outset of treatment. Merlo et al. (2010) used a combined MI and family-based approach to treating pediatric OCD in treatment resistant youth and those results suggest that this approach may accelerate a youth's speed of response to CBT.

*Low Insight or Intellectual Functioning*

Insight involves recognizing that one's obsessions and compulsions are excessive and unreasonable and it varies considerably across individuals. Approximately 36% of adults (Alonso et al., 2008) and more than half (52%) of children are estimated to have low insight into their OCD symptoms (Lewin et al., 2010; Storch et al., 2008d). Furthermore, low insight is associated with greater symptom severity (Bellino, Patria, Ziero, & Bogetto, 2005; Storch et al., 2008d), higher comorbidity rates (Bellino et al., 2005; Lewin et al., 2010; Storch et al., 2008d), low symptom resistance (Alonso et al., 2008), lower cognitive functioning and adaptive behavior (Lewin et al., 2010), and poor treatment outcomes (Alonso et al., 2008).

Individuals with low insight may have difficulty integrating information that is inconsistent with their obsessive beliefs (Tolin, Abramowitz, Kozak, & Foa, 2001), which could render cognitive restructuring ineffective and contribute to decreased CBT response rates (Lewin et al., 2010; Storch et al., 2008d). Therefore, Lewin et al. (2010) suggests reducing the use of cognitive therapy techniques with patients with low insight and placing a greater emphasis on behavioral ones. Additionally, SRI augmentation may help some individuals with low insight habituate to exposures more effectively, although research is needed to establish this approach (Foa, Abramowitz, Franklin, & Kozak, 1999).

A primarily behavioral approach to treating OCD is also recommended for individuals with intellectual disabilities and borderline intellectual functioning. In a recent case series, Pence, Aldea, Sulkowski, and Storch (2010) modified a CBT treatment protocol to treat adults with borderline intellectual functioning. Modifications included increasing parental involvement in treatment, simplifying language used in session, reducing the use of cognitive therapy techniques, and the addition of a contingency management and role-playing strategies with caregivers. Following these modifications, all three patients in this case series experienced reductions in their OCD symptoms at post-treatment. Similarly, Ellis, Ala'i-Rosales, Glenn, Rosales-Ruiz, and Greenspoon (2006) highlight the importance of a therapist modeling therapeutic techniques (e.g., exposure tasks) and providing social rewards (e.g., positive attention) in session to motivate children with intellectual disabilities to participate in exposures. Further, Anderson and Morris (2006) recommended using visuals (e.g., charts, graphs, pictures) when providing psychoeducation to youth with cognitive limitations as well as including caregivers in treatment as much as possible to increase treatment generalization.

*Biological Factors*

Specific biological events can engender or exacerbate OCD symptoms. Pediatric autoimmune neuropsychiatric disorders associated with streptococcus (PANDAS) have received increased attention over the past decade due to advances in identification and treatment of the condition in children (see Martino, Defazio, & Giovannoni, 2009 for review). In contrast to other presentations of OCD, the onset of PANDAS is rapid and various symptoms associated with the syndrome (e.g., obsessive-compulsive behavior, tics, irritability/agitation, hyperactivity, impaired attention control) emerge following an autoimmune response to exposure to streptococcus infection. In addition to displaying anxiety and repetitive behaviors, youth with PANDAS often display neurological dysfunction, excessive motor activity, and impaired executive functioning abilities that are not related to the presence of a premorbid or comorbid condition (e.g., tic disorder).

If a child's clinical presentation suggests PANDAS, a physician can verify the presence of streptococcal infection and treat the infection accordingly, which may involve antibiotic therapy and/or immune-modulatory treatments (e.g., interventions that purport to interrupt the autoimmune response to streptococcal bacteria). Although research on psychological treatments for PANDAS is nascent, a study by Storch et al. (2006) provides preliminary support for treating youth with PANDAS-related OCD using CBT. Six out of seven participants were treatment responders following 14 intensive CBT sessions and these youth maintained their gains at three-month follow-up. Therefore, individuals with PANDAS may benefit from combined medical and psychological treatments and the efficacy of CBT for OCD appears to be independent from the etiology of symptoms.

## Conclusions and Future Directions

Cognitive-behavioral therapy is a safe, effective, and durable treatment for OCD in children and adults. As a first-line treatment, a number of alternative formats have emerged (e.g., intensive CBT, group-based CBT) that each have specific advantages and may be similarly effective. However, the number of trained CBT practitioners is limited and not all patients respond favorably to treatment.

Therefore, efforts are underway to personalize and augment CBT to address treatment-interfering factors such as the presence of comorbid psychopathology, poor insight and treatment motivation, low cognitive functioning, and biological factors (e.g., PANDAS) that can engender or exacerbate OCD symptoms.

Despite the treatment's established efficacy, improving and augmenting CBT remains an exciting area of clinical and research attention, especially for improving outcomes for difficult to treat and treatment refractory cases. For example, D-cycloserine (DCS), an antibiotic that initially was used as a treatment for tuberculosis, has recently been used to facilitate fear extinction and exposure therapy (Norberg et al., 2008) with some success in adult (Kushner et al., 2007; Wilhelm, et al., 2008) and pediatric OCD samples (Storch et al., 2010). Although results from a meta-analysis suggest that DCS did not result in superior post-treatment results compared to CBT without DCS augmentation, results of this analysis also indicate that DCS augmentation was associated with increases in the speed and efficiency by which patients experienced reductions in anxiety (Norberg et al., 2008). Thus, the use of DCS in conjunction with CBT may be a promising approach for facilitating early treatment gains and reducing premature dropout.

In addition to DCS augmentation, other novel approaches to delivering CBT or enhancing its effectiveness have been developed over the past several decades. The delivery of CBT has been tailored for different settings (e.g., school, community mental health center) and populations (e.g., children, adults). Overall, considerable growth has been observed in the dissemination of CBT as well as its research support. However, room for growth still exists in these important respects as well as for further refinement of this efficacious treatment.

## References

Abramowitz, J. S., & Foa, E. B. (2000). Does comorbid major depressive disorder influence outcome of exposure and response prevention for OCD? *Behavior Therapy, 31,* 795-800.

Abramowitz, J. S., Franklin, M. E., Street, G. P., Kozak, M. J., & Foa, E, B. (2000). Effects of comorbid depression on response to treatment for obsessive-compulsive disorder. *Behavior Therapy, 31,* 517-538.

Abramowitz, J. S., Whiteside, S. P., & Deacon, B. J. (2005). The effectiveness of treatment for pediatric obsessive compulsive disorder: A meta-analysis. *Behavior Therapy, 36,* 55-63.

Ale, C. M., & Krackow, E. (2012). Concurrent treatment of early childhood OCD and ODD: A case illustration. *Clinical Case Studies, 10*(4), 312.

Alonso, P., Menchon, J. M., Segalas, C., Jaurrieta, N., Jimenez-Murcia, S., Cardoner, N., . . . Vallejo, J. (2008). Clinical implications of insight assessment in obsessive-compulsive disorder. *Comprehensive Psychiatry*, *49*(3), 305-312.

American Psychiatric Association (2000). *Diagnostic and statistical manual of mental disorders - fourth edition – text revision.* Washington, DC.

American Psychological Association Task Force on Psychological Intervention Guidelines. (1995). *Template for developing guidelines: Interventions for mental disorders and psychological aspects of physical disorders.* Washington, DC: American Psychological Association.

Anderson, S., & Morris, J. (2006). Cognitive behaviour therapy for people with Asperger syndrome. *Behavioural and Cognitive Psychotherapy*, *34*, 293–303.

Andersson, E., Enander, J., Andren, P., Hedman, E., Ljotsson, B., Hursti, T., . . . Ruck, C. (2012). Internet-based cognitive behaviour therapy for obsessive-compulsive disorder: A randomized controlled trial. *Psychological Medicine*, 1-11.

AuBuchon, P. G., & Malatesta, V. J. (1994). Obsessive compulsive patients with comorbid personality disorder: Associated problems and response to a comprehensive behavior therapy. *Journal of Clinical Psychiatry*, *55*(10), 448-453.

Barrett, P., Healy-Farrell, L., & March, J. S. (2004). Cognitive-behavioral family treatment of childhood obsessive-compulsive disorder: A controlled trial. *Journal of the American Academy of Child and Adolescent Psychiatry*, *43*(1), 46-62.

Bellino, S., Patria, L., Ziero, S., & Bogetto, F. (2005). Clinical picture of obsessive-compulsive disorder with poor insight: A regression model. *Psychiatry Research*, *136*(2-3), 223-231.

Deacon, B. J., & Abramowitz, J. S. (2004). Cognitive and behavioral treatments for anxiety disorders: A review of meta-analytic findings. *Journal of Clinical Psychology*, *60*(4), 429-441.

deHaan, E. (2006). Effective treatment of OCD? *Journal of the American Academy of Child and Adolescent Psychiatry*, *45*, 383-384.

Diefenbach, G. J., Abramowitz, J. S., Norberg, M. M., & Tolin, D. F. (2007). Changes in quality of life following cognitive-behavioral therapy for obsessive-compulsive disorder. *Behaviour Research and Therapy*, *45*(12), 3060-3068.

Douglass, H. M., Moffitt, T. E., Dar, R., McGee, R., & Silva, P. (1995). Obsessive-compulsive disorder in a birth cohort of 18-year-olds: Prevalence and predictors. *Journal of the American Academy of Child and Adolescent Psychiatry*, *34*(11), 1424-1431.

Dreessen, L., Hoekstra, R., & Arntz, A. (1997). Personality disorders do not influence the results of cognitive and behavior therapy for obsessive compulsive disorder. *Journal of Anxiety Disorders*, *11*(5), 503-521.

Eddy, K. T., Dutra, L., Bradley, R., & Westen, D. (2004). A multidimensional meta-analysis of psychotherapy and pharmacotherapy for obsessive–compulsive disorder. *Clinical Psychology Review*, *24*, 1011–1030.

Eisen, J. L., Mancebo, M. A., Pinto, A., Coles, M. E., Pagano, M. E., Stout, R., & Rasmussen, S. A. (2006). Impact of obsessive-compulsive disorder on quality of life. *Comprehensive Psychiatry, 47,* 270–275.

Ellis, E. M., Ala'i-Rosales, S. S., Glenn, S. S., Rosales-Ruiz, J., & Greenspoon, J. (2006). The effects of graduated exposure, modeling, and contingent social attention on tolerance to skin care products with two children with autism. *Research in Developmental Disabilities, 27*(6), 585-598.

Foa, E. B., Abramowitz, J. S., Franklin, & M. E., Kozak, M. J. (1999). Feared consequences, fixity of belief, and treatment outcome in patients with obsessive-compulsive disorder. *Behavior Therapy, 30,* 717-724.

Foa, E. B., & Kozak, M. J. (1985). Treatment of anxiety disorders: Implications for psychopathology. In A. H. Tuma & J. D. Maser (Eds.), *Anxiety and the anxiety disorders* (pp. 451-452). Hillsdale, NJ: Erlbaum.

Foa, E. B., Kozak, M. J., Steketee, G. S., & McCarthy, P. R. (1992). Treatment of depressive and obsessive-compulsive symptoms in OCD by imipramine and behaviour therapy. *British Journal of Clinical Psychology, 31 (Pt 3),* 279-292.

Foa, E. B., Liebowitz, M. R., Kozak, M. J., Davies, S., Campeas, R., Franklin, M. E., . . . Tu, X. (2005). Randomized, placebo-controlled trial of exposure and ritual prevention, clomipramine, and their combination in the treatment of obsessive-compulsive disorder. *American Journal of Psychiatry, 162*(1), 151-161.

Franklin, M. E., Sapyta, J., Freeman, J. B., Khanna, M., Compton, S., Almirall, D . . . March, J. S. (2011). Cognitive behavior therapy augmentation of pharmacotherapy in pediatric obsessive-compulsive disorder: The Pediatric OCD Treatment Study II (POTS II) randomized controlled trial. *JAMA, 306,* 1224-1232.

Freeman, J. B., Garcia, A. M., Coyne, L., Ale, C., Przeworski, A., Himle, M., . . . Leonard, H. L. (2008). Early childhood OCD: Preliminary findings from a family-based cognitive-behavioral approach. *Journal of the American Academy of Child and Adolescent Psychiatry, 47*(5), 593-602.

Fricke, S., Moritz, S., Andresen, B., Hand, I., Jacobsen, M., Kloss, M., & Rufer, M. (2006). Do personality disorders predict negative treatment outcome in obsessive-compulsive disorders? A prospective 6-month follow-up study. *European Psychiatry, 21,* 319-324.

Fritzler, B. K., Hecker, J. E., & Losee, M. C. (1997). Self-directed treatment with minimal therapist contact: Preliminary findings for obsessive-compulsive disorder. *Behaviour Research and Therapy, 35*(7), 627-631.

Gershuny, B. S., Baer, L., Jenike, M. A., Minichiello, W. E., & Wilhelm, S. (2002). Comorbid posttraumatic stress disorder: Impact on treatment outcome for obsessive-compulsive disorder. *American Journal of Psychiatry, 159*(5), 852-854.

Ginsburg, G. S., Burstein, M., Becker, K. D., Drake, & K. L. (2011). Treatment of obsessive compulsive disorder in young children: An intervention model and case series. *Child and Family Behavior Therapy, 32*(2), 97-122.

Greist, J. H., Marks, I. M., Baer, L., Kobak, K. A., Wenzel, K. W., Hirsch, M. J., . . . Clary, C. M. (2002). Behavior therapy for obsessive-compulsive disorder guided by a computer or by a clinician compared with relaxation as a control. *Journal of Clinical Psychiatry, 63*(2), 138-145.

Himle, J. A., Fischer, D. J., Van Etten, M. L., Janeck, A. S., & Hanna, G. L. (2003). Group behavioral therapy for adolescents with tic-related and non-tic-related obsessive-compulsive disorder. *Depression and Anxiety, 17*(2), 73-77.

Hiss, H., Foa, E. B., & Kozak, M. J. (1994). Relapse prevention program for treatment of obsessive-compulsive disorder. *Journal of Consulting and Clinical Psychology, 62*(4), 801-808.

Jónsson, H., & Hougaard, E. (2009). Group cognitive behavioural therapy for obsessive-compulsive disorder: A systematic review and meta-analysis. *Acta Psychiatrica Scandinavica, 119*(2), 98-106.

Jónsson, H., Hougaard, E., & Bennedsen, B. E. (2011). Randomized comparative study of group versus individual cognitive behavioural therapy for obsessive compulsive disorder. *Acta Psychiatrica Scandinavica, 123*(5), 387-397.

Kessler, R. C., Berglund, P., Demler, O., Jin, R., Merikangas, K. R., & Walters, E. E. (2005). Lifetime prevalence and age-of-onset distributions of DSM-IV disorders in the National Comorbidity Survey Replication. *Archives of General Psychiatry, 62*(6), 593-602.

Keeley, M. L., Storch, E. A., Merlo, L. J., & Geffken, G. R. (2008). Clinical predictors of response to cognitive-behavioral therapy for obsessive-compulsive disorder. *Clinical Psychology Review, 28*(1), 118-130.

Kushner, M. G., Kim, S. W., Donahue, C., Thuras, P., Adson, D., Kotlyar, M., . . . Foa, E. B. (2007). D-cycloserine augmented exposure therapy for obsessive-compulsive disorder. *Biological Psychiatry, 62*(8), 835-838.

Lehmkuhl, H. D., Storch, E. A., Rahman, O., Freeman, J., Geffken, G. R., Murphy, T. K. (2007). Just say no: Sequential parent management training and cognitive-behavioral therapy for a child with comorbid disruptive behavior and obsessive-compulsive disorder. *Clinical Case Studies, 8*, 48-58.

Lewin, A. B., Bergman, R. L., Peris, T. S., Chang, S., McCracken, J. T., & Piacentini, J. (2010). Correlates of insight among youth with obsessive-compulsive disorder. *Journal of Child Psychology and Psychiatry, 51*(5), 603-611.

Maltby, N., & Tolin, D. F. (2005). A brief motivational intervention for treatment-refusing OCD patients. *Cognitive and Behaviour Therapy, 34*(3), 176-184.

Mancuso, E., Faro, A., Joshi, G., & Geller, D. A. (2010). Treatment of pediatric obsessive-compulsive disorder: A review. *Journal of Child and Adolescent Psychopharmacology, 20*(4), 299-308.

March, J. S. (1995). Cognitive-behavioral psychotherapy for children and adolescents with OCD: A review and recommendations for treatment. *Journal of the American Academy of Child and Adolescent Psychiatry, 34*(1), 7-18.

March, J. S., Franklin, M. E., Leonard, H., Garcia, A., Moore, P., Freeman, J., Foa, E. (2007). Tics moderate treatment outcome with sertraline but not cognitive-behavior therapy in pediatric obsessive-compulsive disorder. *Biological Psychiatry, 61*, 344-347.

March, J. S., Franklin, M., Nelson, A., & Foa, E. (2001). Cognitive-behavioral psychotherapy for pediatric obsessive-compulsive disorder. *Journal of Clinical Child Psychology, 30*(1), 8-18.

Martino, D., Defazio, G., & Giovannoni, G. (2009). The PANDAS subgroup of tic disorders and childhood-onset obsessive-compulsive disorder. *Journal of Psychosomatic Research, 67*(6), 547-557.

McKay, D., Storch, E. A., Nelson, B., Morales, M., &Moretz, M. W. (2009). Obsessive-compulsive disorder in children and adolescents: Treating difficult cases. In D. McKay & E. A. Storch (Eds.). *Cognitive-behavior therapy for children: treating complex and refractory cases.* New York, NY: Springer.

Merlo, L. J., Storch, E. A., Lehmkuhl, H. D., Jacob, M. L., Murphy, T. K., Goodman, W. K., & Geffken, G. R. (2010). Cognitive behavioral therapy plus motivational interviewing improves outcome for pediatric obsessive-compulsive disorder: a preliminary study. *Cognitve and Behaviour Therapy, 39*(1), 24-27.

Miller, W. R., & Rollnick, S. (2002). *Motivational interviewing: Preparing people for change.* New York: Guilford Press.

Minichiello, W. E., Baer L., & Jenike M. A., (1987). Schizotypal personality disorder: A poor prognostic indicator for behaviour therapy in the treatment of obsessive compulsive disorder. *Journal of Anxiety Disorders, 1*, 273–276.

Norberg, M. M., Krystal, J. H., & Tolin, D. F. (2008). A meta-analysis of D-cycloserine and the facilitation of fear extinction and exposure therapy. *Biological Psychiatry, 63*(12), 1118-1126.

O'Leary, E. M., Barrett, P., & Fjermestad, K. W. (2009). Cognitive-behavioral family treatment for childhood obsessive-compulsive disorder: A 7-year follow-up study. *Journal of Anxiety Disorders, 23*(7), 973-978.

Pediatric OCD Treatment Study Team. (2004). Cognitive behavior therapy, sertraline, and their combination for children and adolescents with obsessive-compulsive disorder. *JAMA, 292*, 1969–1976.

Pence, S. L., Jr., Aldea, A., Sulkowski, M. L., & Storch, E. A. (2010). Cognitive behavioral therapy in adults with obsessive-compulsive disorder and borderline intellectual functioning: A case series of three patients. *Journal of Developmental and Physical Disabilities, 23,* 71–85.

Pence, S. R., Storch, E. A., & Geffken, G. R. (2010). Intense CBT: The effectiveness of intensive cognitive behavior therapy: A case study in pediatric obsessive compulsive disorder. *Annals of the American Psychotherapy Association,* 13(1), 58-61.

Pence, S. L., Jr., Sulkowski, M. L., Jordan, C., & Storch, E. A. (2010). When exposures go wrong: Troubleshooting guidelines for managing difficult scenarios that arise in exposure-based treatment for obsessive-compulsive disorder. *American Journal of Psychotherapy, 64*(1), 39-53.

Piacentini, J., March, J. S.,& Franklin, M. E. (2006). Cognitive-behavior therapy for youth with obsessive-compulsive disorder. In P. C. Kendall (Ed.), *Child and adolescent therapy, third edition.* New York, NY: Guilford.

Rector, N. A., Cassin, S. E., & Richter, M. A. (2009). Psychological treatment of obsessive-compulsive disorder in patients with major depression: A pilot randomized controlled trial. *Canadian Journal of Psychiatry, 54,* 846-851.

Renshaw, K. D., Steketee, G., & Chambless, D. L. (2005). Involving family members in the treatment of OCD. *Cognitive Behaviour Therapy, 34*(3), 164-175.

Rosa-Alcázar, A., Sánchez-Meca, J., Gómez-Conesa, A., & Marín-Martínez, F. (2008). Psychological treatment of obsessive-compulsive disorder: A meta-analysis. *Clinical Psychology Review, 28*(8), 1310-1325.

Salkovskis, P. M. (1985). Obsessional-compulsive problems: A cognitive-behavioural analysis. *Behaviour Research and Therapy, 23*(5), 571-583.

Simpson, H. B., Huppert, J. D., Petkova, E., Foa, E. B., & Liebowitz, M. R. (2006). Response versus remission in obsessive-compulsive disorder. *Journal of Clinical Psychiatry, 67*(2), 269-276.

Simpson, H. B., Zuckoff, A. M., Maher, M. J., Page, J. R., Franklin, M. E., Foa, E. B., . . . Wang, Y. (2010). Challenges using motivational interviewing as an adjunct to exposure therapy for obsessive-compulsive disorder. *Behaviour Research and Therapy, 48*(10), 941-948.

Simpson, H. B., Zuckoff, A., Page, J. R., Franklin, M. E., & Foa, E. B. (2008). Adding motivational interviewing to exposure and ritual prevention for obsessive-compulsive disorder: An open pilot trial. *Cognitive and Behaviour Therapy, 37*(1), 38-49.

Sloman, G. M., Gallant, J., & Storch, E. A. (2007). A school-based treatment model for pediatric obsessive-compulsive disorder. *Child Psychiatry and Human Development, 38*(4), 303-319.

Steketee, G., Chambless, D. L., & Tran, G. Q. (2001). Effects of axis I and II comorbidity on behavior therapy outcome for obsessive-compulsive disorder and agoraphobia. *Comprehensive Psychiatry, 42*(1), 76-86.

Steketee, G., & Van Noppen, B. (2003). Family approaches to treatment for obsessive compulsive disorder. *Journal of Family Psychotherapy, 14*(4), 55-71.

Stewart, R. E., & Chambless, D. L. (2009). Cognitive-behavioral therapy for adult anxiety disorders in clinical practice: a meta-analysis of effectiveness studies. *Journal of Consulting and Clinical Psychology, 77*(4), 595-606.

Storch, E. A., Caporino, N. E., Morgan, J. R., Lewin, A. B., Rojas, A., Brauer, L., . . . Murphy, T. K. (2011). Preliminary investigation of web-camera delivered cognitive-behavioral therapy for youth with obsessive-compulsive disorder. *Psychiatry Research, 189*(3), 407-412.

Storch, E. A., Geffken, G. R., Merlo, L. J., Mann, G., Duke, D., Munson, M., . . . Goodman, W. K. (2007). Family-based cognitive-behavioral therapy for pediatric obsessive-compulsive disorder: Comparison of intensive and weekly approaches. *Journal of the American Academy of Child and Adolescent Psychiatry, 46*(4), 469-478.

Storch, E. A., Lewin, A. B., Farrell, L., Aldea, M. A., Reid, J., Geffken, G. R., & Murphy, T. K. (2010). Does cognitive-behavioral therapy response among adults with obsessive-compulsive disorder differ as a function of certain comorbidities? *Journal of Anxiety Disorders, 24*(6), 547-552.

Storch, E. A., Merlo, L. J., Larson, M. J., Geffken, G. R., Lehmkuhl, H. D., Jacob, M. L., . . . Goodman, W. K. (2008c). Impact of comorbidity on cognitive-behavioral therapy response in pediatric obsessive-compulsive disorder. *Journal of the American Academy of Child and Adolescent Psychiatry, 47*(5), 583-592.

Storch, E. A., Merlo, L. J., Lehmkuhl, H., Geffken, G. R., Jacob, M., Ricketts, E., . . . Goodman, W. K. (2008b). Cognitive-behavioral therapy for obsessive-compulsive disorder: a non-randomized comparison of intensive and weekly approaches. *Journal of Anxiety Disorders, 22*(7), 1146-1158.

Storch, E. A., Milsom, V. A., Merlo, L. J., Larson, M., Geffken, G. R., Jacob, M. L., . . . Goodman, W. K. (2008d). Insight in pediatric obsessive-compulsive disorder: Associations with clinical presentation. *Psychiatry Research, 160*(2), 212-220.

Storch, E. A., Murphy, T. K., Geffken, G. R., Mann, G., Adkins, J., Merlo, L. J., . . . Goodman, W. K. (2006). Cognitive-behavioral therapy for PANDAS-related obsessive-compulsive disorder: Findings from a preliminary waitlist controlled open trial. *Journal of the American Academy of Child and Adolescent Psychiatry, 45*(10), 1171-1178.

Storch, E. A., Murphy, T. K., Goodman, W. K., Geffken, G. R., Lewin, A. B., Henin, A., . . . Geller, D. A. (2010). A preliminary study of D-cycloserine augmentation of cognitive-behavioral therapy in pediatric obsessive-compulsive disorder. *Biological Psychiatry, 68*(11), 1073-1076.

Storch, E. A., Murphy, T. K., Lack, C. W., Geffken, G. R., Jacob, M. L., & Goodman, W. K. (2008a). Sleep-related problems in pediatric obsessive-compulsive disorder. *Journal of Anxiety Disorders, 22*(5), 877-885.

Sulkowski, M. L., Wingfield, R. J., Jones, D., & Coulter, W. A. (2011). Response to intervention and interdisciplinary collaboration: Joining hands to support children and families. *Journal of Applied School Psychology, 27*, 1–16.

Tolin, D. F., Abramowitz, J. S., Kozak, M. J., & Foa, E. B. (2001). Fixity of belief, perceptual aberration, and magical ideation in obsessive-compulsive disorder. *Journal of Anxiety Disorders, 15*(6), 501-510.

Tolin, D. F., Diefenbach, G. J., & Gilliam, C. M. (2011). Stepped care versus standard cognitive-behavioral therapy for obsessive-compulsive disorder: A preliminary study of efficacy and costs. *Depression and Anxiety, 28*(4), 314-323.

Tolin, D. F., Maltby, N., Diefenbach, G. J., Hannan, S. E., & Worhunsky, P. (2004). Cognitive-behavioral therapy for medication nonresponders with obsessive-compulsive disorder: A wait-list-controlled open trial. *Journal of Clinical Psychiatry, 65*(7), 922-931.

van Oppen, P., & Arntz, A. (1994). Cognitive therapy for obsessive-compulsive disorder. *Behaviour Research and Therapy, 32*(1), 79-87.

Watson, H. J., & Rees, C. S. (2008). Meta-analysis of randomized, controlled treatment trials for pediatric obsessive-compulsive disorder. *Journal of Child Psychology and Psychiatry, 49*(5), 489-498.

Wilhelm, S., Buhlmann, U., Tolin, D. F., Meunier, S. A., Pearlson, G. D., Reese, H. E., . . . Rauch, S. L. (2008). Augmentation of behavior therapy with D-cycloserine for obsessive-compulsive disorder. *American Journal of Psychiatry, 165*(3), 335-341.

Wilhelm, S., & Steketee, G. S. (2006). *Cognitive therapy for obsessive-compulsive disorder: A guide for professionals.* Oakland, CA: New Harbinger Publications.

Wilhelm, S., Steketee, G., Fama, J. M., Buhlmann, U., Teachman, B. A., & Golan, E. (2009). Modular cognitive therapy for obsessive-compulsive disorder: A wait-list controlled trial. *Journal of Cognitive Psychotherapy, 23*(4), 294-305.

Zohar, J., Hermesh, H., Weizman, A., Voet, H., & Gross-Isseroff, R. (1999). Orbitofrontal cortex dysfunction in obsessive-compulsive disorder? I. Alternation learning in obsessive-compulsive disorder: Male-female comparisons. *European Neuropsychopharmacology, 9*(5), 407-413.

# Chapter Six

# Pharmacotherapy in the Treatment of Obsessive-Compulsive Disorder

Erika L. Nurmi & Roy Eyal

Obsessive-compulsive disorder (OCD) is a common and often significantly disabling chronic mental illness. OCD is characterized by the presence of distressing and intrusive obsessions, "recurrent and persistent thoughts, impulses, or images"; coupled with compulsions, "repetitive behaviors or mental acts… aimed at preventing or reducing distress or preventing some dreaded event or situation."[1]

---

### Clinical Sidebar – Typical OCD

Charlie is a 10 year boy with history of normal development and no history of psychiatric treatment who was brought to an evaluation after his parents became concerned about his increasing fears of contamination. Over the previous few months Charlie started spending more and more time washing his hands, showering, and smelling his hands. He explains, "I have to wash them and then make sure that they are really clean. If I smell anything bad, I have to wash them again." He worries that if he does not wash his hands he will get sick with serious illness, including AIDS and cancer. At times, he has thoughts he describes as "mean," such as hoping his sister gets a bad grade or thinking that his parents got into a car crash. He washes his hands after having one of these thoughts, even though, when pressed, he knows this will not help decrease the likelihood of these events happening.

---

**Etiology.** The pathophysiology underlying OCD remains poorly understood. Family aggregation and twins studies support a substantial genetic contribution to its etiology, especially pediatric-onset OCD, but no specific genes have been definitely proven to increase OCD risk.[2] Structural differences in the frontal-subcortical circuits of the brain are also implicated in the etiology of OCD with findings including smaller volume of the orbitofrontal cortex, left anterior cingulate cortex (ACC) and the left and right orbitofrontal cortex (OFC); white matter changes; and a larger volume of the thalamus.[3-5] Since these structures mediate motor activity and behavior, it is reasonable that differences exist between healthy controls and people with OCD; however, causality is not established. Likewise, differences have been found in the levels of certain neurotrophic factors in the brains of people with OCD compared to healthy controls.[6] Environment can also play a role in the development of OCD.[7] Stress in general is a risk factor.[8] Infections may also impart risk for the development of OCD. A putative severe, sudden-onset type of OCD triggered by Group A Streptococcal infection, Pediatric Autoimmune Neuropsychiatric Disorders Associated with Streptococcus (PANDAS), has received increasing attention;[9] however, no clear mechanisms have been solidly confirmed and much controversy remains around the diagnosis, treatment and even existence of PANDAS.[10, 11]

---

### *Clinical Sidebar – Chronic Course and Delays in Treatment*

Georgia is a 73-year-old woman always thought to be odd by her neighbors who frequently see her rummaging through her own trash can and walking in and out of her front door many times before leaving her house. When asked about this she explains that she needs to make sure she turned off her stove and locked the back door before she leaves. She had never been evaluated or treated until her adult granddaughter insisted that she seek treatment after years of frustration related to Georgia calling her up to 20 times daily to make sure she was safe.

---

**Epidemiology.** OCD is common in both childhood and adulthood. Of American adult respondents of the National Comorbidity Survey conducted between 2001 and 2003, the lifetime prevalence and 12-month prevalence was 2.3% and 1.2% respectively.[12, 13] Other studies in populations around the world support this finding and indicate that OCD is experienced in all cultures.[13-21] The incidence of the disorder appears to have a bimodal distribution with one peak in childhood (average age of onset of 10 years)[22] and another peak in adulthood (average age of onset 20 years), with earlier onset for males.[13] While the prevalence of OCD is well below that of some psychiatric illnesses, such as Major Depressive Disorder (29.9% lifetime prevalence),[23] several factors expand the negative impact this illness has on populations. For half or more of affected people, OCD runs a chronic course even when receiving treatment.[24] Pinto and colleagues report "67% rated the course as continuous (with mild variation in intensity of symptoms but with no remission), 23% as waxing and waning (with periods of at least 3 months duration of only subclinical symptoms), 8% as episodic (with periods of complete remission of 3 months or more), and 2% as deteriorative (OCD continues to worsen even with treatment)."[25] In a naturalistic 2 year prospective study of the course of OCD, only 6% of treatment-seeking adult patients achieved remission.[26] Even in controlled treatment studies, 30-50% of patients are found to be "treatment resistant". This makes OCD unusually detrimental even in treatment-seeking populations. Impairment is likely worse in those not receiving treatment. Unfortunately, people generally experience impairing symptoms for many years before seeking treatment. [25]

**Comorbidity.** OCD is highly comorbid with other mental illness. About 9 in 10 people with OCD have comorbid mental illness including very high rates of other anxiety disorders, mood disorders, impulse control and tic disorders and substance use disorders. In adults, >50% have comorbid Major Depressive Disorder.[13] In children, approximately half have comorbid ADHD.[22, 27]

**Assessment.** OCD presents with a range of severity that changes over time and in different situations such as during successful treatment. Over the past decades, several rating scales have been established, but the most widely accepted is the Yale-Brown Obsessive-Compulsive Scale (YBOCS).[28, 29] Recent concerns about the validity of the YBOCS[30] led to an update of this scale,[31] but the original YBOCS and the related Child version, CYBOCS,[32] remain the most commonly reported tools for communicating severity of symptoms and response to treatment in the studies discussed in this review.

---

*Clinical Sidebar – The YBOCS*

The YBOCS is a clinician-rated scale consisting of more than 20 questions with ranked score of 0 points for no symptoms, up to 4 points for extreme symptoms. The score is the sum of the 10 principal questions for a total possible score of 0-40 points. Scores range from sub-clinical (0–7), to mild (8–15), to moderate (16–23), to severe (24–31), to extreme (32–40).

Questions included in the final score include the following:
- Time occupied by obsessive thoughts.
- Interference due to obsessive thoughts.
- Distress associated with obsessive thoughts.
- Resistance against obsessions.
- Degree of control over obsessive thoughts.
- Time spent performing compulsive behaviors.
- Interference due to compulsive behaviors.
- Distress associated with compulsive behaviors.
- Resistance against compulsions.
- Degree of control over compulsive behaviors.

---

To help understand the outcomes of treatment, below are some examples of the changes in symptoms correlated to a specific reduction in YBOCS score:

A **2 point reduction** in total YBOCS score could mean that all symptoms remained the same except: previously patient was "completely and willingly yielding to all compulsions" but now "makes some effort to resist compulsions".

A **4 point reduction** in total YBOCS score could mean that all symptoms remained the same except: reduced time spent performing compulsions from 5 hours to less than 1 hour daily, and patient previously very disturbed by obsessive thoughts but now mildly disturbed.

A **10 point reduction** in to total YBOCS score could mean that for each question the score decreased by one point, for example: reduced time occupied by obsessions from 2 hours daily to 30 minutes daily, and previously "incapacitated" by obsessive thoughts but is now "substantially impaired", and previously "severely disturbed" by obsessive thoughts but is now "moderately disturbed but still manageable", and previously "making some effort to resist obsessions" but is now "trying to resist most of the time", and previously had "not control of obsessive thoughts" but now has "little control", and reduced time spent performing compulsions from 8 hours daily to 5 hours daily, and previously had "definite interference with social or occupation performance" but now has "slight interference" due to compulsive behaviors, and previously "severely disturbed" but compulsive behavior but now is "moderately disturbed", and previously "yielding to almost all compulsions" but now "makes some effort to resist", and previously "little control" over compulsions but now "has moderate control."

**Treatment.** Response to various treatments including psychotherapy, medication, and more, has been measured using standardized scales such as the YBOCS and general assessments such as Clinical Global Impression Scale (CGI). Robust response is the exception in the treatment of OCD; however, studies have found positive effects from both psychotherapy and medication. These results have been reviewed in several recent publications for adult[33-36] and pediatric patients.[22] While the focus of this review is on the use of psychopharmacology for OCD, therapy (particularly using Exposure and Response Prevention [ERP]) is a well-documented, effective treatment for OCD. Though head-to-head comparisons are complicated, therapy including ERP is likely similarly or more effective than medication management alone, and the combination is possibly most effective.[37-39] Therapeutically oriented self-help resources such as computerized therapy may also be an important tool in the treatment of OCD due to the prominent gap in treatment seeking and limited access to trained clinicians.[40, 41]

---

### Clinical Sidebar – Treatment for OCD

John is a 27 year old graduate student. He and his wife recently had their first baby and he is seeking treatment for the first time for distressing thoughts of harming his infant. He has developed a ritual of reentering his infant's room until he crosses the threshold "with a positive thought in my mind." At times this takes more than 5 minutes. He describes many years of other compulsions, which he has successfully hidden from others. At first he says that he does not have time to attend regular therapy and is started on the SSRI, fluvoxamine. After several months, his symptoms have decreased somewhat, but he continues to be frustrated by his symptoms and at times avoids caring for his infant. This is causing increasing conflict with his wife. He starts therapy including ERP with added reduction in symptom impairment. His wife attends several sessions to learn about the process of ERP and now helps him by encouraging him to recognize OCD thoughts and complete exposure-based exercises.

---

## METHODS

This clinically-oriented review focuses on pharmacologic approaches to OCD management. The authors performed PubMed searches for each medication or form of treatment using a title search for the medication name and "Obsessive Compulsive Disorder." The searches were conducted in February and March of 2013 and were limited to Controlled Clinical Trials, Randomized Controlled Trials (RCT), or Clinical Trials; human subjects; and papers published in English. If no such data was available, other types of publications were reviewed such as open studies, non-controlled studies, and case reports. These papers were reviewed and statistics were extracted, where possible, to calculate the Cohen's $d$ Effect Size (ES)[42] and Number Needed to Treat (NNT) for binary outcome (success/failure or response/no response): NNT = 100/(% treatment responders - % control responders).[43]

After reviewing the available literature, the authors determined the level of quality of evidence following the Oxford Centre for Evidence Based Medicine (CEBM) framework to judge the quality of the study and Grade of Recommendation for treatment.[44] *It is important to note that these "grades" do not rate how well the treatments work comparatively, but the level of evidence (evidence grade = EGr) supporting use in OCD.*

### Levels of Evidence, Oxford Centre for Evidence-Based Medicine [44]

The CEBM recommends the following levels for individual studies:

- 1a: Systematic reviews (with homogeneity) of randomized controlled trials
- 1b: Individual randomized controlled trials (with narrow confidence interval)
- 1c: All or none randomized controlled trials
- 2a: Systematic reviews (with homogeneity) of cohort studies
- 2b: Individual cohort study or low quality randomized controlled trials (e.g. <80% follow-up)
- 2c: "Outcomes" Research; ecological studies
- 3a: Systematic review (with homogeneity) of case-control studies
- 3b: Individual case-control study
- 4: Case-series (and poor quality cohort and case-control studies)
- 5: Expert opinion without explicit critical appraisal, or based on physiology, bench research or "first principles"

Treatment is then graded as follows, and referred to as Evidence Grade in this review:

A. consistent level 1 studies
B. consistent level 2 or 3 studies or extrapolations from level 1 studies
C. level 4 studies or extrapolations from level 2 or 3 studies
D. level 5 evidence or troublingly inconsistent or inconclusive studies of any level

---

### Clinical Sidebar – Measures of Clinically Meaningful Effects

*NUMBER NEEDED TO TREAT (NNT)*
NNT is calculated by using this formula: 100 / (% responders to treatment – % responders to control). For example, a study reports that 60% of patients responded to treatment with medication X and 35% of patients responded to placebo. NNT = 100/(60-35) = 4. This means that for every 4 patients treated with medication X, one more patients will respond to treatment than would have responded to placebo.

*EFFECT SIZE*
Effect size is a measure of the response to treatment standardized to the variance in the measure used. This allows for a dimensionless result that can be used to compare treatments in different studies even if different scales of measurement tools are used. An effect size of 0.2 is considered "small," 0.4 "moderate," and 0.8 or above "large."

# RESULTS
## OCD Monotherapy (see Table 1)

TRICYCLIC ANTIDEPRESSANTS
*Clomipramine (Adults: Evidence Grade (EGr) = A, Children and adolescents: EGr = B)*
Clomipramine is a tricyclic antidepressant with strong serotonin reuptake inhibition. A Pubmed search for clinical studies of clomipramine returned 65 publications. Nine of these publications report results from placebo-controlled studies. The largest study by Katz et. al., is a CEBM Level 1b study with N=263, reported strong ES = 1.3 and NNT of 1.7.[45] This robust clinical response was similar to several smaller level 2b studies reviewed with ES ranging from 0.7 to 1.4 and NNT ranging from 1.7 to 3. The consistency of these results over various settings and time, give clomipramine an EGr = A for adults. Two studies reported original data with placebo controls in pediatric patients.[46, 47] DeVeaugh et al in 1991 reported statistically significant results in an N=60 level 2b double-blind parallel group study with NNT=2.3.[46] Data was not available to calculate an ES. This result is supported by a small (N=19) crossover study with ES=0.8.[47] These results support the finding of robust clinical response as in adults, but replication with high quality studies is needed as is reflected in the EGr = B. Like other tricyclic antidepressants, clomipramine has a high potential for side effects, complicating its use and potentially biasing studies by limiting true blinding. In the Katz study, frequency of side effects was dramatically different between the treatment and placebo groups.[45] Clomipramine has an FDA indication for both adult and pediatric OCD.

---

*Clinical Sidebar – Side Effects of Clomipramine*
Side effects are common with clomipramine making tolerability a problem. Like other tricyclic antidepressants, clomipramine has a narrow therapeutic window, so its use is limited in patients with suicide risk. Rates of side effects from Katz et. al. are as follows (CMI = clomipramine, PLA = placebo):

| Side Effect | %CMI | %PLA |
|---|---|---|
| Dry mouth | 83 | 6 |
| Tremor | 57 | 0 |
| Constipation | 46 | 12 |
| Headache | 37 | 35 |
| Increased appetite | 17 | 0 |
| Dizziness | 29 | 6 |
| Ejaculation failure | 16 | 0 |

## Other Tricyclic antidepressants (Adults: EGr = D, Children and adolescents: EGr = D)

In contrast to clomipramine, other tricyclic antidepressants have negative evidence, or evidence against efficacy in the treatment of OCD. One small non-controlled level 4 study of imipramine showed "modest" improvement.[48] A crossover comparison study of children and adolescents compared clomipramine and desipramine, finding that "Clomipramine was clearly superior to desipramine."[49] There is no high quality data supporting the use of tricyclic antidepressants for OCD other than clomipramine.

## SELECTIVE SEROTONIN REUPTAKE INHIBITORS (OVERALL EGr = A)

SSRIs are commonly prescribed antidepressants with a primary mechanism of action likely related to increasing the concentration of serotonin in the synaptic cleft by blocking serotonin reuptake by its transporter. A Cochrane review level 1a publication including 17 studies involving 3,097 adult participants found that, as a group, SSRIs are more effective than placebo as a group. Two meta-analyses of serotonergic medications for treatment of OCD in pediatric patients have been published, and both support the use of SSRIs.[50, 51] Both studies included data from clinical trials of SSRIs and clomipramine, so the results cannot be generalized to SSRIs alone.

## Citalopram (Adults: EGr = B, Children and adolescents: EGr = C)

A PubMed search for clinical studies of citalopram returned 15 publications. Only one article reported original data with a placebo control. With an N = 401, this fixed dose, level 1b study of adults with OCD was statistically significant with moderate effect size and NNT between 3.5 and 6.5.[52] For children and adolescents, data was limited to one level 2b study comparing citalopram to fluoxetine which found no significant difference between groups,[53] and two level 4 open-label cohort studies all suggesting that citalopram is effective and safe.[54, 55] Replications of these studies would add to the strength of evidence. Due to the recent black box warning about an elevated risk of prolonged QT at doses above 40 mg and the frequent need for higher dosing in OCD, cardiac risk of higher citalopram dose may limit its use in OCD.[56]

## Escitalopram (Adults: EGr = B, Children and adolescents: EGr = D)

A Pubmed search for clinical studies of escitalopram returned 7 publications. Only one reported original data with a placebo control. With an N = 341, this fixed dose level 1b study of adults with OCD was statistically significant for 20 mg dosing and approached statistical significance for 10 mg (p=0.052). The effect size was low to moderate with NNT ~ 5.[57] Non-controlled level 2b studies add to the evidence of efficacy for escitalopram;[58, 59] however, replication of a placebo-controlled trial is currently lacking. High dose escitalopram may be more effective and several case series and open label studies have been published to address this question. One found no difference between escitalopram 20 mg and 30 mg.[58] In contrast, an open label cohort study showed added benefit of escitalopram up to 50 mg daily[59]. A retrospective chart review with N=246 corroborated that escitalpram is more effective at higher doses, where best outcomes were achieved with escitalopram doses greater than 40 mg/day. Side effects rates also were higher and no controlled data has been published supporting these findings. No publications include data for escitalopram use in pediatric patients with OCD.

---

***Clinical Sidebar – High dose SSRIs***

With all of the variables involved in clinical trials, it is impossible to design a perfect study. One variable is dose of medication to use. In treatment studies of OCD, SSRIs are generally studied using doses found to be effective in the treatment of Major Depressive Disorder. Some experts believe these doses are too low for the treatment of OCD. A meta-analysis by Bloch et al published in 2009 found that subjects responded best to "high dose" SSRIs, for example escitalopram 30-40 mg, paroxetine 60mg, and fluvoxamine 300-350mg. This finding supports the practice of using high dose SSRIs for OCD if tolerated, as is recommended by the American Psychiatric Association (APA) and the American Academy of Child and Adolescent Psychiatry (AACAP).[60, 61]

| Dose Range Provided in AACAP Guidelines: | |
| --- | --- |
| Clomipramine | 50-200 |
| Fluoxetine | 10-80 |
| Sertaline | 50-200 |
| Fluvoxamine | 50-300 |
| Paroxetine | 10-60 |
| Citalopram | 10-60* |

*An EKG should be obtained when using doses of citalopram exceeding 40 mg due to risk of QT prolongation.

---

### Fluoxetine (Adults: EGr = B, Children and adolescents: EGr = A)

A Pubmed search for clinical studies of fluoxetine returned 38 publications. Three publications reported original data in adults with a placebo control. The largest level 1b study by Tollefson et. al. published in 1994 was statistically significant with P<0.001, NNT=4, and ES 0.8.[62] The oldest published in 1993 by Montgomery et al with N=214 except for responder rates in 40mg and 60mg group, a secondary outcome. Change in YBOCS was only trend level with P=0.059 in the 60mg group with an ES=0.4.[63] It is possible that this study was compromise by the use of too low a dose of fluoxetine. A third study with N=40 found statistical significance with ES=0.4.[64] Two reports involving pediatric subjects provided original data with a placebo control. Geller and colleagues published the largest level 1b study of 103 youth, yielding statistically significant outcomes (p=0.026) with moderate ES = 0.5 and NNT = 4.2.[65] A small level 2b crossover study (N=14) was not statistically significant P=0.17, but supports a conclusion that fluoxetine is effective.[66] Combined with another open label level 2c study of 61 adolescents with positive results,[67] fluoxetine has EGr = A evidence of efficacy for youth. Two small cohort level 4 studies with N=4 and 6 suggest benefit for preschoolers with OCD,[68, 69] but further definitive evidence in this age group is warranted. Fluoxetine has an FDA indication for both adult and pediatric OCD.

---

**Clinical sidebar – What does that Effect Size actually mean?**
In the level 1b study by Tollefson published in 1994, fluoxetine was found to have a large effect size of ~0.8. The average YBOCS score at baseline was ~24. After 13 weeks of treatment, the mean YBOCS score of the placebo group was unchanged from baseline but the mean YBOCS score of the group treated with fluoxetine 60 mg was 17. This endpoint mean YBOCS score was still above the entry criteria for the study, YBOCS score of at least 16, indicating moderate or greater severity. However, a reduction of 7 points indicates significant changes in symptoms (see *Clinical sidebar – YBOCS*).

---

### Fluvoxamine (Adults: EGr = A, Children and adolescents: EGr = B)

A Pubmed search for clinical studies of fluvoxamine returned 31 publications. Seven publications in adults reported original data with a placebo control including 2 level 1b studies with N>150 and generally consistent results with p<0.05, ES of 0.4 and 0.3, and NNT of 3 and 7.[70, 71] Smaller RTCs support these findings. One RTC in pediatric patients (N=120) reported statistical significance with p=0.033, ES=0.3, and NNT of 6; however, the dropout rate was 38%, so this is a level 2b study.[72] A small level 4 study supports that fluvoxamine is effective for OCD in adolescents.[73] Fluvoxamine has an FDA indication for both adult and pediatric OCD.

### Paroxetine (Adults: EGr = A, Children and adolescents: EGr = B)

A Pubmed search for clinical studies of paroxetine returned 17 publications. Three reports in adults analyzed original data with a placebo control including 2 level 1b studies with statistically significant results.[57, 74] These results suggest better response to higher doses. NNT was only calculable in one study with NNT~5. A third study was compromised from high dropout rate,[75] leaving two level 1b studies with positive results. Pediatric data is limited to one level 1b study with p=0.002, NNT=4, and ES=0.4.[76] Paroxetine has an FDA indication for both adult and pediatric OCD.

### Sertraline (Adults: EGr = B, Children and adolescents: EGr = A)

A Pubmed search for clinical studies of sertraline returned 21 publications. Three adult investigations reported original data with a placebo control. One fixed dose level 1b study reported statistical significance after pooling data from the 3 treatment arms with p=0.006. This study found a moderate ES of 0.35 with NNT=11.[77] A second study was negative[78] and the third found statistically positive results only by pooling all the treatment groups, a *post hoc* statistical decision which was not a primary outcome.[79] The quality of this study was also compromised by a 30% dropout rate and was therefore judged to be level 2b. Data was not supplied to calculate ES, but a NNT of 6 was estimated from a graph. Two level 1b studies in children and adolescents have positive consistent results with moderate ES=0.4 and NNT 6, giving sertraline good evidence of modest effect in pediatric patients.[39, 80] High dose sertraline, up to 400 mg, was found to be superior to 200 mg for reducing symptoms, though not for overall response, in a sample of nonresponders to 16 weeks of sertraline 200 mg (N=66).[81] This suggests that higher doses may add benefit. Sertraline has an FDA indication for both adult and pediatric OCD.

### SEROTONIN-NOREPINEPHRINE REUPTAKE INHIBITORS

### Venlafaxine (Adults: EGr = C, Children and adolescents: EGr = D)

A Pubmed search for clinical studies of venlafaxine returned 9 publications. One publication reported original data with a placebo control in adult subjects. This level 2b study with N=30 was not statistically significant; however, some secondary measures favored venlafaxine and the study was compromised by 8 subjects dropping out.[83] One rater-blinded study with N=73 comparing +venlafaxine to clomipramine in adults found equivalent results in both groups, suggesting that venlafaxine is as effective as clomipramine in adults with OCD.[84] A 12 week double-blind comparison with paroxetine with N=150 found equivalent response in all measures[85] contributing fair data to support efficacy of venlafaxine. An open cohort with N=39 reported a response rate of ~70%.[86] There is no published data with pediatric patients. Data supporting the use of other SNRIs in OCD is lacking.

Table 1. Double-Blind Randomized Controlled Trials Supporting Clomipramine and Selective Serotonin Reuptake Inhibitors (SSRIs) for OCD Monotherapy.

| Medication | Publication | Dose | N | Ages | Weeks | Outcome P value | NNT | ES |
|---|---|---|---|---|---|---|---|---|
| Clomipramine **Adults: EGr = A** **CAP: EGr = B** | DeVeaugh 1992 | Up to 200mg | 60 | 10-17 | 10 | <0.05 | 2.3 | NC |
| | Jenike 1989 | Up to 300mg | 27 | Adult | 10 | <0.001 | NC | 1.4 |
| | Flament 1985 | Up to 200mg | 19 | 6-18 | 10 | 0.04 | NC | 0.8 |
| | Katz 1990 | Up to 300mg | 263 | 18-65 | 10 | <0.001 | 1.7 | 1.3 |
| | Foa 2005 | Up to 250mg | 62 | 18-70 | 12 | <0.05 | 3 | 0.7 |
| Citalopram **Adults: EGr = B** **CAP: EGr = C** | Montgomery 2001 | Fixed 20mg /40mg /60mg | 401 | 18-65 | 12 | <0.001 | 4.8 6.5 3.5 | 0.4 0.5 0.7 |
| Escitalopram **Adults: EGr = B CAP: EGr = D** | Stein 2007 | Fixed dose 10mg 20mg | 341 | 18-65 | 12 | =0.052 <0.01 | ~5 | 0.3 0.3 |
| Fluoxetine **Adults: EGr =B** **CAP: EGr = A** | Jenike 1997 | Up to 80mg | 40 | Adult | 10 | 0.03 reported | NC | 0.4 |
| | Riddle 1992 | 20mg | 14 | 8-16 | 8 wk/ 12 wk | 0.17 NS | NC | 0.8 |
| | Tollefson 1994 | Flx 20-60mg | 355 | 15-70 | 13 | <0.001 | 4 | 0.8 |
| | Geller 2001 | Up to 60mg | 103 | 7-17 | 13 | =0.026 | 4.2 | 0.5 |
| | Montgomery 1993 | Fixed 20mg /40mg /60mg | 214 | 18-65 | 8 | NS NS NS=0.059 | 10 4.5 4.8 | 0.2 0.2 0.4 |
| Fluvoxamine **Adults: EGr =A** **CAP: EGr = B** | Riddle 2001 | Up to 200mg | 120 | 8-17 | 10 | 0.033 | 6.2 | 0.3 |
| | Nakatani 2005 | Up to 200mg | 18 | 18-60 | 12 | <0.01 | 3.3 | 0.8 |
| | Jenike 1990 | Up to 300mg | 38 | >18 | 10 | <0.001 | NC | 0.5 |
| | Perse 1987 | Up to 300mg | 20 | 18-60 | 20 | 0.027 | NC | 0.6 |
| | Goodman 1996 | Up to 300mg | 156 | >18 | 10 | 0.013 | 2.9 | 0.5 |
| | Hollinder 2003 | Up to 300mg | 253 | >18 | 10 | 0.001 | 6.7 | 0.3 |
| | Goodman 1989 | Up to 300mg | 42 | Adult | 6-8 | <0.01 | 2.3 | NC |

| Medication | Publication | Dose | N | Ages | Weeks | Outcome P value | NNT | ES |
|---|---|---|---|---|---|---|---|---|
| Paroxetine **Adults: EGr =A** **CAP: EGr = B** | Geller 2004 | Up to 50mg | 203 | 7-17 | 10 | 0.002 | 4.2 | 0.4 |
| | Stein 2007 | 40mg | 231 | 18-65 | 12 | <0.05 | ~5 | 0.5 |
| | Kamijima 2004 | Up to 50mg | 188 | 16-71 | 12 | Reported significant | 4 | 0.7 |
| | Hollander 2003 | Fixed 20mg /40mg /60mg | 348 | >16 | 12 | NS 0.003 <0.001 | NC | NC |
| Sertraline **Adults: EGr =B** **CAP: EGr = A** | Griest 1995 | Fixed 50/100/200 | 325 | >18 | 12 | Pooled 0.006 | 11 | 0.4 |
| | Choinard 1990 | Up to 200mg | 87 | adult | 8 | NS | NC | NC |
| | POTS 2004 | Up to 200mg | 56 | 7-17 | 12 | 0.007 | 6 | 0.4 |
| | Kronig 1999 | UP to 200mg | 167 | >18 | 12 | <0.05 | 6* | NC |
| | March 1998 | Up to 200mg | 187 | 6-17 | 12 | 0.005 | 6.3 | 0.4 |

Abbreviations: EGr = Evidence Grade, CAP = Children and adolescents, ES = Effect Size, NNT = number needed to treat, NS = non-significant, NC = not calculable.


## MONOAMINE OXIDASE INHIBITORS (ADULTS: EGr =D. CHILDREN AND ADOLESCENTS: EGr = D.)

A Pubmed search for clinical studies of phenelzine returned 2 publications. One publication reported original data with a placebo control in adult subjects. In a double-blinded three arm, phenelzine/fluoxetine/placebo, study with phenelzine N=20 and placebo N=21; neither phenelzine nor fluoxetine differed from placebo.[64] In contrast, a double-blind study with N=30 comparing phenelzine with clomipramine found the groups statistically equivalent suggesting efficacy for phenelzine.[87] These studies are judged to be level 2b and are inconsistent, yielding an overall EGr=D. There is no data for pediatric patients. A Pubmed search for clinical studies of clorgyline returned one small double-blind comparison with clomipramine. Only 13 subject entered the treatment protocol of the study and findings supported clomipramine as being superior to clorgyline.[88] A Pubmed search for clinical studies of other MAOIs returned no results.

## OTHER MEDICATIONS

### *Buspirone (Adults: EGr = D, Children and adolescents: EGr = D)*

A Pubmed search for clinical studies of buspirone returned 8 publications. No publications reported original data for monotherapy with a placebo control. A level 2b double-blind comparison study with N=20 found buspirone equivalent to clomipramine.[89] An open label level 2c trial with N=14 found "of 14 patient with OCD who entered an 8-week open trial of buspirone, none improved."[90] No data is available for pediatric patients.

### *Bupropion (Adults: EGr = D, Children and adolescents: EGr = D)*

A Pubmed search for clinical studies of bupropion returned one level 2c open-label outcomes study with N=12.[91] This study reported no benefit from treatment.

### *D-cycloserine (Adults: EGr = B, Children and adolescents: EGr = C)*

D-cycloserine (DCS), a glutamate NMDA receptor partial agonist and anti-mycobacterial agent, was first tested as a learning facilitator in conjunction with CBT due to its potentiation of fear extinction in rodent models.[74] DCS has shown positive results in RCTs of both children[92] and adults,[93, 94] but has not been helpful in all studies,[95] perhaps due to considerable differences in dose and timing across studies. This may be significant due to differential receptor affinities across the dosing range and onset and duration of effects. Since DCS is a partial agonist at the NMDA receptor, it can act as an antagonist at higher doses and reverse desired effects.[96, 97] Indeed, studies employing lower doses (~50mg) have been more successful. The timing of DCS administration is also a critical factor, with positive studies reporting the use of DCS immediately preceding[92, 94] or following[98] exposure therapy. Finally, while single administration is insufficient to produce benefit, prolonged use may cause receptor desensitization and effect reversal.[96] Despite variability in protocols and outcomes, three meta-analyses and a systematic review conclude that DCS is a promising new agent with small to moderate effect sizes.[99-102] Importantly, DCS appears to accelerate the response slope consistently across positive studies, but does not enhance the overall magnitude of response.[93, 94, 103] Nevertheless, a more rapid response induction can minimize patient distress and the significant expense of CBT treatment. A recent finding suggests that the success of the exposures performed while taking DCS may also influence outcomes.[104] While successful exposures may be required for DCS-mediated learning enhancement, unsuccessful exposures may actually inhibit learning. DCS was well-tolerated in all studies with no significant adverse effects, including those in children.[99] Once exposure timing and conditions are better understood, DCS may prove to be a useful adjunct of CBT treatment.

> ### *Clinical Sidebar – Medication or Therapy?*
> One randomized study with N=56 compared sertraline with cognitive behavioral group therapy (CBGT).[82] Since there was no placebo control group, this study is unable to support the efficacy of sertraline alone, however it does contribute to evidence-based treatment decisions. In this study, CBGT was superior to sertraline alone with a NNT=3.6. While this seems like a robustly superior benefit for CBGT, the quality of this study is compromised by the lack of blinding (the subjects and providers know if they are taking medication or in group therapy). A similar study in adolescents supports the conclusion that CBGT is superior to monotherapy with sertraline.[77] The Pediatric OCD Treatment Study (POTS) in 2004 found CBT and sertraline treatment equivalent but the combination superior.

## COMPLEMENTARY AND ALTERNATIVE MEDICINES (ADULTS: EGr = D, CHILDREN AND ADOLESCENTS: EGr = D)

A Pubmed search for clinical studies of *Silybum marianum*, the medicinal plant with common name Milk Thistle (MT), returned one publication. In this 8 week double-blind comparison study with fluoxetine 30 mg daily with N=37 adults, YBOCS scores decreased by ~50% in both groups with no statistical difference suggesting that MT is equivalent to fluoxetine for the treatment of OCD.[97] This study is compromised by incomplete data, high mean YBOCS score at baseline, no control arm, and inconsistencies in the graphs included and the text. No high quality data is available to support the use of MT for OCD. A Pubmed search for clinical studies of *Hypericum perforatum*, the medicinal plant with common name St. John's Wort (SJW), returned two publications. One publication reported original data with a placebo control in adult subjects. With N=60, this level 2b study found no benefit of SJW over placebo on any measures.[98] A Pubmed search for clinical studies of *Echium amoenum*, the medicinal plant with common name Borage (BG), returned one publication.[99] In this 6 week double-blind placebo controlled study with N=40 adults, BG extract was superior to placebo with ES of ~2.0 and p<0.001. This strongly positive study is too small to determine clinical recommendations, but certainly calls for replication. A Pubmed search for clinical studies of inositol returned two publications. One publication reported original data with a placebo control in adult subjects.[100] This double-blind placebo controlled cross over study of N=13 reported statistically significant results with ES = 0.5. While this is a promising finding, this study is too small to determine clinical recommendations.

## Pediatric-Specific Considerations

Similarities in OCD presentation, prevalence and treatment exist across the lifespan; however, important differences in pediatric OCD include a more episodic course, slight male predominance, enriched family histories, and high rates of comorbidity and disinhibition.[22] Common childhood comorbidities such as attention-deficit hyperactivity disorder (ADHD), tic disorders, oppositional-defiant disorder (ODD), and autism spectrum disorders (ASDs) can complicate both CBT and medication treatment.[22] Without appropriate intervention, it is common for pediatric OCD to chronically persist into adulthood.[101] The AACAP Practice Parameters for OCD consider CBT, with or without medication, as the first-line intervention for pediatric OCD.[60] Because family accommodation is common, family involvement in therapy is often essential. As discussed previously, support for most pharmacotherapies in children have paralleled that in adults. While general dosing precautions for pediatric populations apply, such as using lower starting doses or divided doses, similarly high dose SSRIs can be beneficial in youth if tolerated.[60]

## Maintenance and Discontinuation

Based on data suggesting that many patients will tolerate a gradual SSRI taper without worsening of their clinical symptoms,[102] current guidelines advise the continuation of effective treatment for at least 1 year, followed by gradual discontinuation to minimize the risk of relapse.[61, 103] The APA recommends 1–2 years of symptom remission before considering a gradual taper by decrements of 10%–25% every 1–2 months with close observation for symptom return.[61] The value of longer-term treatment should be considered after two or three relapses of at least moderate severity.[60] The inclusion of CBT in treatment may facilitate successful medication discontinuation.[61, 104]

## Treatment Resistance

According to the AACAP, failure of adequate trials of at least two SSRIs or one SSRI and a clomipramine trial and a failure of adequately delivered CBT would constitute treatment resistance.[60] This includes a minimum of 10 weeks of each SSRI or clomipramine at maximum recommended or tolerated doses, with no change in dose for the preceding 3 weeks. CBT nonresponders would be defined as those showing no improvement after 8-10 total sessions of adequate CBT. Strategies to manage treatment resistance include augmentation with a second medication (detailed below) or an increase in the intensity of treatment. Treatment refractory cases after augmentation or intensive therapy would be candidates for brain stimulation and psychosurgical approaches (discussed below).

## Augmentation Agents

Approximately 40–60% of patients with OCD achieve only partial response to first-line treatment with SSRIs,[105] and up to 20% are treatment-resistant, deriving little benefit.[106] Even in those who respond well, a minority of patients reach full symptom remission with optimal SSRI treatment.[107] Augmentation strategies are recommended in those with a partial response to an SSRI trial of adequate dose and duration or poor response to multiple SSRIs. In many cases, CBT augmentation of an SSRI represents the most effective and least harmful option. However, if CBT is not an option or is not successful, many pharmacologic augmentation options have been investigated (Table 2). Augmentation strategies can be classified by the neurotransmitter systems predominantly targeted: serotonergic, dopaminergic, glutamatergic, or those impacting other neurotransmitter systems.

### SEROTONERGIC AGENTS

In addition to its efficacy as monotherapy (discussed above), Clomipramine has shown promise when used as augmentation therapy in case studies in both adults and children[108-110] and in a double-blind randomized trial of augmentation with clomipramine compared to quetiapine in adults.[111] Monitoring for patients taking clomipramine in conjunction with an SSRI should include vigilance for cardiac effects, seizures, and signs of serontonin syndrome. Interactions between clomipramine and SSRIs are important to consider due to cytochrome p450 metabolic enzyme induction or inhibition. Certain combinations can increase side effects due to these interactions (sertraline + clomipramine) and others can minimize them (fluvoxamine + clomipramine) due to effects on the metabolic pathways in clomipramine metabolism.[112]

Serotonin receptor (5-HT) agonists and antagonists have also been a target in OCD augmentation. In a lone single-blind RCT study of mirtazapine (a postsynaptic $5\text{-HT}_2$ and $5\text{-HT}_3$ receptor antagonist) in OCD, overall response was not improved but a shorter latency of response was observed.[113] Two groups have published positive RCTs of fluoxetine augmented with ondansetron or granisetron (5-HT3 antagonists) in Iranian populations.[114, 115] These trials await replication in and generalization to other populations. Two negative double-blind trials of buspirone (a 5HT1A partial agonist) augmentation have been reported.[116, 117]

### DOPAMINERGIC AGENTS

#### Antipsychotics

While antipsychotic monotherapy has little support, augmentation of SSRIs with antipsychotic medications is a common strategy in OCD treatment. In a meta-analysis of 9 placebo-controlled trials, one third of patients failing two prior SRI trials became responders after the addition of an antipsychotic.[118] A second meta-analysis of 12 placebo-controlled trials[119] demonstrated significant benefit of antipsychotic augmentation using standardized criteria of both categorical (responders defined as ≥35% reduction in Y-BOCS score) and continuous (Y-BOCS score differences) outcomes. Overall, reported response rate was 28% versus 13% in the treatment group compared to placebo, with a relative risk of 2.10 (N = 12; n = 394; 95% CI: 1.16–3.80) or ES 0.54 and NNT 5.9; however, specific antipsychotics showed widely variable effects.

In some studies, antipsychotics have demonstrated the greatest benefit for OCD with comorbid tic disorder, which is often resistant to SSRI monotherapy.[120] In Bloch and colleagues' meta-analysis, NNT increased from 5.9 to 2.3 in patients with cormorbid tic disorders.[118] A second meta-analyses one year later did not detect this effect unless dose was considered, with higher doses improving response in trials including subjects with comorbid tic disorders.[121] Antipsychotics have also been proposed for patients with poor insight approaching delusional proportions, but this has not been well studied.[122]

Atypical antipsychotics have received almost exclusive attention in the antipsychotic SSRI augmentation literature. Haloperidol is the only typical antipsychotic with RCT data, showing it to be effective (ES = 0.91, NNT = 3.4), especially when comorbid tics are present.[120] Three positive RCTs have been published on risperidone augmentation of SSRIs using doses ranging from 0.5 to 3 mg for the majority of patients.[123-125] The Dold and colleagues meta-analysis highlighted that risperidone was the only antipsychotic reviewed that demonstrated efficacy using both the continuous change in YBOCS outcome (combined ES = 0.89) and the dichotomous responder criteria of ≥35% decrease in CYBOCS (NNT range across reports = 2.9-3.3). While quetiapine is the most studied neuroleptic in OCD, six controlled trials using doses from 200-600 mg have produced mixed results,[126-131] generating a very small combined ES of 0.18 in the meta-analysis by Dold et al. A comparison study originally claimed superiority of quetiapine over clomipramine in an open-label design but the reverse result emerged in a follow-up RCT.[111, 132] Two RCTs have been published for olanzapine, also with conflicting results,[133, 134] but because one study reported a much larger effect than the other (ES 0.81 vs. 0.29), the olanzapine combined ES cited by Dold et al. was moderate at 0.48. One possible reason for this ES disparity was the use of double the olanzapine dose in the positive trial (10 mg versus 5 mg). In line with a larger olanzapine effect size, a single-blind comparison study using flexible dosing suggested that olanzapine was equivalent to risperidone.[135] Two positive RCTs using doses from 10-15 mg have supported aripiprazole SSRI augmentation,[136, 137] though risperidone was superior to aripiprazole in a single-blind randomized comparison.[138] Only one aripiprazole RCT had been published at the time of the Dold and colleagues meta-analysis, but results of the second trial were similar (ES 1.13 and 1.17 in the Sayyah and

Muscatello studies respectively).[136, 137] While Sayyah et al. did not provide sufficient data to calculate NNT, the Muscatello et al. study yielded a NNT of 2.8. Almost no data is available for ziprasidone augmentation, but one retrospective case review found it to be less effective than quetiapine.[139] A 2010 Cochrane Systematic Review supported risperidone and quetiapine but not olanzapine use in SSRI augmentation treatement for OCD.[140] Given the agreement across multiple RCTs for risperidone and aripiprazole, these both warrant an EGr = A for SSRI augmentation in adult OCD. Conflicting results underscore the need for large, well-designed studies to resolve these inconsistencies limiting quetiapine and olanzapine recommendation (EGr = C). SSRI augmentation studies in pediatric OCD are limited to two positive case series evaluating risperidone and one aripiprazole (EGr = C).[141-143]

Clearly, the family of antipsychotic medications have disparate levels of supporting evidence for efficacy in OCD. Head-to-head trials are warranted to establish clear differences in comparative antipsychotic efficacy in OCD. In both meta-analyses of OCD augmentation agents across 9-12 double-blind, placebo-controlled trials, risperidone and haloperidol showed superior effects over quetiapine and olanzapine.[118, 119] The choice of antipsychotic should be based on the evidence base weighed against known side effects and patient-specific factors including potential impact of metabolic effects, sedation, or extrapyramidal side effects.

Studies have suggested that modest dose antipsychotics are efficacious in OCD.[144] Compared to SRI response latency, a more rapid response can be expected after initiating antipsychotic augmentation; most patients demonstrate response within 4 weeks.[144] While literature examining long-term augmentation is sparse, in light of a chart review reporting relapse of 15/18 patients upon antipsychotic discontinuation,[145] long-term maintenance may be a prudent strategy. Given the substantial metabolic and motor adverse effects associated with long-term use, studies exploring the relationship between duration of post-remission antipsychotic maintenance and relapse risk are sorely needed. Risks and benefits should be carefully weighed in the decision of when to discontinue antipsychotic augmentation.

### Stimulants

The mechanism of stimulant action in OCD is unclear, especially given their known pro-compulsive properties, but may be related to pro-serotonergic effects.[146] Single stimulant doses have been reported to improve OCD-symptoms in very small randomized and case studies and suggest a specificity of effect to dextroamphetamine versus methylphenidate.[146-148] Caffeine control showed slightly greater augmentation effects than dextroamphetamine (58% versus 50% response rate respectively) in a double-blind study, though both groups showed unusually high response rates.[148] These studies should be interpreted with caution due to their small sample sizes and other above noted limitations.

GLUTAMATERGIC AGENTS

A mechanistic role for aberrant glutamate signaling in OCD has been proposed based on increased CSF glutamate in OCD patients,[149] imaging data in both children and adults with OCD,[150-152] animal models with OC behavior,[114, 153] and convergence of genetic data on the glutamate transporter gene (SLC1A1). [154-159]

Medications modulating glutamate neurotransmission are widely used in the management of neurodegenerative and seizure disorders. A number of these have been tested for a possible role in OCD augmentation. **Memantine**, a glutamate NMDA receptor antagonist commonly used in Alzheimer's disease, has support from an open-label,[160] a single blind,[161] and a double-blind randomized controlled trial in adults,[162] and a single case-study in an adolescent.[163] Data from a case study[164] and small open-label studies in children[165] and adults[166] support continued investigation of riluzole, a negative modulator of glutamatergic transmission, in SSRI augmentation. **Riluzole** use, however, is limited by high rates of transaminitis and pancreatitis. **Ketamine**, a noncompetitive antagonist of the glutamate NMDA receptor, used as either monotherapy or augmentation therapy produced only a transient effect lasting hours to days in an open-label study of 10 subjects with treatment-resistant OCD.[167]

Many antiepileptic drugs modulating glutamate transmission have some support in SSRI augmentation in OCD. **Topiramate** attenuates excitatory neurotransmission through effects on ion channels and glutamate and GABA signaling, and is supported by a case series[168] and two small RCTs,[169, 170] one of which had large tolerability issues with high resultant dropout and demonstrated effects on only obsession subscales but not compulsion or overall response scores. Augmentation with **lamotrigine**, another negative modulator of glutamatergic transmission, is supported by success in 1 of 4 patients in an open-label case series[171] and a subsequent small RCT.[172] **Gabapentin** and **pregabalin**, which appear to regulate excitatory neurotransmission through effects on voltage-dependent calcium channels, have support for accelerated response[173] and reduction in compulsions[174] respectively in open-label studies. **N-acetylcysteine (NAC)**, long used medically as an anti-oxidant in nephro- and hepatotoxicity, also has glutamatergic modulatory effects.[175] NAC has shown encouraging data in OC-related grooming, habit and impulse control disorders,[175] but only a single case study in OCD.[176]

Overall, psychotherapeutics modulating glutamate neurotransmission have been promising augmenting agents to SSRIs in OCD treatment. Other drugs targeting the glutamate system, such as presynaptic metabotropic receptors, are currently in development[177] and will be intriguing to test in OCD. Given the role of glutamatergic signaling in learning and memory, it would be especially interesting to test these medications in combination with CBT.

Table 2. Augmentation Agents: Evidence Grades

| Augmentation Agent | Adults | Children/Adolescents |
|---|---|---|
| **SEROTONERGIC** | | |
| Clomipramine | B | C |
| Mirtazapine | C | D |
| 5-HT3 Antagonists | C | D |
| | | |
| **DOPAMINERGIC** | | |
| *Antipsychotics* | | |
| Haloperidol | B | D |
| Risperidone | A | C |
| Quetiapine | C | D |
| Olanzapine | C | D |
| Aripiprazole | A | C |
| Ziprasidone | D | D |
| | | |
| *Stimulants* | | |
| Dextroamphetamine | C | D |
| | | |
| **GLUTAMATERGIC** | | |
| Memantine | C | D |
| Riluzole | C | C |
| Topiramate | C | D |
| Lamotrigine | C | D |
| Gabapentin/Pregabalin | D | D |
| N-Acetylcysteine (NAC) | D | D |

OTHER TRANSMITTER SYSTEMS

OCD monotherapy with **benzodiazepines**, which facilitate GABA transmission, has produced conflicting results in two RCTs [178, 179] and was ineffective as an augmenting agent in a double-blind RCT.[180] An **opioid agonist** was an effective augmenting agent in a 2-week RCT study of once-weekly morphine[181] but not in a placebo cross-over RCT of the opioid antagonist naltrexone, frequently used to treat related impulse control disorders.[182] Side effects, tolerance, and dependence potential make the use of benzodiazepines and opiates less attractive in OCD augmentation. **Pindolol**, a non-selective beta-adrenergic antagonist with partial agonist and putative 5HT1A antagonist properties, has conflicting data from two RCTs.[183, 184] **Lithium**, a mood stabilizer, was shown to be ineffective as an augmenting agent in an RCT.[185]

## Intensive Treatment Programs

Partial response to pharmacotherapy and CBT or difficulty in adherence to treatment may call for an increase in the intensity of treatment.[61] While inpatient hospitalization may be indicated for safety concerns, unless specialized CBT is available at the facility, hospitalization in a general psychiatric hospital may not be beneficial and may be very difficult for patients to tolerate due to their extensive rituals. However, adult and pediatric specialty programs for OCD, if available, can be highly effective.[61] Increased levels of care range from intensive outpatient and partial hospitalization programs to long-term residential treatment.

> ### *Clinical Sidebar – Intensive Treatment Programs*
> A group of children are enrolled in an intensive outpatient program for severe OCD. Part of the time they perform individualized exposures with a therapist, and the rest of the time they receive group therapy which consists of psychoeducational sessions; relaxation, meditation and mindfulness training; exposure planning and discussion; and group exposure games such as scavenger hunts for provoking items, races to perform difficult tasks, or water gun fights with "contaminated" water. The children provide both compassionate support and healthy competition for each other in tackling tough challenges. Their mood and motivation improve due to the positive effects of socialization that they have lacked due to the severity of their symptoms and relief at feeling less alone knowing that others struggle with similar difficulties. Their parents receive concomitant psychoeducation, training, and support groups.

## Brain Simulation and Psychosurgery
### rTMS

Repetitive transcranial magnetic stimulation (rTMS) therapy applies repetitive pulses of electrical current over the skull, inducing a magnetic field pulse capable of depolarizing underlying neurons ~2 cm deep.[186] This non-invasive therapy with minimal side effects has received considerable enthusiasm in the treatment of depression.[186] While reports have been mixed, studies are complicated by the use of excitatory (high frequency) versus inhibitory (low frequency) rTMS in different brain regions (dorsolateral prefrontal cortex [DLPFC] versus supplemental motor area [SMA] and orbitofrontal cortex). A recent meta-analysis including 10 RCTs of 282 subjects with OCD supported the use of rTMS in OCD with a medium effect size (OR 3.4, p=0.002).[195] This meta-analysis additionally concluded that benefit was achieved with low frequency (inhibitory) stimulation over the SMA or orbitofrontal cortex. While current rTMS coils do not penetrate to the deep brain regions implicated in OCD (e.g., anterior cingulated cortex, orbitofrontal cortex), newly invented deep coils may be more effective in OCD and await testing.[152]

*DBS/ABLATION*

In intractable OCD cases with profound impairment or distress, neurosurgical options for OCD treatment are available on a research basis. The less invasive option involves the implantation of electrodes that provide deep brain stimulation (DBS) of the anterior limb of the internal capsule,[196] the adjacent striatum,[196] the subthalamic nucleus,[197] or the nucleus accumbens.[197] A review of 90 DBS cases reported in the international literature estimated ~50% improvement in OCD, depressive and anxiety symptoms.[198] A recent meta-analysis of five sham-controlled DBS trials enrolling 44 subjects showed small but significant improvement; however significant adverse events were experienced by one third of the patients.[199] Neurosurgical ablation of OCD-related brain structures (e.g., cingulotomy, capsulotomy, subcaudate tractotomy and limbic leucotomy), either by open procedure or stereotactic radiosurgery (γ-knife), is a more invasive, last resort treatment.[200] While controlled studies are limited, review of the uncontrolled studies suggests that at least 50–60% of the patients show a response to surgery.[200] One recent RCT revealed a response rate less than 40%.[201] Patients must be carefully screened and selected prior to undertaking these invasive interventions. These procedures are generally avoided in children, since symptoms may improve over the course of development without surgical intervention.

---

*Clinical Sidebar – The Importance of Working with Family in Pediatric OCD*

Heather is an 8 year old girl with OCD with pervasive obsessional doubt and checking compulsions who enrolls in combined CBT and medication treatment. Her family has taken her out of school due to her anxiety and tantrums whenever she is expected to attend. Her mother has quit her job so that she can help Heather manage at home. Heather refuses to perform any independent action without first asking her mom if it's okay and her mom answering three times "you're okay, you're okay, you're okay." She is frequently unsure if she heard things that her mom said correctly and will make her repeat herself over and over again. She is also unsure if she was correctly heard, so she will make her mother stop and look at her as she repeats something again and again until it feels right. Mom understands that as part of Heather's exposure therapy, she is not to provide reassurance or accommodate the rituals that Heather is practicing. Mom will often give in, however, when she is unable to tolerate Heather becoming more and more upset. During the exposure practice, Heather's mom will often calm her anxious daughter by repeating, "It's going to be okay. Nothing bad is going to happen. I promise."

**Summary and Conclusions**

A variety of agents have been tested in the treatment of OCD as reviewed above. The level of evidence supporting each can be used to outline a recommended treatment algorithm (Figure 1). Due to excellent effectiveness and tolerability, pharmacotherapy of OCD in adults and children should begin with an SSRI. The best evidence supports fluoxetine, paroxetine, and fluvoxamine in adults with good evidence that sertraline, citalopram, and escitalopram are also effective. In children, the best evidence supports the use of fluoxetine, sertraline, fluvoxamine, and paroxetine with evidence that citalopram is also effective. Fluoxetine, sertraline, and fluvoxamine all have FDA indications for both adult and childhood OCD treatment. It is likely that all SSRIs are useful in reducing OCD symptoms; however, head-to-head trials are needed to address whether there are any within class differences in effectiveness. A careful consideration of the evidence in the context of side effect profile and patient-specific factors should guide clinician choice. Comorbidity should be evaluated and addressed in the development of a comprehensive treatment plan and may influence treatment choice. CBT should be considered as a first-line alternative to pharmacotherapy, especially in children, and can be more effective when combined with an SSRI than medication alone. Family education and support can be critical to many patients who seek reassurance and recruit others into their rituals, especially in children. DCS can be added to CBT therapy for a possible hastening of response. Failure of an SSRI warrants a switch to a second SSRI or possibly clomipramine monotherapy, which also has an FDA indication in both adult and pediatric OCD, as an alternative after SSRI treatment failure. A partial SSRI response or treatment resistance should prompt a consideration of augmentation agents. The best evidence supports augmentation with an antipsychotic medication, of which risperidone and aripiprazole have the greatest support in both adults and children. Antipsychotics may be especially helpful in patients with tic disorders, poor insight, or childhood oppositionality. Other options with reasonable evidence include clomipramine and glutamatergic agents, of which memantine has the greatest level of evidence. Intensive treatment programs including intensive outpatient, partial, and residential hospitalization can be beneficial for those not responding fully to outpatient combination treatment with medication and CBT. For those failing all previous treatments, trials of monotherapy or augmentation agents with less evidence may be considered as well as rTMS therapy. For those truly treatment refractory patients with profound distress and impairment, psychosurgery may represent the only option for symptom relief. Data supports the long-term continuation (at least 1 year) of an effective treatment regimen prior to gradual taper with vigilant monitoring. CBT may improve the success of eventual medication discontinuation and long-term remission.

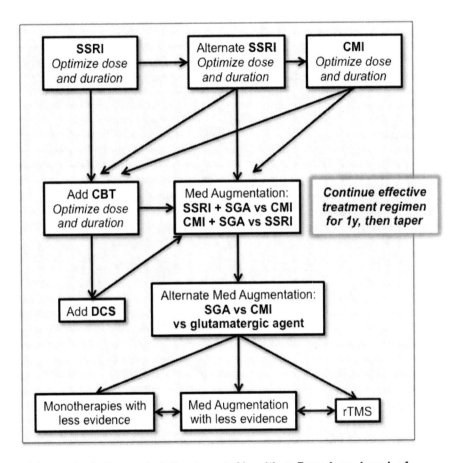

**Figure 1. A Suggested Treatment Algorithm Based on Level of Evidence.** Boxes indicate treatment option and arrows show suggested flow in the case of treatment failure. SSRI = selective serotonin reuptake inhibitor, CMI = clomipramine, CBT = cognitive behavior therapy, SGA = second generation antipsychotic, DCS = d-cycloserine, rTMS = repetitive transcranial magnetic stimulation.

# References

1    American Psychiatric Association. Diagnostic and statistical manual of mental disorders (Revised 4th ed.). Washington, D.C.: American Psychiatric Association, 2000

2    Sakolsky DJ, McCracken JT, Nurmi EL. Genetics of pediatric anxiety disorders. *Child and adolescent psychiatric clinics of North America* 2012; **21**(3): 479-500 [PMID: 22800990 DOI: 10.1016/j.chc.2012.05.010]

3    Chiu CH, Lo YC, Tang HS, Liu IC, Chiang WY, Yeh FC, Jaw FS, Tseng WY. White matter abnormalities of fronto-striato-thalamic circuitry in obsessive-compulsive disorder: A study using diffusion spectrum imaging tractography. *Psychiatry research* 2011; **192**(3): 176-182 [PMID: 21546223 DOI: 10.1016/j.pscychresns.2010.09.009]

4    Rotge JY, Dilharreguy B, Aouizerate B, Martin-Guehl C, Guehl D, Jaafari N, Langbour N, Bioulac B, Tignol J, Allard M, Burbaud P. Inverse relationship between thalamic and orbitofrontal volumes in obsessive-compulsive disorder. *Progress in neuro-psychopharmacology & biological psychiatry* 2009; **33**(4): 682-687 [PMID: 19306905 DOI: 10.1016/j.pnpbp.2009.03.011]

5    Rotge JY, Guehl D, Dilharreguy B, Tignol J, Bioulac B, Allard M, Burbaud P, Aouizerate B. Meta-analysis of brain volume changes in obsessive-compulsive disorder. *Biological psychiatry* 2009; **65**(1): 75-83 [PMID: 18718575 DOI: 10.1016/j.biopsych.2008.06.019]

6    Fontenelle LF, Barbosa IG, Victor Luna J, Pessoa Rocha N, Silva Miranda A, Teixeira AL. Neurotrophic factors in obsessive-compulsive disorder. *Psychiatry research* 2012; **199**(3): 195-200 [PMID: 22494702 DOI: 10.1016/j.psychres.2012.03.034]

7    Fontenelle LF, Hasler G. The analytical epidemiology of obsessive-compulsive disorder: risk factors and correlates. *Progress in neuro-psychopharmacology & biological psychiatry* 2008; **32**(1): 1-15 [PMID: 17689849 DOI: 10.1016/j.pnpbp.2007.06.024]

8    Grisham JR, Fullana MA, Mataix-Cols D, Moffitt TE, Caspi A, Poulton R. Risk factors prospectively associated with adult obsessive-compulsive symptom dimensions and obsessive-compulsive disorder. *Psychological medicine* 2011: 1-12 [PMID: 21672296 DOI: 10.1017/S0033291711000894]

9    Swedo SE, Leonard HL, Garvey M, Mittleman B, Allen AJ, Perlmutter S, Lougee L, Dow S, Zamkoff J, Dubbert BK. Pediatric autoimmune neuropsychiatric disorders associated with streptococcal infections: clinical description of the first 50 cases. *The American journal of psychiatry* 1998; **155**(2): 264-271 [PMID: 9464208]

10   Shulman ST. Pediatric autoimmune neuropsychiatric disorders associated with streptococci (PANDAS): update. *Current opinion in pediatrics* 2009;

21(1):     127-130     [PMID:     19242249     DOI:
10.1097/MOP.0b013e32831db2c4]

11    Swedo SE, Schrag A, Gilbert R, Giovannoni G, Robertson MM, Metcalfe
C, Ben-Shlomo Y, Gilbert DL. Streptococcal infection, Tourette
syndrome, and OCD: is there a connection? PANDAS: horse or zebra?
*Neurology* 2010; **74**(17): 1397-1398; author reply 1398-1399 [PMID:
20421587 DOI: 10.1212/WNL.0b013e3181d8a638]

12    Adam Y, Meinlschmidt G, Gloster AT, Lieb R. Obsessive-compulsive
disorder in the community: 12-month prevalence, comorbidity and
impairment. *Social psychiatry and psychiatric epidemiology* 2012; **47**(3): 339-349
[PMID: 21287144 DOI: 10.1007/s00127-010-0337-5]

13    Ruscio AM, Stein DJ, Chiu WT, Kessler RC. The epidemiology of
obsessive-compulsive disorder in the National Comorbidity Survey
Replication. *Molecular psychiatry* 2010; **15**(1): 53-63 [PMID: 18725912
PMCID: 2797569 DOI: 10.1038/mp.2008.94]

14    Canals J, Hernandez-Martinez C, Cosi S, Voltas N. The epidemiology of
obsessive--compulsive disorder in Spanish school children. *Journal of
anxiety disorders* 2012; **26**(7): 746-752 [PMID: 22858901 DOI:
10.1016/j.janxdis.2012.06.003]

15    Cillicilli AS, Telcioglu M, Askin R, Kaya N, Bodur S, Kucur R. Twelve-
month prevalence of obsessive-compulsive disorder in Konya, Turkey.
*Comprehensive psychiatry* 2004; **45**(5): 367-374 [PMID: 15332200 DOI:
10.1016/j.comppsych.2004.06.009]

16    Grabe HJ, Meyer C, Hapke U, Rumpf HJ, Freyberger HJ, Dilling H, John
U. Prevalence, quality of life and psychosocial function in obsessive-
compulsive disorder and subclinical obsessive-compulsive disorder in
northern Germany. *European archives of psychiatry and clinical neuroscience* 2000;
**250**(5): 262-268 [PMID: 11097170]

17    Mohammadi MR, Ghanizadeh A, Rahgozar M, Noorbala AA, Davidian
H, Afzali HM, Naghavi HR, Yazdi SA, Saberi SM, Mesgarpour B,
Akhondzadeh S, Alaghebandrad J, Tehranidoost M. Prevalence of
obsessive-compulsive disorder in Iran. *BMC psychiatry* 2004; **4**: 2 [PMID:
15018627 PMCID: 362878 DOI: 10.1186/1471-244X-4-2]

18    Subramaniam M, Abdin E, Vaingankar JA, Chong SA. Obsessive--
compulsive disorder: prevalence, correlates, help-seeking and quality of
life in a multiracial Asian population. *Social psychiatry and psychiatric
epidemiology* 2012; **47**(12): 2035-2043 [PMID: 22526825 DOI:
10.1007/s00127-012-0507-8]

19    Tadai T, Nakamura M, Okazaki S, Nakajima T. The prevalence of
obsessive-compulsive disorder in Japan: a study of students using the
Maudsley Obsessional-Compulsive Inventory and DSM-III-R. *Psychiatry
and clinical neurosciences* 1995; **49**(1): 39-41 [PMID: 8608432]

20    Torres AR, Prince MJ, Bebbington PE, Bhugra D, Brugha TS, Farrell M, Jenkins R, Lewis G, Meltzer H, Singleton N. Obsessive-compulsive disorder: prevalence, comorbidity, impact, and help-seeking in the British National Psychiatric Morbidity Survey of 2000. *The American journal of psychiatry* 2006; **163**(11): 1978-1985 [PMID: 17074950 DOI: 10.1176/appi.ajp.163.11.1978]

21    Yoldascan E, Ozenli Y, Kutlu O, Topal K, Bozkurt AI. Prevalence of obsessive-compulsive disorder in Turkish university students and assessment of associated factors. *BMC psychiatry* 2009; **9**: 40 [PMID: 19580658 PMCID: 2719627 DOI: 10.1186/1471-244X-9-40]

22    Geller DA. Obsessive-compulsive and spectrum disorders in children and adolescents. *The Psychiatric clinics of North America* 2006; **29**(2): 353-370 [PMID: 16650713 DOI: 10.1016/j.psc.2006.02.012]

23    Eisen JL, Pinto A, Mancebo MC, Dyck IR, Orlando ME, Rasmussen SA. A 2-year prospective follow-up study of the course of obsessive-compulsive disorder. *The Journal of clinical psychiatry* 2010; **71**(8): 1033-1039 [PMID: 20797381 DOI: 10.4088/JCP.08m04806blu]

24    Kessler RC, Petukhova M, Sampson NA, Zaslavsky AM, Wittchen HU. Twelve-month and lifetime prevalence and lifetime morbid risk of anxiety and mood disorders in the United States. *International journal of methods in psychiatric research* 2012; **21**(3): 169-184 [PMID: 22865617 DOI: 10.1002/mpr.1359]

25    Pinto A, Mancebo MC, Eisen JL, Pagano ME, Rasmussen SA. The Brown Longitudinal Obsessive Compulsive Study: clinical features and symptoms of the sample at intake. *The Journal of clinical psychiatry* 2006; **67**(5): 703-711 [PMID: 16841619 PMCID: 3272757]

26    Schuurmans J, van Balkom AJ, van Megen HJ, Smit JH, Eikelenboom M, Cath DC, Kaarsemaker M, Oosterbaan D, Hendriks GJ, Schruers KR, van der Wee NJ, Glas G, van Oppen P. The Netherlands Obsessive Compulsive Disorder Association (NOCDA) study: design and rationale of a longitudinal naturalistic study of the course of OCD and clinical characteristics of the sample at baseline. *International journal of methods in psychiatric research* 2012; **21**(4): 273-285 [PMID: 23148029 DOI: 10.1002/mpr.1372]

27    Fireman B, Koran LM, Leventhal JL, Jacobson A. The prevalence of clinically recognized obsessive-compulsive disorder in a large health maintenance organization. *The American journal of psychiatry* 2001; **158**(11): 1904-1910 [PMID: 11691699]

28    Goodman WK, Price LH, Rasmussen SA, Mazure C, Delgado P, Heninger GR, Charney DS. The Yale-Brown Obsessive Compulsive Scale. II. Validity. *Archives of general psychiatry* 1989; **46**(11): 1012-1016 [PMID: 2510699]

29    Goodman WK, Price LH, Rasmussen SA, Mazure C, Fleischmann RL, Hill CL, Heninger GR, Charney DS. The Yale-Brown Obsessive Compulsive Scale. I. Development, use, and reliability. *Archives of general psychiatry* 1989; **46**(11): 1006-1011 [PMID: 2684084]

30    Sulkowski ML, Storch EA, Geffken GR, Ricketts E, Murphy TK, Goodman WK. Concurrent validity of the Yale-Brown Obsessive-Compulsive Scale-Symptom Checklist. *Journal of clinical psychology* 2008; **64**(12): 1338-1351 [PMID: 18942133 DOI: 10.1002/jclp.20525]

31    Storch EA, Larson MJ, Price LH, Rasmussen SA, Murphy TK, Goodman WK. Psychometric analysis of the Yale-Brown Obsessive-Compulsive Scale Second Edition Symptom Checklist. *Journal of anxiety disorders* 2010; **24**(6): 650-656 [PMID: 20471199 DOI: 10.1016/j.janxdis.2010.04.010]

32    Scahill L, Riddle MA, McSwiggin-Hardin M, Ort SI, King RA, Goodman WK, Cicchetti D, Leckman JF. Children's Yale-Brown Obsessive Compulsive Scale: reliability and validity. *Journal of the American Academy of Child and Adolescent Psychiatry* 1997; **36**(6): 844-852 [PMID: 9183141 DOI: 10.1097/00004583-199706000-00023]

33    Stein DJ, Koen N, Fineberg N, Fontenelle LF, Matsunaga H, Osser D, Simpson HB. A 2012 evidence-based algorithm for the pharmacotherapy for obsessive-compulsive disorder. *Current psychiatry reports* 2012; **14**(3): 211-219 [PMID: 22527872 DOI: 10.1007/s11920-012-0268-9]

34    Fineberg NA, Brown A, Reghunandanan S, Pampaloni I. Evidence-based pharmacotherapy of obsessive-compulsive disorder. *The international journal of neuropsychopharmacology / official scientific journal of the Collegium Internationale Neuropsychopharmacologicum* 2012; **15**(8): 1173-1191 [PMID: 22226028 DOI: 10.1017/S1461145711001829]

35    Fenske JN, Schwenk TL. Obsessive compulsive disorder: diagnosis and management. *American family physician* 2009; **80**(3): 239-245 [PMID: 19621834]

36    Walsh KH, McDougle CJ. Psychotherapy and medication management strategies for obsessive-compulsive disorder. *Neuropsychiatric disease and treatment* 2011; **7**: 485-494 [PMID: 21931490 PMCID: 3173031 DOI: 10.2147/NDT.S13205]

37    de Haan E, Hoogduin KA, Buitelaar JK, Keijsers GP. Behavior therapy versus clomipramine for the treatment of obsessive-compulsive disorder in children and adolescents. *Journal of the American Academy of Child and Adolescent Psychiatry* 1998; **37**(10): 1022-1029 [PMID: 9785713]

38    Foa EB, Liebowitz MR, Kozak MJ, Davies S, Campeas R, Franklin ME, Huppert JD, Kjernisted K, Rowan V, Schmidt AB, Simpson HB, Tu X. Randomized, placebo-controlled trial of exposure and ritual prevention, clomipramine, and their combination in the treatment of obsessive-compulsive disorder. *The American journal of psychiatry* 2005; **162**(1): 151-161 [PMID: 15625214 DOI: 10.1176/appi.ajp.162.1.151]

39      Pediatric O. C. D. Treatment Study Team. Cognitive-behavior therapy, sertraline, and their combination for children and adolescents with obsessive-compulsive disorder: the Pediatric OCD Treatment Study (POTS) randomized controlled trial. *JAMA : the journal of the American Medical Association* 2004; **292**(16): 1969-1976 [PMID: 15507582 DOI: 10.1001/jama.292.16.1969]

40      Moritz S, Wittekind CE, Hauschildt M, Timpano KR. Do it yourself? Self-help and online therapy for people with obsessive-compulsive disorder. *Current opinion in psychiatry* 2011; **24**(6): 541-548 [PMID: 21897252 DOI: 10.1097/YCO.0b013e32834abb7f]

41      Tumur I, Kaltenthaler E, Ferriter M, Beverley C, Parry G. Computerised cognitive behaviour therapy for obsessive-compulsive disorder: a systematic review. *Psychotherapy and psychosomatics* 2007; **76**(4): 196-202 [PMID: 17570957 DOI: 10.1159/000101497]

42      McGough JJ, Faraone SV. Estimating the size of treatment effects: moving beyond p values. *Psychiatry* 2009; **6**(10): 21-29 [PMID: 20011465 PMCID: 2791668]

43      Kraemer HC, Kupfer DJ. Size of treatment effects and their importance to clinical research and practice. *Biological psychiatry* 2006; **59**(11): 990-996 [PMID: 16368078 DOI: 10.1016/j.biopsych.2005.09.014]

44      Oxford Centre for Evidence-based Medicine. Levels of Evidence. In: Bob Phillips CB, Dave Sackett, Doug Badenoch, Sharon Straus, Brian Haynes, Martin Dawes, Jeremy Howick, ed. Oxford, England, March 2009.

45      Katz RJ, DeVeaugh-Geiss J, Landau P. Clomipramine in obsessive-compulsive disorder. *Biological psychiatry* 1990; **28**(5): 401-414 [PMID: 2207219]

46      DeVeaugh-Geiss J, Moroz G, Biederman J, Cantwell D, Fontaine R, Greist JH, Reichler R, Katz R, Landau P. Clomipramine hydrochloride in childhood and adolescent obsessive-compulsive disorder--a multicenter trial. *Journal of the American Academy of Child and Adolescent Psychiatry* 1992; **31**(1): 45-49 [PMID: 1537780 DOI: 10.1097/00004583-199201000-00008]

47      Flament MF, Rapoport JL, Berg CJ, Sceery W, Kilts C, Mellstrom B, Linnoila M. Clomipramine treatment of childhood obsessive-compulsive disorder. A double-blind controlled study. *Archives of general psychiatry* 1985; **42**(10): 977-983 [PMID: 3899048]

48      Volavka J, Neziroglu F, Yaryura-Tobias JA. Clomipramine and imipramine in obsessive-compulsive disorder. *Psychiatry research* 1985; **14**(1): 85-93 [PMID: 3887445]

49      Leonard HL, Swedo SE, Rapoport JL, Koby EV, Lenane MC, Cheslow DL, Hamburger SD. Treatment of obsessive-compulsive disorder with clomipramine and desipramine in children and adolescents. A double-

blind crossover comparison. *Archives of general psychiatry* 1989; **46**(12): 1088-1092 [PMID: 2686576]

50  Geller DA, Biederman J, Stewart SE, Mullin B, Martin A, Spencer T, Faraone SV. Which SSRI? A meta-analysis of pharmacotherapy trials in pediatric obsessive-compulsive disorder. *The American journal of psychiatry* 2003; **160**(11): 1919-1928 [PMID: 14594734]

51  Watson HJ, Rees CS. Meta-analysis of randomized, controlled treatment trials for pediatric obsessive-compulsive disorder. *Journal of child psychology and psychiatry, and allied disciplines* 2008; **49**(5): 489-498 [PMID: 18400058 DOI: 10.1111/j.1469-7610.2007.01875.x]

52  Montgomery SA, Kasper S, Stein DJ, Bang Hedegaard K, Lemming OM. Citalopram 20 mg, 40 mg and 60 mg are all effective and well tolerated compared with placebo in obsessive-compulsive disorder. *International clinical psychopharmacology* 2001; **16**(2): 75-86 [PMID: 11236072]

53  Alaghband-Rad J, Hakimshooshtary M. A randomized controlled clinical trial of citalopram versus fluoxetine in children and adolescents with obsessive-compulsive disorder (OCD). *European child & adolescent psychiatry* 2009; **18**(3): 131-135 [PMID: 19190958 DOI: 10.1007/s00787-007-0634-z]

54  Mukaddes NM, Abali O, Kaynak N. Citalopram treatment of children and adolescents with obsessive-compulsive disorder: a preliminary report. *Psychiatry and clinical neurosciences* 2003; **57**(4): 405-408 [PMID: 12839522 DOI: 10.1046/j.1440-1819.2003.01139.x]

55  Thomsen PH. Child and adolescent obsessive-compulsive disorder treated with citalopram: findings from an open trial of 23 cases. *Journal of child and adolescent psychopharmacology* 1997; **7**(3): 157-166 [PMID: 9466233]

56  Sheeler RD, Ackerman MJ, Richelson E, Nelson TK, Staab JP, Tangalos EG, Dieser LM, Cunningham JL. Considerations on safety concerns about citalopram prescribing. *Mayo Clinic proceedings Mayo Clinic* 2012; **87**(11): 1042-1045 [PMID: 23018033 PMCID: 3532688 DOI: 10.1016/j.mayocp.2012.07.009]

57  Stein DJ, Andersen EW, Tonnoir B, Fineberg N. Escitalopram in obsessive-compulsive disorder: a randomized, placebo-controlled, paroxetine-referenced, fixed-dose, 24-week study. *Current medical research and opinion* 2007; **23**(4): 701-711 [PMID: 17407626 DOI: 10.1185/030079907X178838]

58  Dougherty DD, Jameson M, Deckersbach T, Loh R, Thompson-Hollands J, Jenike M, Keuthen NJ. Open-label study of high (30 mg) and moderate (20 mg) dose escitalopram for the treatment of obsessive-compulsive disorder. *International clinical psychopharmacology* 2009; **24**(6): 306-311 [PMID: 19730388 DOI: 10.1097/YIC.0b013e32833119d8]

59  Rabinowitz I, Baruch Y, Barak Y. High-dose escitalopram for the treatment of obsessive-compulsive disorder. *International clinical*

*psychopharmacology* 2008; **23**(1): 49-53 [PMID: 18090508 DOI: 10.1097/YIC.0b013e3282f0f0c5]

60    American Academy of Child and Adolescent Psychiatry. Practice parameter for the assessment and treatment of children and adolescents with obsessive-compulsive disorder. *Journal of the American Academy of Child and Adolescent Psychiatry* 2012; **51**(1): 98-113 [PMID: 22176943 DOI: 10.1016/j.jaac.2011.09.019]

61    Koran LM, Hanna GL, Hollander E, Nestadt G, Simpson HB, American Psychiatric A. Practice guideline for the treatment of patients with obsessive-compulsive disorder. *The American journal of psychiatry* 2007; **164**(7 Suppl): 5-53 [PMID: 17849776]

62    Tollefson GD, Rampey AH, Jr., Potvin JH, Jenike MA, Rush AJ, kominguez RA, Koran LM, Shear MK, Goodman W, Genduso LA. A multicenter investigation of fixed-dose fluoxetine in the treatment of obsessive-compulsive disorder. *Archives of general psychiatry* 1994; **51**(7): 559-567 [PMID: 8031229]

63    Montgomery SA, McIntyre A, Osterheider M, Sarteschi P, Zitterl W, Zohar J, Birkett M, Wood AJ. A double-blind, placebo-controlled study of fluoxetine in patients with DSM-III-R obsessive-compulsive disorder. The Lilly European OCD Study Group. *European neuropsychopharmacology : the journal of the European College of Neuropsychopharmacology* 1993; **3**(2): 143-152 [PMID: 8364350]

64    Jenike MA, Baer L, Minichiello WE, Rauch SL, Buttolph ML. Placebo-controlled trial of fluoxetine and phenelzine for obsessive-compulsive disorder. *The American journal of psychiatry* 1997; **154**(9): 1261-1264 [PMID: 9286186]

65    Geller DA, Hoog SL, Heiligenstein JH, Ricardi RK, Tamura R, Kluszynski S, Jacobson JG, Fluoxetine Pediatric OCDST. Fluoxetine treatment for obsessive-compulsive disorder in children and adolescents: a placebo-controlled clinical trial. *Journal of the American Academy of Child and Adolescent Psychiatry* 2001; **40**(7): 773-779 [PMID: 11437015]

66    Riddle MA, Scahill L, King RA, Hardin MT, Anderson GM, Ort SI, Smith JC, Leckman JF, Cohen DJ. Double-blind, crossover trial of fluoxetine and placebo in children and adolescents with obsessive-compulsive disorder. *Journal of the American Academy of Child and Adolescent Psychiatry* 1992; **31**(6): 1062-1069 [PMID: 1429406 DOI: 10.1097/00004583-199211000-00011]

67    Jenike MA, Buttolph L, Baer L, Ricciardi J, Holland A. Open trial of fluoxetine in obsessive-compulsive disorder. *The American journal of psychiatry* 1989; **146**(7): 909-911 [PMID: 2787123]

68    Coskun M, Zoroglu S. Efficacy and safety of fluoxetine in preschool children with obsessive-compulsive disorder. *Journal of child and adolescent*

*psychopharmacology* 2009; **19**(3): 297-300 [PMID: 19519265 DOI: 10.1089/cap.2008.055]

69      Ercan ES, Kandulu R, Akyol Ardic U. Preschool children with obsessive-compulsive disorder and fluoxetine treatment. *European child & adolescent psychiatry* 2012; **21**(3): 169-172 [PMID: 22271063 DOI: 10.1007/s00787-012-0244-2]

70      Goodman WK, Kozak MJ, Liebowitz M, White KL. Treatment of obsessive-compulsive disorder with fluvoxamine: a multicentre, double-blind, placebo-controlled trial. *International clinical psychopharmacology* 1996; **11**(1): 21-29 [PMID: 8732310]

71      Hollander E, Koran LM, Goodman WK, Greist JH, Ninan PT, Yang H, Li D, Barbato LM. A double-blind, placebo-controlled study of the efficacy and safety of controlled-release fluvoxamine in patients with obsessive-compulsive disorder. *The Journal of clinical psychiatry* 2003; **64**(6): 640-647 [PMID: 12823077]

72      Riddle MA, Reeve EA, Yaryura-Tobias JA, Yang HM, Claghorn JL, Gaffney G, Greist JH, Holland D, McConville BJ, Pigott T, Walkup JT. Fluvoxamine for children and adolescents with obsessive-compulsive disorder: a randomized, controlled, multicenter trial. *Journal of the American Academy of Child and Adolescent Psychiatry* 2001; **40**(2): 222-229 [PMID: 11211371 DOI: 10.1097/00004583-200102000-00017]

73      Neziroglu F, Yaryura-Tobias JA, Walz J, McKay D. The effect of fluvoxamine and behavior therapy on children and adolescents with obsessive-compulsive disorder. *Journal of child and adolescent psychopharmacology* 2000; **10**(4): 295-306 [PMID: 11191690]

74      Hollander E, Allen A, Steiner M, Wheadon DE, Oakes R, Burnham DB, Paroxetine OCDSG. Acute and long-term treatment and prevention of relapse of obsessive-compulsive disorder with paroxetine. *The Journal of clinical psychiatry* 2003; **64**(9): 1113-1121 [PMID: 14628989]

75      Kamijima K, Murasaki M, Asai M, Higuchi T, Nakajima T, Taga C, Matsunaga H. Paroxetine in the treatment of obsessive-compulsive disorder: randomized, double-blind, placebo-controlled study in Japanese patients. *Psychiatry and clinical neurosciences* 2004; **58**(4): 427-433 [PMID: 15298657 DOI: 10.1111/j.1440-1819.2004.01278.x]

76      Geller DA, Wagner KD, Emslie G, Murphy T, Carpenter DJ, Wetherhold E, Perera P, Machin A, Gardiner C. Paroxetine treatment in children and adolescents with obsessive-compulsive disorder: a randomized, multicenter, double-blind, placebo-controlled trial. *Journal of the American Academy of Child and Adolescent Psychiatry* 2004; **43**(11): 1387-1396 [PMID: 15502598 DOI: 10.1097/01.chi.0000138356.29099.f1]

77      Greist J, Chouinard G, DuBoff E, Halaris A, Kim SW, Koran L, Liebowitz M, Lydiard RB, Rasmussen S, White K, et al. Double-blind parallel comparison of three dosages of sertraline and placebo in

outpatients with obsessive-compulsive disorder. *Archives of general psychiatry* 1995; **52**(4): 289-295 [PMID: 7702445]

78    Chouinard G, Goodman W, Greist J, Jenike M, Rasmussen S, White K, Hackett E, Gaffney M, Bick PA. Results of a double-blind placebo controlled trial of a new serotonin uptake inhibitor, sertraline, in the treatment of obsessive-compulsive disorder. *Psychopharmacology bulletin* 1990; **26**(3): 279-284 [PMID: 2274626]

79    Kronig MH, Apter J, Asnis G, Bystritsky A, Curtis G, Ferguson J, Landbloom R, Munjack D, Riesenberg R, Robinson D, Roy-Byrne P, Phillips K, Du Pont IJ. Placebo-controlled, multicenter study of sertraline treatment for obsessive-compulsive disorder. *Journal of clinical psychopharmacology* 1999; **19**(2): 172-176 [PMID: 10211919]

80    March JS, Biederman J, Wolkow R, Safferman A, Mardekian J, Cook EH, Cutler NR, Dominguez R, Ferguson J, Muller B, Riesenberg R, Rosenthal M, Sallee FR, Wagner KD, Steiner H. Sertraline in children and adolescents with obsessive-compulsive disorder: a multicenter randomized controlled trial. *JAMA : the journal of the American Medical Association* 1998; **280**(20): 1752-1756 [PMID: 9842950]

81    Ninan PT, Koran LM, Kiev A, Davidson JR, Rasmussen SA, Zajecka JM, Robinson DG, Crits-Christoph P, Mandel FS, Austin C. High-dose sertraline strategy for nonresponders to acute treatment for obsessive-compulsive disorder: a multicenter double-blind trial. *The Journal of clinical psychiatry* 2006; **67**(1): 15-22 [PMID: 16426083]

82    Sousa MB, Isolan LR, Oliveira RR, Manfro GG, Cordioli AV. A randomized clinical trial of cognitive-behavioral group therapy and sertraline in the treatment of obsessive-compulsive disorder. *The Journal of clinical psychiatry* 2006; **67**(7): 1133-1139 [PMID: 16889458]

83    Yaryura-Tobias JA, Neziroglu FA. Venlafaxine in obsessive-compulsive disorder. *Archives of general psychiatry* 1996; **53**(7): 653-654 [PMID: 8660133]

84    Albert U, Aguglia E, Maina G, Bogetto F. Venlafaxine versus clomipramine in the treatment of obsessive-compulsive disorder: a preliminary single-blind, 12-week, controlled study. *The Journal of clinical psychiatry* 2002; **63**(11): 1004-1009 [PMID: 12444814]

85    Denys D, van der Wee N, van Megen HJ, Westenberg HG. A double blind comparison of venlafaxine and paroxetine in obsessive-compulsive disorder. *Journal of clinical psychopharmacology* 2003; **23**(6): 568-575 [PMID: 14624187 DOI: 10.1097/01.jcp.0000095342.32154.54]

86    Hollander E, Friedberg J, Wasserman S, Allen A, Birnbaum M, Koran LM. Venlafaxine in treatment-resistant obsessive-compulsive disorder. *The Journal of clinical psychiatry* 2003; **64**(5): 546-550 [PMID: 12755657]

87    Vallejo J, Olivares J, Marcos T, Bulbena A, Menchon JM. Clomipramine versus phenelzine in obsessive-compulsive disorder. A controlled clinical

trial. *The British journal of psychiatry : the journal of mental science* 1992; **161**: 665-670 [PMID: 1422616]

88    Insel TR, Murphy DL, Cohen RM, Alterman I, Kilts C, Linnoila M. Obsessive-compulsive disorder. A double-blind trial of clomipramine and clorgyline. *Archives of general psychiatry* 1983; **40**(6): 605-612 [PMID: 6342562]

89    Pato MT, Pigott TA, Hill JL, Grover GN, Bernstein S, Murphy DL. Controlled comparison of buspirone and clomipramine in obsessive-compulsive disorder. *The American journal of psychiatry* 1991; **148**(1): 127-129 [PMID: 1984696]

90    Jenike MA, Baer L. An open trial of buspirone in obsessive-compulsive disorder. *The American journal of psychiatry* 1988; **145**(10): 1285-1286 [PMID: 3048120]

91    Vulink NC, Denys D, Westenberg HG. Bupropion for patients with obsessive-compulsive disorder: an open-label, fixed-dose study. *The Journal of clinical psychiatry* 2005; **66**(2): 228-230 [PMID: 15705009]

92    Storch EA, Murphy TK, Goodman WK, Geffken GR, Lewin AB, Henin A, Micco JA, Sprich S, Wilhelm S, Bengtson M, Geller DA. A preliminary study of D-cycloserine augmentation of cognitive-behavioral therapy in pediatric obsessive-compulsive disorder. *Biological psychiatry* 2010; **68**(11): 1073-1076 [PMID: 20817153 PMCID: 3034091 DOI: 10.1016/j.biopsych.2010.07.015]

93    Kushner MG, Kim SW, Donahue C, Thuras P, Adson D, Kotlyar M, McCabe J, Peterson J, Foa EB. D-cycloserine augmented exposure therapy for obsessive-compulsive disorder. *Biological psychiatry* 2007; **62**(8): 835-838 [PMID: 17588545 DOI: 10.1016/j.biopsych.2006.12.020]

94    Wilhelm S, Buhlmann U, Tolin DF, Meunier SA, Pearlson GD, Reese HE, Cannistraro P, Jenike MA, Rauch SL. Augmentation of behavior therapy with D-cycloserine for obsessive-compulsive disorder. *The American journal of psychiatry* 2008; **165**(3): 335-341; quiz 409 [PMID: 18245177 DOI: 10.1176/appi.ajp.2007.07050776]

95    Storch EA, Merlo LJ, Bengtson M, Murphy TK, Lewis MH, Yang MC, Jacob ML, Larson M, Hirsh A, Fernandez M, Geffken GR, Goodman WK. D-cycloserine does not enhance exposure-response prevention therapy in obsessive-compulsive disorder. *International clinical psychopharmacology* 2007; **22**(4): 230-237 [PMID: 17519647 DOI: 10.1097/YIC.0b013e32819f8480]

96    Chasson GS, Buhlmann U, Tolin DF, Rao SR, Reese HE, Rowley T, Welsh KS, Wilhelm S. Need for speed: evaluating slopes of OCD recovery in behavior therapy enhanced with d-cycloserine. *Behaviour research and therapy* 2010; **48**(7): 675-679 [PMID: 20362975 DOI: 10.1016/j.brat.2010.03.007]

97 Sayyah M, Boostani H, Pakseresht S, Malayeri A. Comparison of Silybum marianum (L.) Gaertn. with fluoxetine in the treatment of Obsessive-Compulsive Disorder. *Progress in neuro-psychopharmacology & biological psychiatry* 2010; **34**(2): 362-365 [PMID: 20035818 DOI: 10.1016/j.pnpbp.2009.12.016]

98 Kobak KA, Taylor LV, Bystritsky A, Kohlenberg CJ, Greist JH, Tucker P, Warner G, Futterer R, Vapnik T. St John's wort versus placebo in obsessive-compulsive disorder: results from a double-blind study. *International clinical psychopharmacology* 2005; **20**(6): 299-304 [PMID: 16192837]

99 Sayyah M, Boostani H, Pakseresht S, Malaieri A. Efficacy of aqueous extract of Echium amoenum in treatment of obsessive-compulsive disorder. *Progress in neuro-psychopharmacology & biological psychiatry* 2009; **33**(8): 1513-1516 [PMID: 19737592 DOI: 10.1016/j.pnpbp.2009.08.021]

100 Fux M, Levine J, Aviv A, Belmaker RH. Inositol treatment of obsessive-compulsive disorder. *The American journal of psychiatry* 1996; **153**(9): 1219-1221 [PMID: 8780431]

101 Stewart SE, Geller DA, Jenike M, Pauls D, Shaw D, Mullin B, Faraone SV. Long-term outcome of pediatric obsessive-compulsive disorder: a meta-analysis and qualitative review of the literature. *Acta psychiatrica Scandinavica* 2004; **110**(1): 4-13 [PMID: 15180774 DOI: 10.1111/j.1600-0447.2004.00302.x]

102 Kordon A, Kahl KG, Broocks A, Voderholzer U, Rasche-Rauchle H, Hohagen F. Clinical outcome in patients with obsessive-compulsive disorder after discontinuation of SRI treatment: results from a two-year follow-up. *European archives of psychiatry and clinical neuroscience* 2005; **255**(1): 48-50 [PMID: 15538591 DOI: 10.1007/s00406-004-0533-y]

103 Bandelow B, Sher L, Bunevicius R, Hollander E, Kasper S, Zohar J, Moller HJ, Care WTFoMDiP, Wfsbp Task Force on Anxiety Disorders OCD, Ptsd. Guidelines for the pharmacological treatment of anxiety disorders, obsessive-compulsive disorder and posttraumatic stress disorder in primary care. *International journal of psychiatry in clinical practice* 2012; **16**(2): 77-84 [PMID: 22540422 DOI: 10.3109/13651501.2012.667114]

104 Hembree EA, Riggs DS, Kozak MJ, Franklin ME, Foa EB. Long-term efficacy of exposure and ritual prevention therapy and serotonergic medications for obsessive-compulsive disorder. *CNS spectrums* 2003; **8**(5): 363-371, 381 [PMID: 12766692]

105 Pallanti S, Hollander E, Bienstock C, Koran L, Leckman J, Marazziti D, Pato M, Stein D, Zohar J, International Treatment Refractory OCDC. Treatment non-response in OCD: methodological issues and operational definitions. *The international journal of neuropsychopharmacology / official scientific*

*journal of the Collegium Internationale Neuropsychopharmacologicum* 2002; **5**(2): 181-191 [PMID: 12135542 DOI: doi:10.1017/S1461145702002900]

106    Bloch MH, McGuire J, Landeros-Weisenberger A, Leckman JF, Pittenger C. Meta-analysis of the dose-response relationship of SSRI in obsessive-compulsive disorder. *Molecular psychiatry* 2010; **15**(8): 850-855 [PMID: 19468281 PMCID: 2888928 DOI: 10.1038/mp.2009.50]

107    Simpson HB, Huppert JD, Petkova E, Foa EB, Liebowitz MR. Response versus remission in obsessive-compulsive disorder. *The Journal of clinical psychiatry* 2006; **67**(2): 269-276 [PMID: 16566623]

108    Figueroa Y, Rosenberg DR, Birmaher B, Keshavan MS. Combination treatment with clomipramine and selective serotonin reuptake inhibitors for obsessive-compulsive disorder in children and adolescents. *Journal of child and adolescent psychopharmacology* 1998; **8**(1): 61-67 [PMID: 9639080]

109    Marazziti D, Golia F, Consoli G, Presta S, Pfanner C, Carlini M, Mungai F, Catena Dell'osso M. Effectiveness of long-term augmentation with citalopram to clomipramine in treatment-resistant OCD patients. *CNS spectrums* 2008; **13**(11): 971-976 [PMID: 19037176]

110    Pallanti S, Quercioli L, Paiva RS, Koran LM. Citalopram for treatment-resistant obsessive-compulsive disorder. *European psychiatry : the journal of the Association of European Psychiatrists* 1999; **14**(2): 101-106 [PMID: 10572334]

111    Diniz JB, Shavitt RG, Fossaluza V, Koran L, Pereira CA, Miguel EC. A double-blind, randomized, controlled trial of fluoxetine plus quetiapine or clomipramine versus fluoxetine plus placebo for obsessive-compulsive disorder. *Journal of clinical psychopharmacology* 2011; **31**(6): 763-768 [PMID: 22020357 DOI: 10.1097/JCP.0b013e3182367aee]

112    Flament MF, Geller D, Irak M, Blier P. Specificities of treatment in pediatric obsessive-compulsive disorder. *CNS spectrums* 2007; **12**(2 Suppl 3): 43-58 [PMID: 17277723]

113    Pallanti S, Quercioli L, Bruscoli M. Response acceleration with mirtazapine augmentation of citalopram in obsessive-compulsive disorder patients without comorbid depression: a pilot study. *The Journal of clinical psychiatry* 2004; **65**(10): 1394-1399 [PMID: 15491244]

114    Askari N, Moin M, Sanati M, Tajdini M, Hosseini SM, Modabbernia A, Najand B, Salimi S, Tabrizi M, Ashrafi M, Hajiaghaee R, Akhondzadeh S. Granisetron adjunct to fluvoxamine for moderate to severe obsessive-compulsive disorder: a randomized, double-blind, placebo-controlled trial. *CNS drugs* 2012; **26**(10): 883-892 [PMID: 22873680 DOI: 10.2165/11635850-000000000-00000]

115    Soltani F, Sayyah M, Feizy F, Malayeri A, Siahpoosh A, Motlagh I. A double-blind, placebo-controlled pilot study of ondansetron for patients with obsessive-compulsive disorder. *Human psychopharmacology* 2010; **25**(6): 509-513 [PMID: 20737524 DOI: 10.1002/hup.1145]

116    Pigott TA, L'Heureux F, Hill JL, Bihari K, Bernstein SE, Murphy DL. A double-blind study of adjuvant buspirone hydrochloride in clomipramine-treated patients with obsessive-compulsive disorder. *Journal of clinical psychopharmacology* 1992; **12**(1): 11-18 [PMID: 1552034]

117    Grady TA, Pigott TA, L'Heureux F, Hill JL, Bernstein SE, Murphy DL. Double-blind study of adjuvant buspirone for fluoxetine-treated patients with obsessive-compulsive disorder. *The American journal of psychiatry* 1993; **150**(5): 819-821 [PMID: 8480832]

118    Bloch MH, Landeros-Weisenberger A, Kelmendi B, Coric V, Bracken MB, Leckman JF. A systematic review: antipsychotic augmentation with treatment refractory obsessive-compulsive disorder. *Molecular psychiatry* 2006; **11**(7): 622-632 [PMID: 16585942 DOI: 10.1038/sj.mp.4001823]

119    Dold M, Aigner M, Lanzenberger R, Kasper S. Antipsychotic augmentation of serotonin reuptake inhibitors in treatment-resistant obsessive-compulsive disorder: a meta-analysis of double-blind, randomized, placebo-controlled trials. *The international journal of neuropsychopharmacology / official scientific journal of the Collegium Internationale Neuropsychopharmacologicum* 2012: 1-18 [PMID: 22932229 DOI: 10.1017/S1461145712000740]

120    McDougle CJ, Goodman WK, Leckman JF, Lee NC, Heninger GR, Price LH. Haloperidol addition in fluvoxamine-refractory obsessive-compulsive disorder. A double-blind, placebo-controlled study in patients with and without tics. *Archives of general psychiatry* 1994; **51**(4): 302-308 [PMID: 8161290]

121    Skapinakis P, Papatheodorou T, Mavreas V. Antipsychotic augmentation of serotonergic antidepressants in treatment-resistant obsessive-compulsive disorder: a meta-analysis of the randomized controlled trials. *European neuropsychopharmacology : the journal of the European College of Neuropsychopharmacology* 2007; **17**(2): 79-93 [PMID: 16904298 DOI: 10.1016/j.euroneuro.2006.07.002]

122    Goodwin G, Fleischhacker W, Arango C, Baumann P, Davidson M, de Hert M, Falkai P, Kapur S, Leucht S, Licht R, Naber D, O'Keane V, Papakostas G, Vieta E, Zohar J. Advantages and disadvantages of combination treatment with antipsychotics ECNP Consensus Meeting, March 2008, Nice. *European neuropsychopharmacology : the journal of the European College of Neuropsychopharmacology* 2009; **19**(7): 520-532 [PMID: 19411165 DOI: 10.1016/j.euroneuro.2009.04.003]

123    Erzegovesi S, Guglielmo E, Siliprandi F, Bellodi L. Low-dose risperidone augmentation of fluvoxamine treatment in obsessive-compulsive disorder: a double-blind, placebo-controlled study. *European neuropsychopharmacology : the journal of the European College of Neuropsychopharmacology* 2005; **15**(1): 69-74 [PMID: 15572275 DOI: 10.1016/j.euroneuro.2004.04.004]

124    Hollander E, Baldini Rossi N, Sood E, Pallanti S. Risperidone augmentation in treatment-resistant obsessive-compulsive disorder: a double-blind, placebo-controlled study. *The international journal of neuropsychopharmacology / official scientific journal of the Collegium Internationale Neuropsychopharmacologicum* 2003; **6**(4): 397-401 [PMID: 14604454 DOI: 10.1017/S1461145703003730]

125    McDougle CJ, Epperson CN, Pelton GH, Wasylink S, Price LH. A double-blind, placebo-controlled study of risperidone addition in serotonin reuptake inhibitor-refractory obsessive-compulsive disorder. *Archives of general psychiatry* 2000; **57**(8): 794-801 [PMID: 10920469]

126    Atmaca M, Kuloglu M, Tezcan E, Gecici O. Quetiapine augmentation in patients with treatment resistant obsessive-compulsive disorder: a single-blind, placebo-controlled study. *International clinical psychopharmacology* 2002; **17**(3): 115-119 [PMID: 11981352]

127    Kordon A, Wahl K, Koch N, Zurowski B, Anlauf M, Vielhaber K, Kahl KG, Broocks A, Voderholzer U, Hohagen F. Quetiapine addition to serotonin reuptake inhibitors in patients with severe obsessive-compulsive disorder: a double-blind, randomized, placebo-controlled study. *Journal of clinical psychopharmacology* 2008; **28**(5): 550-554 [PMID: 18794652 DOI: 10.1097/JCP.0b013e318185e735]

128    Vulink NC, Denys D, Fluitman SB, Meinardi JC, Westenberg HG. Quetiapine augments the effect of citalopram in non-refractory obsessive-compulsive disorder: a randomized, double-blind, placebo-controlled study of 76 patients. *The Journal of clinical psychiatry* 2009; **70**(7): 1001-1008 [PMID: 19497245 DOI: 10.4088/JCP.08m04269]

129    Carey PD, Vythilingum B, Seedat S, Muller JE, van Ameringen M, Stein DJ. Quetiapine augmentation of SRIs in treatment refractory obsessive-compulsive disorder: a double-blind, randomised, placebo-controlled study [ISRCTN83050762]. *BMC psychiatry* 2005; **5**: 5 [PMID: 15667657 PMCID: 547907 DOI: 10.1186/1471-244X-5-5]

130    Denys D, de Geus F, van Megen HJ, Westenberg HG. A double-blind, randomized, placebo-controlled trial of quetiapine addition in patients with obsessive-compulsive disorder refractory to serotonin reuptake inhibitors. *The Journal of clinical psychiatry* 2004; **65**(8): 1040-1048 [PMID: 15323587]

131    Fineberg NA, Sivakumaran T, Roberts A, Gale T. Adding quetiapine to SRI in treatment-resistant obsessive-compulsive disorder: a randomized controlled treatment study. *International clinical psychopharmacology* 2005; **20**(4): 223-226 [PMID: 15933483]

132    Diniz JB, Shavitt RG, Pereira CA, Hounie AG, Pimentel I, Koran LM, Dainesi SM, Miguel EC. Quetiapine versus clomipramine in the augmentation of selective serotonin reuptake inhibitors for the treatment of obsessive-compulsive disorder: a randomized, open-label trial. *Journal of*

*psychopharmacology* 2010; **24**(3): 297-307 [PMID: 19164490 DOI: 10.1177/0269881108099423]

133 Bystritsky A, Ackerman DL, Rosen RM, Vapnik T, Gorbis E, Maidment KM, Saxena S. Augmentation of serotonin reuptake inhibitors in refractory obsessive-compulsive disorder using adjunctive olanzapine: a placebo-controlled trial. *The Journal of clinical psychiatry* 2004; **65**(4): 565-568 [PMID: 15119922]

134 Shapira NA, Ward HE, Mandoki M, Murphy TK, Yang MC, Blier P, Goodman WK. A double-blind, placebo-controlled trial of olanzapine addition in fluoxetine-refractory obsessive-compulsive disorder. *Biological psychiatry* 2004; **55**(5): 553-555 [PMID: 15023585 DOI: 10.1016/j.biopsych.2003.11.010]

135 Maina G, Pessina E, Albert U, Bogetto F. 8-week, single-blind, randomized trial comparing risperidone versus olanzapine augmentation of serotonin reuptake inhibitors in treatment-resistant obsessive-compulsive disorder. *European neuropsychopharmacology : the journal of the European College of Neuropsychopharmacology* 2008; **18**(5): 364-372 [PMID: 18280710 DOI: 10.1016/j.euroneuro.2008.01.001]

136 Muscatello MR, Bruno A, Pandolfo G, Mico U, Scimeca G, Romeo VM, Santoro V, Settineri S, Spina E, Zoccali RA. Effect of aripiprazole augmentation of serotonin reuptake inhibitors or clomipramine in treatment-resistant obsessive-compulsive disorder: a double-blind, placebo-controlled study. *Journal of clinical psychopharmacology* 2011; **31**(2): 174-179 [PMID: 21346614 DOI: 10.1097/JCP.0b013e31820e3db6]

137 Sayyah M, Sayyah M, Boostani H, Ghaffari SM, Hoseini A. Effects of aripiprazole augmentation in treatment-resistant obsessive-compulsive disorder (a double blind clinical trial). *Depression and anxiety* 2012; **29**(10): 850-854 [PMID: 22933237 DOI: 10.1002/da.21996]

138 Selvi Y, Atli A, Aydin A, Besiroglu L, Ozdemir P, Ozdemir O. The comparison of aripiprazole and risperidone augmentation in selective serotonin reuptake inhibitor-refractory obsessive-compulsive disorder: a single-blind, randomised study. *Human psychopharmacology* 2011; **26**(1): 51-57 [PMID: 21308781 DOI: 10.1002/hup.1169]

139 Savas HA, Yumru M, Ozen ME. Quetiapine and ziprasidone as adjuncts in treatment-resistant obsessive-compulsive disorder: a retrospective comparative study. *Clinical drug investigation* 2008; **28**(7): 439-442 [PMID: 18544004]

140 Komossa K, Depping AM, Meyer M, Kissling W, Leucht S. Second-generation antipsychotics for obsessive compulsive disorder. *Cochrane database of systematic reviews* 2010(12): CD008141 [PMID: 21154394 DOI: 10.1002/14651858.CD008141.pub2]

141 Fitzgerald KD, Stewart CM, Tawile V, Rosenberg DR. Risperidone augmentation of serotonin reuptake inhibitor treatment of pediatric

obsessive compulsive disorder. *Journal of child and adolescent psychopharmacology* 1999; **9**(2): 115-123 [PMID: 10461822]

142    Masi G, Pfanner C, Millepiedi S, Berloffa S. Aripiprazole augmentation in 39 adolescents with medication-resistant obsessive-compulsive disorder. *Journal of clinical psychopharmacology* 2010; **30**(6): 688-693 [PMID: 21105283]

143    Thomsen PH. Risperidone augmentation in the treatment of severe adolescent OCD in SSRI-refractory cases: a case-series. *Annals of clinical psychiatry : official journal of the American Academy of Clinical Psychiatrists* 2004; **16**(4): 201-207 [PMID: 15702568]

144    Arumugham SS, Reddy JY. Augmentation strategies in obsessive-compulsive disorder. *Expert review of neurotherapeutics* 2013; **13**(2): 187-203 [PMID: 23368806 DOI: 10.1586/ern.12.160]

145    Maina G, Albert U, Ziero S, Bogetto F. Antipsychotic augmentation for treatment resistant obsessive-compulsive disorder: what if antipsychotic is discontinued? *International clinical psychopharmacology* 2003; **18**(1): 23-28 [PMID: 12490771 DOI: 10.1097/01.yic.0000047784.24295.2b]

146    Joffe RT, Swinson RP, Levitt AJ. Acute psychostimulant challenge in primary obsessive-compulsive disorder. *Journal of clinical psychopharmacology* 1991; **11**(4): 237-241 [PMID: 1680885]

147    Woolley JB, Heyman I. Dexamphetamine for obsessive-compulsive disorder. *The American journal of psychiatry* 2003; **160**(1): 183 [PMID: 12505824]

148    Koran LM, Aboujaoude E, Gamel NN. Double-blind study of dextroamphetamine versus caffeine augmentation for treatment-resistant obsessive-compulsive disorder. *The Journal of clinical psychiatry* 2009; **70**(11): 1530-1535 [PMID: 19573497 DOI: 10.4088/JCP.08m04605]

149    Chakrabarty K, Bhattacharyya S, Christopher R, Khanna S. Glutamatergic dysfunction in OCD. *Neuropsychopharmacology : official publication of the American College of Neuropsychopharmacology* 2005; **30**(9): 1735-1740 [PMID: 15841109 DOI: 1300733 [pii] 10.1038/sj.npp.1300733]

150    MacMaster FP, O'Neill J, Rosenberg DR. Brain imaging in pediatric obsessive-compulsive disorder. *Journal of the American Academy of Child and Adolescent Psychiatry* 2008; **47**(11): 1262-1272 [PMID: 18827717 PMCID: 2696312 DOI: 10.1097/CHI.0b013e318185d2be S0890-8567(08)60118-5 [pii]]

151    Maina G, Rosso G, Zanardini R, Bogetto F, Gennarelli M, Bocchio-Chiavetto L. Serum levels of brain-derived neurotrophic factor in drug-naive obsessive-compulsive patients: a case-control study. *Journal of affective disorders* 2010; **122**(1-2): 174-178 [PMID: 19664825 DOI: S0165-0327(09)00334-6 [pii] 10.1016/j.jad.2009.07.009]

152     O'Neill J, Piacentini JC, Chang S, Levitt JG, Rozenman M, Bergman L, Salamon N, Alger JR, McCracken JT. MRSI correlates of cognitive-behavioral therapy in pediatric obsessive-compulsive disorder. *Progress in neuro-psychopharmacology & biological psychiatry* 2012; **36**(1): 161-168 [PMID: 21983143 DOI: S0278-5846(11)00276-4 [pii] 10.1016/j.pnpbp.2011.09.007]

153     Wu K, Hanna GL, Rosenberg DR, Arnold PD. The role of glutamate signaling in the pathogenesis and treatment of obsessive-compulsive disorder. *Pharmacol Biochem Behav* 2012; **100**(4): 726-735 [PMID: 22024159 DOI: S0091-3057(11)00329-7 [pii] 10.1016/j.pbb.2011.10.007]

154     Samuels J, Wang Y, Riddle MA, Greenberg BD, Fyer AJ, McCracken JT, Rauch SL, Murphy DL, Grados MA, Knowles JA, Piacentini J, Cullen B, Bienvenu OJ, 3rd, Rasmussen SA, Geller D, Pauls DL, Liang KY, Shugart YY, Nestadt G. Comprehensive family-based association study of the glutamate transporter gene SLC1A1 in obsessive-compulsive disorder. *Am J Med Genet B Neuropsychiatr Genet* 2011; **156B**(4): 472-477 [PMID: 21445956 PMCID: 3082623 DOI: 10.1002/ajmg.b.31184]

155     Wendland JR, Moya PR, Timpano KR, Anavitarte AP, Kruse MR, Wheaton MG, Ren-Patterson RF, Murphy DL. A haplotype containing quantitative trait loci for SLC1A1 gene expression and its association with obsessive-compulsive disorder. *Archives of general psychiatry* 2009; **66**(4): 408-416 [PMID: 19349310 PMCID: 2775716 DOI: 66/4/408 [pii] 10.1001/archgenpsychiatry.2009.6]

156     Shugart YY, Wang Y, Samuels JF, Grados MA, Greenberg BD, Knowles JA, McCracken JT, Rauch SL, Murphy DL, Rasmussen SA, Cullen B, Hoehn-Saric R, Pinto A, Fyer AJ, Piacentini J, Pauls DL, Bienvenu OJ, Riddle MA, Liang KY, Nestadt G. A family-based association study of the glutamate transporter gene SLC1A1 in obsessive-compulsive disorder in 378 families. *Am J Med Genet B Neuropsychiatr Genet* 2009; **150B**(6): 886-892 [PMID: 19152386 DOI: 10.1002/ajmg.b.30914]

157     Stewart SE, Fagerness JA, Platko J, Smoller JW, Scharf JM, Illmann C, Jenike E, Chabane N, Leboyer M, Delorme R, Jenike MA, Pauls DL. Association of the SLC1A1 glutamate transporter gene and obsessive-compulsive disorder. *Am J Med Genet B Neuropsychiatr Genet* 2007; **144B**(8): 1027-1033 [PMID: 17894418 DOI: 10.1002/ajmg.b.30533]

158     Dickel DE, Veenstra-VanderWeele J, Cox NJ, Wu X, Fischer DJ, Van Etten-Lee M, Himle JA, Leventhal BL, Cook EH, Jr., Hanna GL. Association testing of the positional and functional candidate gene SLC1A1/EAAC1 in early-onset obsessive-compulsive disorder. *Archives of general psychiatry* 2006; **63**(7): 778-785 [PMID: 16818867 DOI: 63/7/778 [pii] 10.1001/archpsyc.63.7.778]

159 Arnold PD, Sicard T, Burroughs E, Richter MA, Kennedy JL. Glutamate transporter gene SLC1A1 associated with obsessive-compulsive disorder. *Archives of general psychiatry* 2006; **63**(7): 769-776 [PMID: 16818866 DOI: 63/7/769 [pii] 10.1001/archpsyc.63.7.769]

160 Aboujaoude E, Barry JJ, Gamel N. Memantine augmentation in treatment-resistant obsessive-compulsive disorder: an open-label trial. *Journal of clinical psychopharmacology* 2009; **29**(1): 51-55 [PMID: 19142108 DOI: 10.1097/JCP.0b013e318192e9a4]

161 Stewart SE, Jenike EA, Hezel DM, Stack DE, Dodman NH, Shuster L, Jenike MA. A single-blinded case-control study of memantine in severe obsessive-compulsive disorder. *Journal of clinical psychopharmacology* 2010; **30**(1): 34-39 [PMID: 20075645 DOI: 10.1097/JCP.0b013e3181c856de]

162 Ghaleiha A, Entezari N, Modabbernia A, Najand B, Askari N, Tabrizi M, Ashrafi M, Hajiaghaee R, Akhondzadeh S. Memantine add-on in moderate to severe obsessive-compulsive disorder: randomized double-blind placebo-controlled study. *Journal of psychiatric research* 2013; **47**(2): 175-180 [PMID: 23063327 DOI: 10.1016/j.jpsychires.2012.09.015]

163 Hezel DM, Beattie K, Stewart SE. Memantine as an augmenting agent for severe pediatric OCD. *The American journal of psychiatry* 2009; **166**(2): 237 [PMID: 19188297 DOI: 10.1176/appi.ajp.2008.08091427]

164 Pittenger C, Kelmendi B, Wasylink S, Bloch MH, Coric V. Riluzole augmentation in treatment-refractory obsessive-compulsive disorder: a series of 13 cases, with long-term follow-up. *Journal of clinical psychopharmacology* 2008; **28**(3): 363-367 [PMID: 18480706 DOI: 10.1097/JCP.0b013e3181727548]

165 Grant P, Lougee L, Hirschtritt M, Swedo SE. An open-label trial of riluzole, a glutamate antagonist, in children with treatment-resistant obsessive-compulsive disorder. *Journal of child and adolescent psychopharmacology* 2007; **17**(6): 761-767 [PMID: 18315448 DOI: 10.1089/cap.2007.0021]

166 Coric V, Taskiran S, Pittenger C, Wasylink S, Mathalon DH, Valentine G, Saksa J, Wu YT, Gueorguieva R, Sanacora G, Malison RT, Krystal JH. Riluzole augmentation in treatment-resistant obsessive-compulsive disorder: an open-label trial. *Biological psychiatry* 2005; **58**(5): 424-428 [PMID: 15993857 DOI: 10.1016/j.biopsych.2005.04.043]

167 Bloch MH, Wasylink S, Landeros-Weisenberger A, Panza KE, Billingslea E, Leckman JF, Krystal JH, Bhagwagar Z, Sanacora G, Pittenger C. Effects of ketamine in treatment-refractory obsessive-compulsive disorder. *Biological psychiatry* 2012; **72**(11): 964-970 [PMID: 22784486 DOI: 10.1016/j.biopsych.2012.05.028]

168 Van Ameringen M, Mancini C, Patterson B, Bennett M. Topiramate augmentation in treatment-resistant obsessive-compulsive disorder: a

retrospective, open-label case series. *Depression and anxiety* 2006; **23**(1): 1-5 [PMID: 16178009 DOI: 10.1002/da.20118]

169     Mowla A, Khajeian AM, Sahraian A, Chohedri AH, Kashkoli F. Topiramate Augmentation in Resistant OCD: A Double-Blind Placebo-Controlled Clinical Trial. *CNS spectrums* 2010 [PMID: 21632011]

170     Berlin HA, Koran LM, Jenike MA, Shapira NA, Chaplin W, Pallanti S, Hollander E. Double-blind, placebo-controlled trial of topiramate augmentation in treatment-resistant obsessive-compulsive disorder. *The Journal of clinical psychiatry* 2011; **72**(5): 716-721 [PMID: 20816027 DOI: 10.4088/JCP.09m05266gre]

171     Kumar TC, Khanna S. Lamotrigine augmentation of serotonin re-uptake inhibitors in obsessive-compulsive disorder. *The Australian and New Zealand journal of psychiatry* 2000; **34**(3): 527-528 [PMID: 10881981]

172     Bruno A, Mico U, Pandolfo G, Mallamace D, Abenavoli E, Di Nardo F, D'Arrigo C, Spina E, Zoccali RA, Muscatello MR. Lamotrigine augmentation of serotonin reuptake inhibitors in treatment-resistant obsessive-compulsive disorder: a double-blind, placebo-controlled study. *Journal of psychopharmacology* 2012; **26**(11): 1456-1462 [PMID: 22351381 DOI: 10.1177/0269881111431751]

173     Onder E, Tural U, Gokbakan M. Does gabapentin lead to early symptom improvement in obsessive-compulsive disorder? *European archives of psychiatry and clinical neuroscience* 2008; **258**(6): 319-323 [PMID: 18297416 DOI: 10.1007/s00406-007-0798-z]

174     Oulis P, Mourikis I, Konstantakopoulos G. Pregabalin augmentation in treatment-resistant obsessive-compulsive disorder. *International clinical psychopharmacology* 2011; **26**(4): 221-224 [PMID: 21460732 DOI: 10.1097/YIC.0b013e3283466657]

175     Dean O, Giorlando F, Berk M. N-acetylcysteine in psychiatry: current therapeutic evidence and potential mechanisms of action. *Journal of psychiatry & neuroscience : JPN* 2011; **36**(2): 78-86 [PMID: 21118657 PMCID: 3044191 DOI: 10.1503/jpn.100057]

176     Lafleur DL, Pittenger C, Kelmendi B, Gardner T, Wasylink S, Malison RT, Sanacora G, Krystal JH, Coric V. N-acetylcysteine augmentation in serotonin reuptake inhibitor refractory obsessive-compulsive disorder. *Psychopharmacology* 2006; **184**(2): 254-256 [PMID: 16374600 DOI: 10.1007/s00213-005-0246-6]

177     Bhattacharyya S, Chakraborty K. Glutamatergic dysfunction--newer targets for anti-obsessional drugs. *Recent patents on CNS drug discovery* 2007; **2**(1): 47-55 [PMID: 18221217]

178     Hollander E, Kaplan A, Stahl SM. A double-blind, placebo-controlled trial of clonazepam in obsessive-compulsive disorder. *The world journal of biological psychiatry : the official journal of the World Federation of Societies of Biological Psychiatry* 2003; **4**(1): 30-34 [PMID: 12582975]

179    Hewlett WA, Vinogradov S, Agras WS. Clomipramine, clonazepam, and clonidine treatment of obsessive-compulsive disorder. *Journal of clinical psychopharmacology* 1992; **12**(6): 420-430 [PMID: 1474179]

180    Crockett BA, Churchill E, Davidson JR. A double-blind combination study of clonazepam with sertraline in obsessive-compulsive disorder. *Annals of clinical psychiatry : official journal of the American Academy of Clinical Psychiatrists* 2004; **16**(3): 127-132 [PMID: 15517844]

181    Koran LM, Aboujaoude E, Bullock KD, Franz B, Gamel N, Elliott M. Double-blind treatment with oral morphine in treatment-resistant obsessive-compulsive disorder. *The Journal of clinical psychiatry* 2005; **66**(3): 353-359 [PMID: 15766302]

182    Amiaz R, Fostick L, Gershon A, Zohar J. Naltrexone augmentation in OCD: a double-blind placebo-controlled cross-over study. *European neuropsychopharmacology : the journal of the European College of Neuropsychopharmacology* 2008; **18**(6): 455-461 [PMID: 18353618 DOI: 10.1016/j.euroneuro.2008.01.006]

183    Dannon PN, Sasson Y, Hirschmann S, Iancu I, Grunhaus LJ, Zohar J. Pindolol augmentation in treatment-resistant obsessive compulsive disorder: a double-blind placebo controlled trial. *European neuropsychopharmacology : the journal of the European College of Neuropsychopharmacology* 2000; **10**(3): 165-169 [PMID: 10793318]

184    Mundo E, Guglielmo E, Bellodi L. Effect of adjuvant pindolol on the antiobsessional response to fluvoxamine: a double-blind, placebo-controlled study. *International clinical psychopharmacology* 1998; **13**(5): 219-224 [PMID: 9817627]

185    McDougle CJ, Price LH, Goodman WK, Charney DS, Heninger GR. A controlled trial of lithium augmentation in fluvoxamine-refractory obsessive-compulsive disorder: lack of efficacy. *Journal of clinical psychopharmacology* 1991; **11**(3): 175-184 [PMID: 1820757]

186    Slotema CW, Blom JD, Hoek HW, Sommer IE. Should we expand the toolbox of psychiatric treatment methods to include Repetitive Transcranial Magnetic Stimulation (rTMS)? A meta-analysis of the efficacy of rTMS in psychiatric disorders. *The Journal of clinical psychiatry* 2010; **71**(7): 873-884 [PMID: 20361902 DOI: 10.4088/JCP.08m04872gre]

187    Blom RM, Figee M, Vulink N, Denys D. Update on repetitive transcranial magnetic stimulation in obsessive-compulsive disorder: different targets. *Current psychiatry reports* 2011; **13**(4): 289-294 [PMID: 21547545 PMCID: 3128260 DOI: 10.1007/s11920-011-0205-3]

188    Mantovani A, Simpson HB, Fallon BA, Rossi S, Lisanby SH. Randomized sham-controlled trial of repetitive transcranial magnetic stimulation in treatment-resistant obsessive-compulsive disorder. *The international journal of neuropsychopharmacology / official scientific journal of the Collegium Internationale*

*Neuropsychopharmacologicum* 2010; **13**(2): 217-227 [PMID: 19691873 DOI: 10.1017/S1461145709990435]

189    Greenberg BD, Gabriels LA, Malone DA, Jr., Rezai AR, Friehs GM, Okun MS, Shapira NA, Foote KD, Cosyns PR, Kubu CS, Malloy PF, Salloway SP, Giftakis JE, Rise MT, Machado AG, Baker KB, Stypulkowski PH, Goodman WK, Rasmussen SA, Nuttin BJ. Deep brain stimulation of the ventral internal capsule/ventral striatum for obsessive-compulsive disorder: worldwide experience. *Molecular psychiatry* 2010; **15**(1): 64-79 [PMID: 18490925 DOI: 10.1038/mp.2008.55]

190    Blomstedt P, Sjoberg RL, Hansson M, Bodlund O, Hariz MI. Deep Brain Stimulation in the Treatment of Obsessive-Compulsive Disorder. *World neurosurgery* 2012 [PMID: 23044000 DOI: 10.1016/j.wneu.2012.10.006]

191    Greenberg BD, Rauch SL, Haber SN. Invasive circuitry-based neurotherapeutics: stereotactic ablation and deep brain stimulation for OCD. *Neuropsychopharmacology : official publication of the American College of Neuropsychopharmacology* 2010; **35**(1): 317-336 [PMID: 19759530 PMCID: 3055421 DOI: 10.1038/npp.2009.128]

Chapter Seven

# Novel Treatment Approaches to Obsessive-Compulsive Disorder

Erin Rabideau, Linda Herbert, Emily Ach, and Heather Yardley

Obsessive compulsive disorder (OCD) involves excessive or exaggerated worry about threatening or non-threatening stimuli paired with rituals believed to reduce the anxiety. The worry and rituals associated with OCD impair social and emotional functioning as well as prevent completion of necessary daily tasks (Piacentini et al., 2003). Approximately 20-40% of patients with OCD experience treatment refractory symptoms, meaning that they do not experience a relief in OCD symptoms in response to typical pharmacological and cognitive-behavioral therapy techniques, and may experience years of persistent debilitating symptoms that impede their daily functioning (Aouizerate et al., 2006; Mian, Campos, Sheth, & Eskandar, 2010). For these patients, alternative treatment strategies must be considered. The present paper reviews innovative treatments for OCD in three areas: augmentation of traditional CBT with ERP, medication, and surgical intervention.

Cognitive-behavioral therapy (CBT) using exposure and response-prevention (ERP) has been widely acknowledged as the treatment of choice for adults and youth with obsessive compulsive disorder (OCD; Abramowitz, 1997; Abramowitz, Foa, & Franklin, 2003; Abramowitz, Whiteside, & Deacon, 2006; Foa et al., 2005; Storch et al., 2007a; Storch, Mariaskin, & Murphy, 2009). Treatment involves activating obsessional distress through prolonged and repeated exposures to cues related to an individual's obsessions and compulsions. The continued exposure to increasingly feared stimuli (in vivo and/or imagined) while being prevented from engaging in compensatory rituals, leads to habituation to the cues and attenuation of the drive to engage in rituals (Franklin, & Foa, 2008).

ERP treatment for youth with OCD is similar to the treatment for adults with OCD, with the common addition of increased family involvement in treatment. Family involvement is critical to the success of ERP treatment in youth because youth often lack the self-awareness and behavioral regulation to take full advantage of CBT techniques (Storch, Mariaskin, & Murphy, 2009). Including a child's family in treatment allows the family to move away from activities that enable the child's symptoms and begin supporting the child's ability to cope with his/her obsessions and compulsions (Storch, Mariaskin, & Murphy, 2009).

In light of findings that 20-40% of individuals with OCD do not respond to the first line approach of exposure and response prevention (Aouizerate et al., 2006; Mian, Campos, Sheth, & Eskandar, 2010), this group is referred to as non-responders. This may be due in part to a subset of these "non-responders" not having had access to effectively trained therapists which may compromise treatment integrity and effectiveness. In an effort to address the needs of these individuals, a number of alternative treatment strategies have emerged. These include both novel approaches to treatment (e.g., novel medications, surgery) as well as the use of alternative techniques (e.g., virtual reality, motivational interviewing) to augment standard treatment protocols. The remainder of this paper will outline the most common and promising of these approaches.

## Augmentation of CBT

*Virtual Reality*

Treatment for OCD involves gradual exposure to feared stimuli, but it is not always possible or feasible for an individual to be exposed to a feared stimulus (e.g., wild animals, crowds) in a controlled therapeutic environment. Although in vivo exposures are generally recommended (Geffken, Pincus, & Zelikovsky, 1999), imaginal exposures have been used successfully in treatment (i.e., Leahy & Holland, 2000). Recent studies have examined the use of virtual reality (VR) as a method of imagined exposure treatment delivery (e.g. Graziano, Callueng, & Geffken, 2010; Kim, Kim, Kim, Roh, & Kim, 2009). VR is a real-time, computer-generated world comprised of graphics, sounds, and other sensory modalities with which the individual can interact, and has been shown to successfully increase anxiety in patients with OCD during exposures (Kim et al., 2009). VR-based exposure treatment provides a more realistic experience of the feared stimuli compared to an imaginal exposure and may be more easily implemented in the therapy office than in vivo exposure. This technology also allows the therapist to see and control what the patient is viewing during the exposure, which enables the therapist to tailor the VR treatment to patients' specific obsessive/compulsive cues and provides access to exposures that would not otherwise be possible. Graziano and colleagues (2010) used VR successfully in treating an 11-year-old male with emetophobia (fear of vomiting), a fear that would typically be difficult to simulate in a real world setting.

*Motivational Interviewing*

Individuals with OCD who begin treatment may not obtain the full benefit of treatment because they may terminate treatment early or do not adhere to treatment recommendations after termination (Simpson, Huppert et al., 2006; Sookman & Steketee, 2007; Simpson, Zuckoff, Page et al., 2008). Motivational interviewing (MI) has commonly been used to treat or enhance treatment for patients who struggle with change (Miller & Rollnick, 2002). It is an empirically supported, client-centered, goal-oriented treatment approach for enhancing an individual's intrinsic motivation to change by exploring and resolving ambivalence in hopes of increasing adherence to treatment (Miller, 2006; Miller & Rollnick, 2002). Simpson and colleagues (2008) found that integrating MI techniques into the standard ERP protocol was feasible and promising for inclusion in future controlled trials, and MI has been successfully used to supplement ERP treatment as a way to enhance treatment gains in several studies (Westra & Dozois, 2006). In a small trial, Maltby and Tolin (2005) reported that the addition of four sessions of MI prior to standard CBT treatment increased ERP entry among OCD patients who had previously refused treatment. Others have reported that adding MI and thought mapping to CBT group treatment provided greater symptom reduction and rates of remission than the CBT group alone at post-treatment and 3-month follow up (Meyer, Souza, Heldt et al., 2010). The addition of an MI component to treatment with children with OCD is also promising. A randomized controlled clinical trial, conducted by Merlo and colleagues (2010), in which pediatric patients received either CBT with an MI component or standard CBT with psychoeducation, demonstrated that patients who received MI not only exhibited fewer symptoms of OCD at the end of treatment than patients who received standard CBT, but the magnitude of the decrease in symptoms was greater and the average amount of time to treatment completion shorter, which provides compelling evidence that MI could be a crucial component in treatment for OCD among pediatric patients.

However, not all studies have found greater reductions in OCD symptoms as a result of MI-enhanced treatment when compared to standard care. Simpson et al. (2010) conducted a controlled trial in which patients were randomized to either MI-enhanced ERP or standard ERP. Both groups experienced clinically significant decreases in OCD symptoms, but there were no differences between groups. The authors suggested that MI enhancement may not provide additional gain for patients who already want to decrease their symptoms and are willing to engage in therapy (Simpson et al., 2010). Together, the majority of these data offer support for the use of MI techniques in conjunction with standard CBT treatment; however, further research is warranted to determine whether MI may serve to increase adherence and promote positive treatment outcomes globally among individuals with OCD, or whether there are individuals differences that may indicate for whom MI enhancement will be most beneficial.

*Self-Guided Treatments*

Unfortunately, a number of barriers exist that hinder individuals with OCD from receiving treatment (Morgan, Lack, & Storch, 2010). Individuals with OCD are often reluctant to seek out formal medical and/or psychological treatment for the disorder. Leon, Portera and Weissman (1995) found that only 20% of individuals with OCD sought treatment with a mental health professional. Furthermore, many mental health professionals lack adequate training or may be reluctant to effectively treat individuals with ERP (Valderhaug, Gotestam, & Larsson, 2004). OCD sufferers may also encounter financial obstacles to treatment (Leonard et al., 1993) and/or their symptoms may serve as a barrier to treatment (Adams, Waas, March, & Smith, 1994). Additionally, medical providers are often not familiar with the symptoms or presentation associated with OCD and individuals may suffer symptoms without appropriate diagnosis or treatment (Storch, 2005). Therefore, a number of CBT-based self-guided therapeutic techniques have been examined as possible treatment options for individuals with OCD.

Mataix-Cols and Marks (2006a) performed a review of the literature on CBT-based self-guided treatments, such as bibliotherapy, telecare, self-help groups, and computer-based self-help for individuals with OCD. The results indicated support for computer-based ERP both with and without brief, scheduled support from a clinician. There was also support for patient engagement in ERP with instruction from a clinician delivered live by phone. Little support was reported for bibliotherapy due to the scarcity of research examining this mode of treatment and the nature of the study designs, exhibiting low sample sizes and no controlled trials. Fritzler and colleagues (1997) examined bibliotherapy as a treatment for OCD in 9 patients, and found that the participants experienced significant symptom improvement after self-guided treatment using a self-help book in addition to 5 traditional CBT sessions over 12 weeks. However, no other trails examining bibliotherapy were identified. A similar paucity of research exists in the literature examining self-help groups, which is small and inconclusive (Mataix-Cols & Marks, 2006a).

*Computer-Based Interventions*

One method of self-guided treatment that has been considered is computer-based intervention in the place of traditional psychotherapy (Morgan, Lack, & Storch, 2010). These interventions may reduce the need for one-on-one treatment with a mental health profession, which reduces the cost of treatment overall and makes treatment accessible in areas in which qualified professionals are scarce. Currently, these interventions show promise in treating OCD symptoms, particularly in those whom may otherwise unable to access evidence-based treatment (Morgan, Lack, & Storch, 2010).

Baer, Minichiello, and Jenike (1987) as well as by Baer, Minichiello, Jenike, and Holland (1988) first investigated computer-based interventions for OCD with OC-CHECK, which was used as an augmentation of individual face-to-face ERP therapy using hand-held computer devices. Baer and Greist (1997) further investigated computer-based treatments for OCD with the BT STEPS program, which is an interactive computerized voice response system designed to aid a patient in understanding, assessing, and developing and implementing a treatment plan for his/her OCD symptoms across nine "steps" with supplemental work in a partnered workbook. The program utilized the conceptualization of OCD symptoms from ERP in order to develop an appropriate treatment plan for remediation. Among the participants 71% rated their lives as greatly improved after finishing the program. Several studies have further tested and investigated extensions and refinements of the BT (behavioral therapy) STEPS program with similar results (e.g., Greist et al., 1998; Bachofen et al., 1999; Nakagawa et al., 2000). Greist and colleagues (2002) performed a randomized control trial comparing groups receiving either the BT STEPS treatment program, traditional face-to-face CBT for OCD, or systematic relaxation lead by an audio tape and manual. The results indicated that individuals in both treatment groups receiving either the BT STEPS or traditional CBT experienced significantly higher reductions in OCD symptoms compared to the relaxation group. However, the traditional CBT group exhibited significantly higher reductions in OCD symptoms compared to the BT STEPS treatment group. Kim and colleagues (2008) used a similar approach as the BT STEPS program creating a virtual reality exposure task designed to target "checking" behaviors. The results indicated that the exposure task elicited sufficient anxiety to warrant investigation as a possible alternative to face-to-face exposure tasks in future studies. Although this literature is still developing, a number of other studies have also examined the utility of computer-based treatments (e.g., Turner, Heyman, Futh, & Lovell, 2009; Taylor & Luce, 2003; Lovel, Fullalove, Garyey, & Brooker, 2000).

While acknowledging the encouraging results of self-guided treatments for individuals with OCD, Mataix-Cols and Marks (2006b) conclude that the guidance of a clinician may constitute an additional asset in treatment. In their review of the self-guided treatment literature, Mataix-Cols and Marks (2006a,b) observed that many of the treatment protocols included the support of a therapist in-person and/or over the phone. Furthermore, participant adherence and outcomes were augmented by the scheduled support of a therapist. Although a computer may deliver many of the components of effective ERP treatment, the literature indicates that the support of a clinician is an important part of treatment for which a computer is not a sufficient substitute. This was particularly evident in the study performed by Kenwright and colleagues (2005), in which the self-guided BT STEPS treatment group, which also received scheduled clinician support over the phone, adhered better to the ERP protocol, delivered on the computer program and in the workbook, and also experienced greater symptom reduction than other studies examining the effect of the BT STEPS program alone. However, utilization of self-help techniques can enhance treatment and reduce the cost of mental healthcare Mataix-Cols & Marks, 2006b). Tolin, Diefenbach, and Gilliam (2011) examined a stepped ERP approach to care, in which all OCD clients begin with low-cost/low-intensity treatments and reserve high-cost/high intensity interventions for those who do not respond to the low-cost/low-intensity treatments. The results indicated that a stepped approach was as efficacious and more cost-effective compared to traditional CBT. This may be an effective way of incorporating both types of effective treatment approaches in a way that is responsive to the needs of each client. Further research ought to examine the long-term efficacy and feasibility of the stepped ERP approach to OCD treatment.

## Medication Augmentation

*Serotonin Reuptake Inhibitors*

Several studies have examined the effectiveness of enhancing ERP treatment of OCD with either the serotonin reuptake inhibitor (SRI) clomipramine or selective serotonin reuptake inhibitors (SSRIs; Clomipramine Collaborative Group, 1991; The Pediatric OCD Treatment Study (POTS) Team, 2004; Foa et al., 2005; Greist et al., 1995; Goodman et al., 1989a; Hollander et al., 2003; Tollefson et al., 1994; Montgomery, Kasper, Stein, Hedegaard, & Bang, 2001). The POTS Team compared the treatment outcomes in youth with OCD with ERP, sertraline, and a combination therapy. There were mixed findings regarding whether ERP alone or ERP combined with sertraline was more effective (The POTS Team, 2004). Although several SRIs and SSRIs have been studied in the treatment of OCD, clomipramine is considered to be the most widely studied and most efficacious medication in treating the symptoms associated with OCD. However, some studies have questioned whether these drugs contribute to significant symptom reduction beyond that accomplished by ERP alone. Foa and colleagues (2005) performed a randomized, placebo-controlled protocol examining the effectiveness of clomipramine, ERP, and the combination of these treatments in adults with OCD ($n = 122$); and concluded that, although all three conditions were effective in treating OCD, monotherapy with clomipramine and the combined treatment were not superior to ERP alone. Taken together, these studies indicate that SRIs and SSRIs have been shown to, at best, modestly augment the effect of ERP in adults and youth with OCD.

156

*D-cycloserine*

Recent translational research has examined the N-methyl-D-aspartate (NMDA) receptor involved with fear extinction in the amygdala and identified D-cycloserine (DCS), an NMDA partial agonist, as a psychopharmacological way of enhancing the extinction of learned fears, which is a critical component of ERP treatment in individuals with OCD (Davis, Ressler, Rothbaum, & Richardson, 2006; Norberg, Krystal, & Tolin, 2008). DCS acts as a partial agonist on the glycine binding cite on the NMDA receptor body, which facilitates the binding of glutamate to the NMDA receptor when stimulated (Norberg, Krystal, & Tolin, 2008). Through this action, DCS modulates the excitation of the NMDA receptors (via the binding of glutamate) by facilitating the NMDA receptor's function at approximately 60% of the efficacy of glycine when ambient glycine levels are low, and 40-50% of the efficacy of glycine when glycine levels are high. Hence, DCS may improve the efficacy of treatment for OCD by either enhancing neuroplasticity, aiding in unlearning obsessional cues, by facilitating NMDA-receptor functioning, and/or by dampening NMDA-receptor functioning, interrupting the reconsolidation of obsessional cues, based on the level of ambient glycine surrounding the receptor (Norberg, Krystal, & Tolin, 2008).

The inclusion of DCS in the treatment of OCD affects ERP therapy by increasing its speed and efficiency through the modulation of neuroplasicity (Norberg, Krystal, & Tolin, 2008). Several studies have demonstrated the therapeutic effect of the additions of DCS to ERP therapy in both adults and youth (Davis, Ressler, Rothbaum, & Richardson, 2006; Storch et al., 2007b; Storch et al., 2010; Wilhelm et al., 2008). Kushner and colleagues (2007) compared treatment outcomes of 15 adults receiving combined ERP and DCS treatment against 17 adults who received a placebo instead of the DCS treatment. The results indicated that individuals who received the DCS treatment required fewer exposure sessions to make therapeutic gains and had a lower rate of attrition than the placebo group. Kushner and colleagues reported that significant extinction in obsession-related distress was observed in 4 sessions of exposure therapy with DCS treatment. Additionally, Wilhelm and colleagues (2008) performed a randomized, double-blind, controlled trial examining combined ERP and DCS treatment for adults with OCD and found that the individuals who received the DCS treatment had experienced significantly more improvement in symptoms midway through treatment and reported significantly less depression symptoms at post-treatment than the placebo-controlled group. Although these results are encouraging, Storch and colleagues (2007b) performed a similar study with 24 adults and found no significant group differences between the DCS and control groups. However, the authors acknowledged several methodological issues that may have influenced the results.

DCS has also been shown to be an effective addition to ERP treatment in pediatric OCD (Storch et al., 2010). Storch and colleagues (2010) compared a combined DCS and ERP treatment with a placebo-controlled group of ($n$ = 15 per group) youth with OCD (aged 8-17). The results indicated that the DCS treatment group experienced small-to-moderate treatment effects, which were not significantly different than the control group. Although these results support the general direction of the effect of DCS on ERP treatment, more research must be conducted to examine the efficacy of a combination DCS and ERP treatment approach in pediatric OCD.

*Neurosurgical Interventions*

For treatment reactive patients, several neurosurgical treatments have been developed to induce alterations in brain activity in targeted areas of the brain that have been implicated in the pathogenesis of OCD symptoms. Neuroimaging studies suggest that patients with OCD experience abnormal functioning along several feedback loops in the brain. OCD symptoms are most likely present when there is hyperactivity in the orbitofrontal cortex- thalamus (CT) loop or hypoactivity along the cortico-striato-thalamocortical (CSTC) circuit (Koppell & Greenberg, 2008; Mian et al., 2010; Shah, Pesiridou, Baltuch, Malone, & O'Reardon, 2008). Included in these loops are the orbitofrontal cortex (OFC), an area of the brain that is involved in the emotional processing of environmental stimuli and generation of affective and behavioral responses, the anterior cingulate cortex (ACC), which plays an integral role in the detection of threatening stimuli and regulation of autonomic and neuroendocrine responses, and the caudate nucleus of the basal ganglia, an area that regulates the transmission of information regarding worry (Aouizerate et al., 2006; Koppell & Greenberg, 2008; Ruck et al., 2008). Neurosurgical interventions designed to decrease OCD symptomatology typically focus on one or more of these brain structures.

*Stereotactic Ablative Neurosurgery*

Ablative neurosurgeries that create purposeful lesions in the brain have been conducted to treat obsessive-compulsive disorder since the early 1940s, with four primary procedures reaching prominence: anterior capsulotomies, anterior cingulotomies, subcaudate tractotomies, and limbic leucotomies (Aouizerate et al., 2006; Shah et al., 2008). Each ablative neurosurgical intervention is designed to reduce OCD symptoms by interrupting the neural pathways in the brain that are responsible for symptoms. Patients with treatment refractory OCD have typically responded well to ablative neurosurgical procedures, with symptom reduction rates ranging from 30-80% (Aouizerate et al., 2006; Greenberg, Rauch, & Haber,

2010; Shah et al., 2008). Anterior capsulotomies, in particular, tend to be the most effective at sustained symptom reduction (Greenberg et al., 2010).

The earliest ablative neurosurgical interventions were conducted under general anesthesia and required clinical estimation when localizing the target area of the brain; however, recent advances in medical technology have led to the development of less invasive surgical techniques and more precise identification of targeted brain structures (Greenberg et al., 2010; Lopes et al., 2009). Modern ablative neurosurgical procedures are preceded by stereotaxis, or functional imaging of the brain, which identifies the specific location of targeted brain structures for each patient and allows for minimal disruption of surrounding brain tissue, and concomitantly, fewer adverse side effects (Kondziolka, Flickinger, & Hudak, 2011; Lopes et al., 2009; Shah et al., 2008). Current capsulotomy techniques involve minimal invasive surgery because they are completed by either radiofrequency thermolesion, a procedure during which the patient receives local anesthesia followed by the insertion and heating of electrodes at targeted brain sites, or gamma-knife radiosurgery, a technique that does not require anesthesia, but instead creates lesions in targeted neural circuits by firing g-radiation from a stereotactic gamma radiation unit (Aouizerate et al., 2006; Kondziolka et al., 2011; Lopes et al., 2009; Ruck et al., 2008).

Studies examining the long-term outcomes of ablative neurosurgical interventions have demonstrated stable reductions in OCD symptoms (as measured on the Yale Brown Obsessive Compulsive Scale [Y-BOCS; Goodman et al., 1989b; 1989c]) within about two months of intervention and documented neurobiological changes in both the OFC and ACC (Cecconi et al., 2008; Kondziolka et al., 2011; Lopes et al., 2009). Patients who undergo these surgeries tend to experience consistent symptom reduction because brain lesions are permanent. However, most patients continue to receive pharmacological and/or therapeutic treatment after neurosurgery in order to sustain and further decrease their OCD symptoms. Side effects are possible and usually manifest as alterations in mood and/or executive functioning. Most adverse side effects are the result of high doses of radiation or lesions that affect non-targeted brain structures; thus, further refinement of these procedures is warranted (Cecconi et al., 2008; Ruck et al., 2008). Finally, research regarding the effectiveness of ablative neurosurgery is limited by the ethical implications that prohibit the implementation of sham-controlled clinical trials.

*Deep Brain Stimulation*

Another intervention designed to reduce OCD symptomatology by altering the brain circuits implicated in OCD is deep brain stimulation (DBS), a procedure that delivers high-frequency current to targeted brain circuits, without causing extraneous neuronal damage, in order to either heighten or dampen their activity (Abelson, Curtis, Sagher, Albucher, Harrigan, Taylor et al., 2005; Doughtery, 2010; Greenberg et al., 2010). Patients who receive DBS undergo general anesthesia for the surgical implantation of brain 'leads', multiple electrode contacts, and a neurostimulator (Greenberg, Malone, Friehs, Rezai, Kubu, Malloy et al., 2006; Greenberg et al., 2010). After patients heal from surgery, they undergo multiple weekly treatments during which the brain 'leads' are turned on or off (Greenberg et al., 2006; Greenberg et al., 2010). The first of the three areas of the brain that are most frequently targeted for DBS are the anterior limb of the internal capsule (ALIC). This area is targeted due to the effectiveness of anterior capsulotomies, as described previously. The second is the nucleus accumbens (NAc) because of its central location in the midbrain and concomitant involvement in the connection between the limbic system and the basal ganglia (Tass, et al., 2003). Finally, the subtalamic nucleus (STN) is targeted for its role in basal ganglia circuitry (Figee, Mantione, van den Munckof, Schuurman, & Denys, 2010; Haynes & Mallet, 2010; Mian et al., 2010).

Numerous studies assessing the effectiveness of DBS for treatment refractory OCD have found significant reductions in OCD symptoms as measured by the Y-BOCS and increases in global functioning as rated by clinicians and patients (Aouizerate et al., 2006; Goodman, Foote, Greenberg, Ricciuti, Bauer, Ward et al., 2010; Greenberg et al., 2006; Mallet et al., 2008). Preliminary neuroimaging studies reveal functional changes in the CTSC brain circuits as well (Figee et al., 2010). Although the exact mechanism of DBS is not fully understood, Denys, Mantione, Figee, van den Munckhof, Koerselman, Westenberg, and colleagues (2010) have noted a specific pattern of treatment response observed in many of their patients: depressive symptoms tend to decrease within seconds, followed by anxiety symptoms within minutes, obsessions within days, and compulsions within weeks to months.

DBS has rapidly gained prominence as a neurosurgical intervention for OCD for multiple reasons. Neuroimaging has led to increasingly precise identification of the brain structures to be targeted, which allows for minimal damage to non-affected portions of the brain, and, in contrast to stereotactic ablative neurosurgery, DBS is not permanent because brain 'leads' can be turned on or off or surgically removed if needed (Figee et al., 2010; Haynes & Mallet, 2010; Mian et al., 2010). Sham-controlled DBS trials are possible as well and have been used to demonstrate DBS's effectiveness and contributed to the awarding of FDA approval under a humanitarian device exemption (IDE) (Burdick & Foote, 2011; Dougherty, 2010; Goodman et al., 2010). That being said, similar to patients who receive ablative neurosurgical intervention, patients who receive DBS frequently continue to receive psychiatric and psychological treatment following intervention. Additionally, adverse side effects, although rare, do occur and have ranged from hypomania to headaches to hemorrhages and implant site infections (Goodman et al., 2010; Greenberg et al., 2006).

*Repetitive Transcranial Magnetic Stimulation*

An additional neurosurgical intervention designed to reduce OCD symptomatology through the direct alteration of the neurocircuitry of the brain is repetitive transcranial magnetic stimulation (rTMS), a procedure that involves the non-invasive electromagnetic stimulation of targeted areas of the brain's cortex over the course of multiple sessions (Dougherty, 2010). Weak electrical stimulation is delivered via rTMS coils to specific areas of the brain that have been identified by neuroimaging techniques, such as functional magnetic resonance imaging (fMRI). Targeted areas of the brain typically include the dorsolateral prefrontal cortex and/or the supplementary motor cortex (SMA), due to their proposed association with the generation of OCD symptoms (Mantovani, Simpson, Fallon, Rossi, & Lisanby, 2009; Mantovani, Westin, & Hirsch, 2009; Sachdev, Loo, Mitchell, McFarquhar, & Malhi, 2007).

Both open trials and sham-controlled studies of rTMS reveal promising, but mixed, findings. Several studies demonstrated significant, sustained decreases in OCD symptoms among multiple patients after rTMS (Greenberg et al., 1997; Mantovani et al., 2009; Mantovani et al., 2009; Sachdev, McBridge, Loo, Mitchell et al., 2001). Other studies have found less support for rTMS, however, leading researchers to suggest that the most effective rTMS procedures are highly localized (Mantovani et al., 2009; Prasko, Paskova, Zalesky, Novak et al., 2006, Sachdev et al., 2007). Of the current neurosurgical interventions for treatment refractory OCD, rTMS is the least invasive because it does not require surgery or anesthesia and its effects are reversible. However, treatment is time intensive and lengthy, adverse side effects (such as seizures, headaches, scalp pains, and fainting) have been noted, and continued pharmacological and cognitive-behavioral therapies are recommended (Sachdev et al., 2007).

## Treatment Considerations and Future Directions

Many individuals with OCD continue to experience symptoms and impairment despite undergoing CBT with ERP (e.g., Mian, Campos, Sheth, & Eskandar, 2010). Thus, clinicians and researchers have begun to examine alternative treatment options. Given some of the barriers to maximally effective CBT, such as motivation for treatment and ability to complete realistic exposures in session, therapists have incorporated techniques from other therapies. For example, MI has begun to show promise in terms of actively engaging individuals in treatment and helping to reduce barriers (Westra & Dozois, 2006). Additionally, clinicians are using technology within session to improve quality of exposure. VR is being used to enhance the experience of exposure while allowing clinicians to maintain appropriate control (e.g., Kim et al., 2009). While these strategies have been shown to be effective, continued experimentation with other methodologies and components from treatments (i.e., telehealth interventions) should be conducted to further improve treatment outcomes. Additionally, augmenting CBT with medications such as SRIs (POTS, 2004) and DCS (e.g., Storch et al., 2007b) have demonstrated promising but mixed results. Research should examine the addition of other types of medications to currently prescribed ones to examine the additive benefits of medications in controlled clinical trials as case studies have shown promise (e.g., Storch, Lehmkuhl, Geffken, Touchton, & Murphy, 2007).

Stereotactic ablative neurosurgery, DBS, and rTMS are promising interventions that have successfully reduced OCD symptoms and improved global functioning among patients with treatment refractory OCD. As our knowledge about the brain structures that contribute to the pathogenesis of OCD increases and neurosurgical procedures and neuroimaging are further refined, our ability to develop effective, non-invasive neurosurgical procedures for OCD will be enhanced. For example, researchers are beginning to study low-intensity focused ultrasound pulsation as a new OCD treatment, based on its success in other areas (Bystritsky, Korb, Douglas, Cohen, Melega, Melgaonkar et al., 2011), and, due to the heterogeneity of OCD symptoms, other researchers are developing studies to improve our understanding of the brain circuits that are related to specific subtypes of OCD, such as perfectionism and hoarding (Denys et al., 2011; Koppell and Greenberg, 2008).

Despite the success of neurosurgical interventions for OCD, these treatments continue to be an intervention of last resort. Patients whose symptoms improve with cognitive-behavioral therapy and/or pharmacological intervention should not be considered for these treatments because of the potential adverse side effects and intense nature of these treatments (i.e., multiple weekly sessions, surgical requirements; Figee et al., 2010; Haynes & Mallet, 2010; Mian et al., 2010). Furthermore, neurosurgical interventions are not a be-all and end-all treatment for OCD. Most patients who receive these treatments continue to attend psychiatry, psychology, and neurology appointments in order to monitor symptom progression and side effects. That being said, for patients who experience severe, treatment refractory OCD, neurosurgical interventions are a viable treatment option and should be considered.

# References

Abelson, J.L., Curtis, G.C., Sagher, O., Albucher, R.C., Harrigan, M., Taylor, S.F. et al. (2005). Deep brain stimulation for refractory obsessive-compulsive disorder. *Biological Psychiatry, 57*, 510-516.

Abramowitz, J. S. (1997). Effectiveness of psychological and pharmacological treatments for obsessive-compulsive disorder: a quantitative review. *Journal of Consulting and Clinical Psychology, 65*(1), 44-52.

Abramowitz, J. S., Foa, E. B., & Franklin, M. E. (2003). Exposure and ritual prevention for obsessive-compulsive disorder: effects of intensive versus twice-weekly sessions. *Journal of Consulting and Clinical Psychology, 71*, 394–398.

Adams, G.B., Waas, G.A., March, J.S. & Smith, M.C. (1994). Obsessive compulsive disorder in children and adolescents: The role of school psychologists in identification, assessment, and treatment. *School Psychology Quarterly, 9*, 274-294.

Abramowitz, J. S., Whiteside, S. P., & Deacon, B. J. (2006). The effectiveness of treatment for pediatric obsessive-compulsive disorder: a meta-analysis. *Behavior Therapy, 36*, 55-63.

Aouizerate, B., Rotge, J-Y., Martin-Guehl, C., Cuny, E., Rougier, A., Guehl, D. et al. (2006). A systematic review of psychosurgical treatments for obsessive-compulsive disorder: Does deep brain stimulation represent the future trend in psychosurgery? *Clinical Neuropsychiatry, 3*(6), 391-403.

Bachofen, M., Nakagawa, A., Marks, 1. M., Park, J.-M., Greist, J. H., Baer, L., et al. (1999). Home self assessment and self-treatment of obsessive-compulsive disorder using a manual and a computer conducted telephone interview: Replication of a U.K.-U.S. study. *Journal of Clinical Psychiatry, 60*, 545- 549.

Baer, L., & Greist, J. H. (1997). An interactive computer-administered self-assessment and self help program for behavior therapy. *Journal of Clinical Psychiatry, 58*(S12), 23-27.

Baer, L., Minichiello, W. E., & Jenike, M. A. (1987). Use of a portable-computer program in the behavioral treatment of obsessive-compulsive disorder. *American Journal of Psychiatry, 144*, 1101.

Baer, L., Minichiello, W. E., Jenike, M. A., & Holland, A. (1988). Use of a portable computer program to assist behavioral treatment in a case of obsessive-compulsive disorder. *Journal of Behavior Therapy and Psychiatry, 19*, 237-240.

Burdick, A.P. & Foote, K.D. (2011). Advancing deep brain stimulation for obsessive-compulsive disorder. *Expert Reviews in Neurotherapy, 11*(3), 341-344.

Bystritsky, A., Korb, A.S., Douglas, P.K., Cohen, M.S., Melega, W.P., Melgaonkar, A.P. et al. (2011). A review of low-intensity focused ultrasound pulsation. *Brain Stimulation, 4*, 125-136.

Cecconi, J.O., Lopes, A.C., Duran, F.L., Sanots, L.C., Hoexter, M.Q., Gentil, A.F. et al. (2008). Gamma ventral capsulotomy for treatment of resistant obsessive-compulsive disorder: A structural MRI pilot prospective study. *Neuroscience Lettes, 447*, 138-142.

Clomipramine Collaborative Group. (1991). Clomipramine in the treatment of patients with obsessive-compulsive disorder. *Archives of General Psychiatry, 48*, 730–738.

Davis, M., Ressler, K., Rothbaum, B. O., & Richardson, R. (2006). Effects of d-cycloserine on extinction: translation from preclinical to clinical work. *Biological Psychiatry, 60*, 369-375.

Denys, D., Mantione, M., Figee, M., van den Munckhok, P., Koerselman, F., Westenberg, H. et al. (2010). Deep brain stimulation of the nucleus accumbens for treatment-refractory obsessive-compulsive disorder. *Archives of General Psychiatry, 67*(10), 1061-1068.

Dougherty, D.D. (2010). Deep brain stimulation. *Psychiatric Annals, 40*(10), 458-459.

Figee, M., Mantione, M., van den Munckhof, P., Schuurman, R., & Denys, D. (2010). Targets for deep brain stimulation in obsessive-compulsive disorder. *Psychiatric Annals, 40*(10), 492-498.

Franklin, M. E., Abramowitz, J. S., Kozak, M. J., Levitt, J. T., & Foa, E. B. (2000). Effectiveness of exposure and ritual prevention for obsessive–compulsive disorder: Randomized compared with nonrandomized samples. *Journal of Consulting and Clinical Psychology, 68*, 594–602.

Fritzler BK, Hecker JE, Losee MC. Self-directed treatment with minimal therapist contact: preliminary findings from obsessive–compulsive disorder. *Behaviour Research and Therapy, 35*, 627–31.

Franklin, M. E., & Foa, E. B. (2008). Obsessive-compulsive disorder. In D. H. Barlow (Ed.), *Clinical handbook of psychological disorders (pp. 164-215)*. New York, NY: The Guilford Press.

Foa, E. B., Liebowitz, M. R., Kozak, M. J., Davies, S., Campeas, R., . . . Tu, X. (2005). Randomized, placebo-controlled trial of exposure and ritual prevention, clomipramine, and their combination in the treatment of obsessive-compulsive disorder. *American Journal of Psychiatry, 162*, 151–161.

Geffken, G. R., Pincus, D. B., & Zelikovsky, N. (1999). Obsessive compulsive disorder in children and adolescents: review of background, assessment, and treatment. *Journal of Psychological Practice, 5*, 15–31.

Goodman, W.K., Foote, K.D., Greenberg, B.D., Ricciuti, N., Bauer, R., Ward, H. et al. (2010). Deep brain stimulation for intractable obsessive compulsive disorder: Pilot study using a blinded, staggered-onset design. *Biological Psychiatry, 67*, 535-542.

Goodman, W. K., Price, L. H., Rassmussen, S. A., Delgado, P. L., Heninger, G. R., & Charney, D. S. (1989a). Efficacy of fluvoxamine in obsessive-compulsive disorder: a double-blind comparison with placebo. *Archives of General Psychiatry*, 46, 36–44.

Goodman, W. K., Price L. H., Rasmussen, S. A., Mazure, C., Fleischmann, R. L., Hill, C. L. et al. (1989 b). The Yale–Brown obsessive–compulsive scale-Idevelopment, use, and reliability. *Archives of General Psychiatry*, 46, 1006–1011.

Goodman, W. K., Price L. H., Rasmussen, S. A., Mazure, C., Delgado, P., Heninger, G. R. et al. The Yale–Brown obsessive–compulsive scale-II-validity. (1989c) *Archives of General Psychiatry*, 46, 1012–1016.

Graziano, P., Callueng, C., & Geffken, G.. (2010). Cognitive-Behavioral Treatment of an 11-Year-Old Male Presenting With Emetophobia: A Case Study. *Clinical Case Studies*, 9, 411-425.

Greenberg, B.D., Malone, D.A., Friehs, G.M., Rezai, A.R., Kubu, C.S., Malloy, P.F. et al. (2006). Three-year outcomes in deep brain stimulation for highly resistant obsessive-compulsive disorder. *Neurpsychopharmacology*, 31, 2384-2393.

Greenberg, B.D., Rauch S.L., & Haber, S.N. (2010). Invasive circuitry-based neurotherapeutics: Stereotactic ablation and deep brain stimulation for OCD. *Neuropsychopharmacology*, 35, 317-336.

Greist, J. H., Chouinard, G., DuBoff ,E., Halaris, A., Kim, S. W., . . . Sikes, C. (1995) Double-blind parallel comparison of three dosages of sertraline and placebo in outpatients with obsessive-compulsive disorder. *Archives of General Psychiatry*, 52, 289–295.

Greist, J. H., Marks, I. M., Baer, L., Kobak, K. A., Wenzel, K. W., Hirsch, M. J., et al. (2002). Behaviour therapy for obsessive compulsive disorder guided by a computer or by a clinician compared with relaxation as a control. *Journal of Clinical Psychiatry*, 63, 138–45.

Greist, J. H., Marks, I. M., Baer, L., Parkin, J. R., Manzo, P. A., Mantle, J. M., et al. (1998). Self treatment for obsessive-compulsive disorder using a manual and a computerized telephone interview: A U.S.-U.K. study. *MD Computing*, 15, 149-157. PMid:9617085

Haynes, W.I.A. & Mallet, L. (2010). High-frequency stimulation of deep brain structures in obsessive-compulsive disorder: The search for a valid circuit. *European Journal of Neuroscience*, 32, 1118-1127.

Hollander, E., Allen, A., Steiner, M., Wheadon, D. E., Oakes, R., Burnham, D. B., & Paroxetine OCD Study Group. (2003). Acute and long-term treatment and prevention of relapse of obsessive-compulsive disorder with paroxetine. *Journal of Clinical Psychiatry*, 64, 1113–1121.

Kim, K., Kim, C.H., Cha, K.R., Park, J., Han, K., Kim, Y.K., et al. (2008). Anxiety provocation and measurement using virtual reality in patients with obsessive- compulsive disorder. *Cyberpsychology and Behavior*, 11, 37-41.

Kim, K., Kim, C., Kim, S., Roh, D., Kim, S (2009). Virtual reality for obsessive-compulsive disorder: past and the future. *Psychiatry Investig.*; 6, 115-21.

Kondziolka, D., Flickinger, J.C., & Hudak, R. (2011). Results following gamma knife radiosurgical anterior capsulotomies for obsessive compulsive disorder. *Neurosurgery, 68*, 28-33.

Kuskner, M. G., Kim, S. W., Donahue, C., Thuras, P., Adson, D., . . . Foa, E. (2007). D-cycloserine augmented exposure therapy for obsessive-compulsive disorder. *Biological Psychiatry, 62*, 835-838.

Koppell, B.H. & Greenberg, B.D. (2008). Anatomy and physiology of the basal ganglia: Implications for DBS in psychiatry. *Neuroscience and Biobehavioral Reviews, 32*, 308-422.

Leahy, R.L. & Holland, S.J. (2000). *Treatment Plans and Interventions for Depression and Anxiety Disorders, Volume 1*. New York, NY: Guilford Press.

Leon, A. C., Portera, L., & Weissman, M. M. (1995). The social costs of anxiety disorders. *British Journal of Psychiatry, 166*(S27), 19-22. PMid:7894871

Leonard, H.L., Swedo, S.E., Lenane, M.C., Rettew, D.C., Hamburger, S.D., Bartko, U. & Rapoport, J.L. (1993). A 2- to 7-year follow-up study of 54 obsessive compulsive children and adolescents. *Archives of General Psychiatry, 50*, 429-439.

Lopes, A.C., Greenberg, B.D., Noren, G., Canteras, M.M., Busatto, G.F., de Mathis, M.E. et al. (2009). Treatment of resistant obsessive-compulsive disorder with ventral capsular/ventral striatal gamma capsulotomoy: A pilot prospective study. *Journal of Neuropsychiatry and Clinical Neuroscience, 21*(4), 381-392.

Lovell, K., Fullalove, L., Garyey, R., & Brooker, C. (2000). Telephone treatment of obsessive-compulsive disorder. *Behavioural and Cognitive Psychotherapy, 28*, 87-91.

Mallet, L., Polosan, M., Jaafari, N., Baup, N., Welter, M., Fontaine, D. et al. (2008). Subthalamic nucleus stimulation in severe obsessive-compulsive disorder. *The New England Journal of Medicine, 359*(20), 2121-2134.

Maltby, N. & Tolin, D.F. (2005). A brief motivational intervention for treatment refusing OCD patients. *Cognitive Behaviour Therapy, 34*, 176-184.

Mantovani, A., Simpson, H.B., Fallon, B.A., & Rossi, S. (2009). Randomized sham-controlled trial of repetitive transcranial magnetic stimulation in treatment-resistant obsessive-compulsive disorder. *International Journal of Neuropsychopharmacology, 13*, 217-227.

Mantovani, A., Westin, G., & Hirsch, J. (2010). Functional magnetic resonance imaging guided transcranial magnetic stimulation in obsessive-compulsive disorder. *Biological Psychiatry, 67*, e39-e40.

Mataix-Cols, D., & Marks, I. M. (2006a). Self-help with minimal therapist contact for obsessive–compulsive disorder: a review. *European Psychiatry, 21*, 75–80.

Mataix-Cols, D., & Marks, I. M. (2006b). Self-help for obsessive-compulsive disorder: How much therapist contact is necessary?. *Clinical Neuropsychiatry, 3*(6), 404-409. ISSN: 17244935

Merlo, L.J., Storch, E.A., Lehmkuhl, H.D., Jacob, M.L., Murphy, T.K., Goodman, W.K., & Geffken, G.R. (2010). Cognitive behavioral therapy plus motivational interviewing improves outcome for pediatric obsessive-compulsive disorder: A preliminary study. *Cognitive Behavioral Therapy, 39*(1), 24-27. doi: 913869145 [pii] 10.1080/16506070902831773

Meyer, E., Souza, F., Heldt, E., Knapp, P., Cordioli, A., Shavitt, R.G.,& Leukefeld, C. (2010). A randomized clinical trial to examine enhancing cognitive-behavioral group therapy for obsessive-compulsive disorder with motivational interviewing and thought mapping. *Behavioral and Cognitive Psychotherapy, 38*, 319-336.

Mian, M.K., Campos, M., Sheth, S.A., & Eskandar, E.N. (2010). Deep brain stimulation for obsessive-compulsive disorder: Past, present, and future. *Neurosurgical Focus, 29*(2), E10-19.

Miller, W.R. (2006). Motivational factors in addictive behaviors. In W.R. Miller & K.M. Carroll (Eds.), *Rethinking substance abuse: what science shows, and what we should do about it* (pp. 143-150). New York: Guilford Press.

Miller, W.R. & Rollnick, S. (2002). *Motivational Interviewing* (2nd Ed.). New York: Guilford Press.

Montgomery, S. A., Kasper, S., Stein, D. J., Hedegaard, K., & Bang, L. O. M. (2001). Citalopram 20 mg, 40 mg and 60 mg are all effective and well tolerated compared with placebo in obsessive-compulsive disorder. *International Clinical Psychopharmacology, 16*, 75–86.

Morgan, J., Lack, C., & Storch, E. A. (2010). The utilization of technology in the treatment of obsessive compulsive disorder. In L. V. Berhardt (Ed.) *Advances in Medicine and Biology, Volume 6* (pp. 161-176). Hauppauge, NY: Nova Science Publishers, Inc.

Norberg, M. M., Krystal, J. H., & Tolin, D. F. (2008). A meta-analysis of d-cycloserine and the facilitation of fear extinction and exposure therapy. *Biological Psychology, 63*, 1118-1126.

Piacentini, J., Bergman, R. L., Keller, M., & McCracken, J. (2003). Functional impairment in children and adolescents with obsessive-compulsive disorder. *Journal of Child and Adolescent Psychopharmacology, 13S-1*, S61-S69.

Prasko, J., Paskova, B., Zalesky, R., Novak, T. et al. (2006). The effect of repetitive transcranial magnetic stimulation (rTMA) on symptom in obsessive compulsive disorder: A randomized, double blind, sham-controlled study. *Neuroendocrinology Letters, 27*, 327-332.

Ruck, C., Karlsson, A., Steele, D., Edman, G., Meyerson, B.A., Ericson, K. et al. (2008). Capsulotomy for obsessive-compulsive disorder: Long-term follow-up of 25 patients. *Archives of General Psychiatry, 65*(8), 914-922.

Sachdev, P.S., Loo, C.K., Mitchell, P.B., McFarquhar, T., & Malhi, G.S. (2007). Repetitive transcranial magnetic stimulation for the treatment of obsessive compulsive disorder: A double-blind controlled investigation. *Psychological Medicine, 37*, 1645-1649.

Sachdev, P.S., McBride, R., Loo, C.K., Mitchel, P.B. et al. (2001). Right versus left prefrontal transcranial magnetic stimulation for obsessive-compulsive disorder: A preliminary investigation. *Journal of Clinical Psychiatry, 62*(12), 981-984.

Shah, D.B., Pesiridou, A., Baltuch, G.H., Malone, D.A., & O'Reardon, J.P. (2008). Functional neurosurgery in the treatment of severe obsessive compulsive disorder and major depression: Overview of disease circuits and therapeutic targeting for the clinician. *Psychiatry, 5*(9), 24-33.

Simpson, H.B., Huppert, J.D., Petkova, E., Foa, E.B., & Liebowitz, M.R. (2006). Response versus remission in obsessive-compulsive disorder. *Journal of Clinical Psychiatry, 67,* 269-276

Simpson, H.B., Zuckoff, A.M., Maher, M.J., Page, J.R., Franklin, M.E., Foa, E.B. et al. (2010). Challenges using motivational interviewing as an adjunct to exposure therapy for obsessive-compulsive disorder. *Behavior Ressearch & Therapy, 48*(10), 941-948

Simpson, H., Zuckoff, A., Page, J., Franklin, M., & Foa, E. (2008). Adding Motivational Interviewing to Exposure and Ritual Prevention for Obsessive-Compulsive Disorder: An Open Pilot Trial. *Cognitive Behavioral Therapy, 37,* 38-49.

Sookman, D., & Steketee, G. (2007). Directions in specialized cognitive behavior therapy for resistant obsessive-compusive disorder: theory and practice of two approaches. *Cognitive and Behavioral Practice, 14,* 1-17.

Storch, E. A. (2005). Update on childhood anxiety. *Pediatric Annals,* 34, 78-81.

Storch, E. A., Geffken, G. R., Merlo, L. J., Mann, G., Duke, D., . . . Goodman, W. K. (2007a). Family-based cognitive-behavioral therapy for pediatric obsessive compulsive disorder: comparison of intensive and weekly approaches. *Journal of the American Academy of Child and Adolescent Psychiatry,* 46(4), 469-478.

Storch, E. A., Lehmkuhl, H. D., Geffken, G. R., Touchton, A., & Murphy, T. K. (2007). Aripiprazol augmentation of incomplete treatment response in an adolescent male with obsessive-compulsive disorder. *Depression and Anxiety, 0,* 1-3.

Storch, E. A., Merlo, L. J., Bengtson, M., Murphy, T. K., Lewis, M. H., . . . Goodman, W. K. (2007b). D-cycloserine does not enhance exposure-response prevention therapy in obsessive-compulsive disorder. *International Clinical Psychopharmacology,* 22(4), 230-237.

Storch, E. A., Mariaskin, A., & Murphy, T. K. (2009). Psychotherapy for obsessive-compulsive disorder. *Current Psychiatry Reports,* 11, 296-301.

Storch, E. A., Murphy, T. K., Goodman, W. K., Geffken, G. R., Lewin, A. B., . . . Geller, D. A. (2010). A preliminary study of d-cycloserine augmentation of cognitive-behavioral therapy in pediatric obsessive-compulsive disorder. *Biological Psychiatry,* 68, 1073-1076.

Tass, P. A., Klosterkotter, J., Schneider, F., Lenartz, D., Koulousakis, A., & Sturm,

V. (2003). Obsessive compulsive disorder: Development of demand-controlled deep-brain stimulation with methods from stochastic phase resetting. *Neuropsychopharmacology, 28,* S27-S34.

Taylor, C. B., & Luce, K. H. (2003). Computer- and Internet-based psychotherapy interventions. *Current Directions in Psychological Science,* 12, 18-22.

The Pediatric OCD Treatment Study (POTS) Team. (2004). Cognitive-behavior therapy, sertraline, and their combination for children and adolescents with obsessive-compulsive disorder: the Pediatric OCD Treatment Study (POTS) Randomized Controlled Trial. *Journal of the American Medical Association,* 292(16), 1969-1976.

Tollefson, G. D., Rampey, A. H., Potvin, J. H., Jenike, M. A., Rush, A. J., . . . Genduso, L. A. (1994). A multicenter investigation of fixed dose fluoxetine in the treatment of obsessive-compulsive disorder. *Archives of General Psychiatry,* 51, 559–567.

Tolin, D. F., Diefenbach, G. J., & Gilliam, C. M. (2011). Stepped care versus standard cognitive-behavioral therapy for obsessive-compulsive disorder: a preliminary study of efficacy and costs. *Depression and Anxiety,* 28, 314-323.

Turner, c., Heyman, I., Futh, A., & Lovell, K. (2009). A pilot study of telephone cognitive-behavioural therapy for obsessive-compulsive disorder in young people. *Behavioural and Cognitive Psychotherapy,* 37, 469-474. PMID:19545482

Valderhaug, R., Gotestam, K. G., & Larsson, B. (2004). Clinician's views on management of obsessive compulsive disorders in children and adolescents. *Nordic Journal of Psychiatry,* 58, 125-132.

Walker, D. L., Ressler, K. J., Kwok-Tung, L., & Davis, M. (2002). Facilitation of conditioned fear extinction by systemic administration or intra-amygdala infusions of d-cycloserine as assessed with fear-potentiated startle in rats. *The Journal of Neuroscience,* 22(6), 2343-2351.

Westra, H.A. & Dozois, D.J. (2006). Preparing clients for cognitive behavioral therapy: a randomized pilot study of motivational interviewing for anxiety. *Cognitive Therapy and Research,* 30, 481-498.

Wilhelm, S., Buhlmann, U., Tolin, D. F., Meunier, S. A., Peralson, G. D., . . . Rauch, S. L. (2008). Augmentation of behavior therapy with D-cycloserine for obsessive-compulsive disorder. *American Journal of Psychiatry,* 165, 335-341.

Chapter Eight

# The Impact of Family on the Treatment of Obsessive-Compulsive Disorder

Amanda M. Balkhi, Marni L. Jacob, Adam M. Reid, Melissa S. Munson, Rachel L. Juerhing, Gary R. Geffken, & Joseph P.H. McNamara

Obsessive compulsive disorder (OCD) is characterized by obsessions (i.e. reoccurring thoughts, images, or impulses that cause significant anxiety or distress) or compulsions (i.e. repetitive mental or physical acts that are aimed at preventing or reducing distress that the person feels compelled to perform) that cause significant problems, take up a significant amount of time, or significantly interfere with the person's normal functioning (American Psychiatric Association, Diagnostic and Statistical Manual [*DSM-IV-TR*], 2000). While it is not necessary that both obsessions and compulsions are present in OCD, the majority of individuals with OCD do manifest both sets of symptoms (Foa et al., 1995). The *DSM-IV-TR* also specifies that the person must recognize that the thoughts and behaviors associated with OCD are excessive and unreasonable, although this requirement is not necessary for children. The lifetime prevalence of OCD is estimated at approximately 2% (Flament et al., 1988); however more recent studies have reported prevalence rates as high as 4% in community samples (Maggini et al., 2001; Valleni-Basile et al., 1994; Zohar et al., 1992). Further, studies examining adult OCD symptoms suggest that as many as 80% report symptoms that began prior to 18 years of age (Pauls, Alsobrook, Goodman, Rasmussen, & Leckman, 1995; Riddle, 1998). The onset and course of symptoms of Obsessive-Compulsive Disorder varies significantly with some people experiencing an abrupt onset of symptoms, others experiencing a more insidious onset, and some experiencing a triggering event (Flament et al., 1988). In children, approximately 50% report a major psychosocial event, such as a trauma, preceding the onset of symptoms (Geller et al., 1998).

171

# Etiology

While there is no clearly definitive *cause* of OCD, several theories have been proposed in the literature. Several biological factors are thought to be associated with the development of the disorder, including neurochemical factors such as the dysregulation of serotonin in the brain (Micallef & Blin, 2001). This explanation of the disorder is supported by the effectiveness of serotonergic drugs in treating its symptoms (Abramowitz, Whiteside, & Deacon, 2005). Other biological factors that have been associated with obsessive-compulsive symptoms include structural abnormalities and altered functioning of neurocircuitry in the orbitofrontal cortex, anterior cingulate, thalamus, and basal ganglia (Kang, Kim, & Choi, 2004; Rapoport, 1991), as well as a genetic component in which prevalence rates are higher among those who have first degree relatives with OCD, and concordance rates are higher between monozygotic twins than between dizygotic twins (Nicolini, Arnold, Nestadt, Lanzagorta, & Kennedy, 2009). Further support for the idea that biological factors contribute to the development of OCD comes from research that shows a link between pediatric OCD and group A beta-hemolytic streptococcal infections (GABHS; Swedo et al., 1998). This research suggests that in some cases, autoimmune responses related to the infections are misdirected towards regions of the basal ganglia which cause the appearance of OCD symptoms.

One model of OCD that has fairly wide agreement comes from the cognitive behavioral orientation. In this model, OCD develops from dysfunctional beliefs that become attached to normal thought intrusions, leading to anxiety (Salkovskis, 1985). The anxiety then leads to compulsions, which reduce anxiety, making the intrusions and compulsions more likely to occur in the future. The Obsessive-Compulsive Cognitions Working Group (OCCWG; 1997) proposed six areas of cognition that are thought to lead to these cognitive errors, including: inflated sense of responsibility, over-importance of thoughts, over-concern about controlling thoughts, over-estimation of risk, intolerance of uncertainty, and perfectionism. Errors in these areas are consistently found to occur at higher rates in populations with OCD and are believed to be what lead to anxiety over normal thought intrusions (Barrett & Healy, 2003; Rassin, Merckelbach, Muris, & Spaan, 1999).

## Impact of the Family

Given the aforementioned review about the nature of OCD, the focus of the current discussion will be on the impact of the family on the treatment of OCD. While this impact may seem obvious when thinking of a defiant child with OCD, there are many other aspects of OCD in which the family has an impact. Family members of individuals with OCD often play a role in obsessions and compulsions to the point that they become an integral part of the rituals. Family members may also bring their own psychopathology into the treatment equation which may affect how the patient responds to treatment. They may also be a significant source of support throughout treatment and affect the severity of OCD symptoms in a positive way. The subsequent discussion will explore these various aspects of the impact of the family on OCD treatment.

*Family Accommodation and Involvement in OCD*

When considering the impact of family on treatment of OCD, it is important to consider how family members might be impacted by having a family member with this diagnosis. One of the most common methods by which OCD can affect the family is through accommodation, which refers to how family members may participate in the obsessions and compulsions of an individual's OCD. Specifically, family accommodation may consist of family members completing tasks or chores for the individual with OCD because those activities are often associated with time-consuming rituals if the person completes them independently. It may also consist of participating in rituals (e.g., providing excessive reassurance to alleviate anxiety, having to ensure that family members are clean to prevent contamination to the individual with OCD, participating in a particular routine). Further, family members might alter their lifestyles in some manner, modify their daily routines, or avoid particular situations due to fears that they might trigger symptoms (Farrell & Barrett, 2007). Although these actions are often carried out with good intentions to decrease the anxiety of the individual with OCD and allow the family to function efficiently in day-to-day life, they often aid to maintain the problem and also cause distress for family members involved. Nevertheless, research shows that family accommodation is particularly common and occurs in the vast majority of families of someone with OCD (Calvocoressi et al., 1999; Calvocoressi, Lewis, Harris, & Trufan, 1995).

Research on family accommodation in OCD has increased notably in recent years, likely due to increased awareness of its presence. Studies have evaluated family accommodation in families of youth and adults with OCD and revealed that those with higher levels of family accommodation are associated with worse treatment outcome (Flessner et al., 2011; Merlo, Lehmkuhl, Geffken, & Storch, 2009; Keeley et al., 2008; Peris et al., 2008; Albert et al., 2010; Calvocoressi et al., 1995; Amir, Freshman, & Foa, 2000). Such studies have also found that greater levels of family accommodation tend to be associated with greater OCD severity and impairments in family functioning. Both Steketee (1993) and Barrett and colleagues (2005) found that worse treatment outcome was predicted by higher levels of family dysfunction and negative family interactions. This is supported in recent research in which patients who perceived their relatives as critical or hostile experienced more severe OCD symptoms than those with positive family interactions (Van

Noppen & Steketee, 2009). A cycle can develop between poor family interactions and worsening of OCD symptoms. For example, poor family interactions can lead to increasing levels of hostility which would lead to an increase in stress that would trigger an exacerbation of OCD symptoms. Further, the emotional burden of caring for someone with OCD can be particularly difficult for families of individuals with OCD, as quality of life can suffer due to the presence of family distress and accommodation. For example, Storch and colleagues (2007a) found that in a sample of youth, aged 7-17 years old, family accommodation was positively associated with symptom severity and parent-rated functional impairment. Similarly, Peris and colleagues (2008) found that in youth with OCD, parental involvement in rituals was associated with higher levels of child OCD severity and parental psychopathology, and with lower levels of family organization. Another study found that characteristics of youth with OCD, including severity of compulsions, oppositional behavior, and frequency of washing rituals, along with parental anxiety symptoms, significantly predicted parent accommodation of child symptoms (Flessner et al., 2011).

When considering the research on adults with OCD, one study of adult OCD patients, aged 20-75, found that family accommodation was associated with poor family functioning, rejecting attitudes toward the patient, and family stress (Calvocoressi et al., 1995). Further, Cooper (1996) evaluated the impact of OCD on family members (e.g., parents, spouses, children, fiancés, and siblings) of adults with OCD and found that 75% of family members reported experiencing disruption in their personal life (e.g., loss of leisure time, loss of personal relationships) due to their family member with OCD. Black, Gaffney, Schlosser, and Gabel (1998) found that more than 50% of spouses of adults with OCD reported experiencing disruptions in family/social life and in the caregiver's personal life, whereas Black, Gaffney, Schlosser, and Gabel (2003) found that children of adults with OCD had higher rates of emotional and behavioral problems compared to children of adults from a control group.

The functional impairment and the negative impact upon family has been further documented by Piacentini and colleagues in studies of youth with OCD (Piacentini, Bergman, Keller, & McCracken, 2003; Piacentini, Peris, Bergman, Chang, & Jaffer, 2007). Several other researchers have also recognized the emotional burden and distress that are often experienced by family members of individuals with OCD who may not be sure how to help their loved one (Albert et al., 2010; de Abreu Ramos-Cerqueira, Torres, Torresan, Negreiros, & Vitorino, 2008; Steketee, 1997; Storch et al., 2009). The family member may not want to complete tasks related to compulsions yet may see the visible anxiety exhibited by the person with OCD, so they may accommodate their loved one's OCD to temporarily alleviate anxiety. Unfortunately, this pattern typically results in negative experiences for all involved, and it may reinforce the trend for the person with OCD to seek out the assistance of family members the next time they experience symptoms (Farrell and Barrett, 2007).

The potential impact of OCD upon the family can also be highlighted by studies that examine the familial impact of OCD compared to other forms of psychopathology. For example, Vikas, Avasthi, and Sharan (2011) compared patients with OCD and depression and found that caregivers of individuals with OCD experienced greater impairment and engaged in greater family accommodation compared to caregivers of individuals with depression. Jacob et al. (2012) found that parents of youth with OCD reported significantly greater impairment when compared to parents of youth with other anxiety disorders (i.e., Generalized Anxiety Disorder, Social Phobia, and Separation Anxiety Disorder). Overall, the aforementioned research emphasizes the potential detrimental impact that OCD can have upon one's family.

Although family accommodation can play a role in OCD symptomology, it can also play a role in treatment prognosis. Merlo and colleagues (2009) found that reductions in family accommodation during treatment predicted improvements in treatment outcome, even when controlling for pretreatment OCD severity impairment (Merlo et al., 2009). Accordingly, given the family accommodation and involvement often present in OCD, several treatment approaches recognize the importance of involving family members in treatment (e.g., Barrett, Healy-Farrell, March, 2004; Storch et al., 2007b). Effective treatment should begin by providing family members with psychoeducation regarding the nature of OCD. This is of notable importance because clinical experience has found that family members often display anger towards the individual with OCD and may not understand why it is so difficult for the individual to stop engaging in compulsive behaviors. Additionally, family members may poke fun at the person's OCD rituals. For instance, Hibbs, Hamburger, Lenane, and Rapoport (1991) found significantly higher rates of expressed emotion (i.e., high levels of hostility, emotional over-involvement, and criticism) in families of youth with OCD compared to families of youth without a diagnosis. All of these behaviors may make the person with OCD feel invalidated and guilty if family members are blaming them in some manner for their symptoms. One strategy that may be helpful is to externalize OCD at the outset of treatment so that it is clear among family members that OCD is driving the behavior, not the individual (e.g., *"Annie's OCD is telling her to turn the lights on and off"* versus *"Annie is turning the lights on and off"*). Interventions that involve the family must consider variables specific to each family when discussing appropriate disengagement strategies (Peris et al., 2008).

# Assessment

As discussed above, OCD is a severely debilitating disorder that affects not only the individual with the disorder, but also their family or loved ones. The research discussed above specifically highlights the substantial impact OCD can have on a surrounding family's quality of life, as well as the ways in which a family can contribute, both positively and negatively, to a member's OCD severity and treatment outcome. Despite the growing literature highlighting these family factors, there are only three empirically validated assessment tools that are widely used to help clinicians and researchers quantify these variables. These are discussed below.

The *Family Accommodation Scale* for OCD (FAS-OCD) is a 12-question clinician-rated assessment of how primary caregivers of adults or children with Obsessive-Compulsive Disorder interact with their family member when they are engaging in their rituals or compulsions (Calvocoressi et al., 1995; Calvocoressi et al., 1999; Flessner et al., 2009). Regardless of the informant (clinician-rated, parent-report, youth-report), the FAS has strong psychometric properties (Calvocoressi et al., 1999; Albert et al., 2010; Flessner et al., 2009; Fernandez, Storch Geffken & Murphy, 2006) and high clinical utility in its ability to identify relatives who have elevated obsessive-compulsive symptoms (Calvocoressi et al., 1999), track changes in accommodation during treatment (Merlo et al., 2009), and help identify treatment non-responders (Amir et al., 2000, Storch et al., 2007). Research by Flessner and colleagues (2009) using a sample of youth with OCD identified a two-factor structure of the FAS which consists of avoidance of triggers and involvement in compulsions. However, Albert and colleagues (2010) found a three-factor structure: modification, distress/consequences, and participation. Whereas preliminary research suggests that the factor structure of the FAS varies based on the age of the sample used, it is clear that the FAS taps into several unique constructs related to accommodation that have important clinical utility (Albert et al., 2010). As discussed previously, caregivers are often unaware of the frequency and utility of their accommodating behavior and thus, without proper assessment, many of these OCD perpetuating caregiver-patient interactions may never be addressed. In other words, proper assessment of family accommodation has major implications in terms of treatment outcome (Merlo et al., 2009) and should be properly assessed during the initial evaluation. Overall, this measure is a unique tool that should be utilized by clinicians and researchers as a basic screener to identify families who might benefit from psychoeducation on the consequential effects of family accommodation and accordingly, provide them with alternative strategies to respond to the family member's symptoms.

The *OCD Family Functioning* Scale (OFF) is a 42-item self-report measure of family functioning for children or adults with OCD (Steward et al., 2010). This novel questionnaire assesses the daily life, social, occupational, and emotional impact of an individual's OCD on family members, and it provides a symptom specific impairment rating which is utilized to identify the obsessions and/or compulsions that are most impairing on the family well-being (Steward et al., 2010). Because of its youth, there has been little research confirming the psychometric properties of this measure, but the original article by Steward and colleagues (2010) reports good convergent/divergent validity, test-retest reliability, structural validity, and internal consistency. Similarly, while the clinical utility of this measure is mostly speculation, it is reasonable to hypothesize that clinicians can utilize this assessment tool to measure family impairment and track improvement throughout treatment (as evidenced by high test-retest reliability). Further, by the unique design capturing both family and symptom-specific impairment, clinicians may be able to use the OFF to identify specific symptoms that cause the most impairment and subsequently work with the families to learn adaptive coping strategies in response to these symptoms.

The *Child Obsessive Compulsive Impact Scale* (COIS) is a 56-item parent or child report measure of impairment across several primary domains: school, social, and home/family activities (Piacentini & Jaffer, 1999; Piacentini, Bergman, Keller, & McCracken, 2003). The home/family activities scale of the COIS was the first validated assessment measure for pediatric family impairment caused by OCD. While much less comprehensive than the OFF discussed above and limited to only pediatric OCD populations, the COIS does provide a much more empirically supported assessment of family impairment (Piacentini, Bergman, Keller, & McCracken, 2003; Valderhaug & Ivarsson, 2005). As was speculated with the OFF, the COIS has been found to be treatment sensitive (Storch et al., 2007).

The FAS, OFF, and COIS stand as the primary assessment tools for family factors related to OCD; clearly more research is needed in this domain. The assessment literature, and subsequently the understanding and treatment of OCD, will be advanced as more assessment tools are developed. For instance, there is a specific need for measures of caregiver insight into the maladaptive nature of their loved ones obsessions and compulsions, as well as, resistance to OCD diagnosis (e.g. believing it is not a disorder or fear of the stigma related to OCD). The literature will also benefit from a shift in focus from the parents to the siblings of individuals with OCD in the study of domains such as peer victimization, accommodation, and relationship impairment. In the meantime, clinicians and researchers have several useful family related measures that have successfully been used with individuals with OCD, including parenting stress (Abidin, 1995), patient rejection (Kreisman et al., 1979), perceived criticism (Hooley & Teasdale, 1989), quality of life (Varni, Seid & Kurtin, 2001), and expressed emotion (Van Noppen & Steketee, 2009).

# Treatment

The Pediatric Obsessive-Compulsive Disorder Treatment Study (POTS; POTS Team, 2004) is the first randomized controlled trial to compare pharmacotherapy, cognitive behavioral therapy (CBT), and the combination of the two in the treatment of pediatric OCD (Franklin, Foa, & March, 2003). Results of this study indicated that the combination of medication and CBT was superior to all other conditions and that the CBT and medication alone conditions were both better than placebo, but not significantly different from each other.

Pharmacological treatment is a valid option for OCD, as many randomized, placebo-controlled trials have found many medications to be effective in the treatment of pediatric OCD. The medications most commonly prescribed are the serotonin reuptake inhibitors (SRIs) which include; clomipramine, sertraline, fluoxetine, paroxetine, and fluvoxamine, and the tricyclic antidepressant (TCA) clomipramine (see Masi et al., 2009 for a review). A recent meta-analysis found that all of these medications were superior to placebo, with clomipramine showing relative superiority over the others (Geller et al., 2003).

Cognitive-behavioral therapy (CBT) involving exposure with response prevention (E/RP) is a well-studied treatment for OCD (Abramowitz, Whiteside, & Deacon, 2005), and it is currently the standard behavioral treatment for adults and children with OCD (Watson & Rees, 2008; Williams et al., 2010; Expert Consensus Guidelines; March, Frances, Carpenter, & Kahn, 1997). Cognitive-behavioral therapy encourages patients to develop rational self-talk, and to challenge irrational beliefs about the purpose of their obsessive thoughts and compulsive actions to reduce symptoms (Cartwright-Hatton, Roberts, Chitsabesan, Fothergill, & Harrington, 2004; March, Franklin, Nelson, & Foa, 2001; Stewart et al., 2004). CBT-E/RP combines traditional CBT with a systematic protocol of repeatedly exposing the person to the obsessional fear (e.g., that the bathroom is "contaminated" with germs) while having them resist from engaging in compulsive behaviors to reduce those fears (e.g., excessive hand-washing). As the anxiety starts to come down through the process of habituation and without the engagement in rituals, the individual starts to learn that the fears are excessive and/or irrational and that the compulsive behaviors are not necessary to reduce their anxiety. Some factors, such as comorbidity, family accommodation, and poor insight, have been found to be predictors of poor response to CBT treatment (Storch et al., 2010), although CBT is robust against even these problems the majority of the time.

CBT-E/RP has demonstrated significant improvement rates among children and adults with OCD (Milne, 2008; Vande Voort & Svecova, 2010). While there is some evidence to suggest that CBT alone can work just as well as CBTE/RP

(Butler, Chapman, Forman, & Beck, 2005; Rosa-Alcazar, Sanchez-Meca, Gomez-Conesa, & Marin-Martinez, 2008), the vast majority of research suggests that CBT-E/RP is the superior treatment (Abramowitz, Whiteside, & Deacon, 2005; Barrett, 2000; Rapoport & Inoff-Germain, 2000; Milne, 2008; Vande Voort & Svecova, 2010). Medications, such as SSRIs, can also be used to treat OCD symptoms, but the current research suggests that medication alone is not superior to CBT-E/RP and that the best outcome is likely a combination of the two treatments (Abramowitz et al., 2005; Eddy, Dutra, Bradley, & Western, 2004; Lewin et al., 2005; Van Balkon et al., 1994).

In behavioral treatment, social support has been identified as an important component of treatment success (Renshaw, Steketee, & Chambless, 2005). For adults, this often means asking a spouse or close family member to participate in sessions; doing so is intended to improve family dynamics that could impact treatment and provides a system of social support for the patient (Van Noppen & Steketee, 2003). Research generally supports including family in adult treatment, especially if the patient's spouse is participating (Mehta, 1990; Renshaw et al., 2005). In a review by Steketee and Van Noppen (2003) family stress and symptom accommodation were identified as interdependent variables that negatively affect patient outcomes; thus they recommended incorporating family involvement and training into OCD treatment. This recommendation was echoed by Renshaw and colleagues (2005) who suggested that family should be included in treatment to reduce accommodation by family members and to improve the family's understanding of OCD and CBT-E/RP.

In addition to including spouses and other family members in therapy, incorporating parents into therapy has been a primary focus of family-based treatment of OCD. Parental involvement may target several individual and family factors which influence treatment outcomes. Parental help may be necessary for young children whose cognitive development may limit their ability to engage in psychoeducation or actively participate in cognitive-behavioral treatments (Freeman et al., 2003). Further, approximately 25% of adult patients seeking treatment for OCD live with their parents (Steketee & Van Noppen, 2003). Therefore, parental involvement may also be an important component of treatment for adults as well as children (Mehta, 1990; Renshaw et al., 2005). Unfortunately, there is a paucity of research on the benefits of parental involvement in treatment for OCD. One promising study by O'Leary, Barrett, and Fjermestad (2009) found that 87% of their sample of children who participated in family-based CBT did not meet criteria for a diagnosis of OCD seven years post-treatment. While this study did not examine the long-term effects of parental involvement directly, the authors assert that the results support family involvement in treatment as the gains made from a family-based approach were maintained over the long-term. A major weakness in this area is that few studies have focused on children younger than 8 years of age, an age group that is more likely to be prescribed medication for OCD, and who may be more likely to benefit from parental support (Freeman et al., 2007). The limited research in this age group suggests that family based CBT is effective in decreasing symptoms of OCD and in helping a large number of individuals achieve symptom remission (Freeman et al., 2008).

Family involvement in treatment can target a variety of problems that may limit treatment effectiveness. Higher family dysfunction has been found to predict worse long-term outcomes. Therefore, a focus on family dynamics, possibly taking a "family therapy" approach to treatment, may be beneficial (Barrett, Farrell, Dadds, & Boutler, 2005; Freeman et al., 2009; Renshaw et al., 2005; Stekettee & Van Noppen, 2003; Ginsburg & Schlossberg, 2002; Storch et al., 2007, 2010). Psychoeducation with family members who are unfamiliar with OCD, who engage in accommodation of patients' symptoms, and who may be critical or negative towards the patient has also been recommended as a part of family-based treatment; some research suggests that these skills may be more effectively modeled in a group format where patients receive support from other families in addition to their own (Steketee & Van Noppen, 2003; Barrett, Healthy-Farrell, & March, 2004). Communication training may also encourage positive communication and reduce anger expression, although this has only been an informal part of family treatment (Steketee & Van Noppen, 2003). In the treatment of children, parental anxiety or psychopathology has also been noted as an impediment to treatment and parental anxiety management or concurrent individual therapy is an additional intervention strategy (e.g., Barrett et al., 2004; Diamond & Josephson, 2005; Freeman et al., 2009). Behavior management techniques, not specific to OCD, such as behavior plans, and strategies to manage anxiety and distress, have also been suggested as a point of intervention for young children (Freeman et al., 2003; Rapoport & Inoff-Germain, 2000; Wood, Piacentini, Southam-Gerow, Chu, & Sigman, 2006).

While there is currently no well-established family based treatment for OCD, individual exposure-based CBT may be considered a probably efficacious treatment and family-focused CBT, delivered in an individual or group format, may be considered as possibly efficacious (Barrett, Farrell, Peris, & Piacentini, 2008). Several manualized treatments for OCD have been described in the literature. Many treatment protocols (e.g., Barrett et al., 2004; Farrell, Schlup, & Boschen, 2010; Freeman et al., 2003; Jacqueline & Margo, 2005; POTS Team, 2004) have been adapted from March and Mulle's (1998) manual *How I Ran OCD off My Land*. Components of this manual include cognitive training, mapping OCD, exposure and response prevention, and relapse prevention and generalization of therapy (March et al., 2001).

Formal family-based treatments include *Freedom from Obsession and Compulsions Using Cognitive Behavioral Strategies* (FOCUS; Barrett et al., 2007), which contains structured parent and sibling protocols and may be used in individual or group treatment settings. Treatment is delivered in three components including: (1) psychoeducation, anxiety management, and cognitive therapy, (2) intensive exposure/response prevention, and (3) maintenance of gains and relapse prevention. Child and parent sessions are conducted separately and parent sessions focus on psychoeducation, problem solving skills, reducing parental involvement and accommodation of symptoms, and building family support for exposure and response prevention assignments at home (Barrett et al., 2004).

Marien, Storch, Geffken, and Murphy (2009) utilized an intensive CBT protocol described in Lewin and colleagues (2005) and Storch and colleagues (2007b). In this treatment, at least one parent or caregiver is required to be present at all treatment sessions. Parents are first provided with psychoeducation about OCD and treatment and are then taught to be their child's "therapist" or "coach," so that they may effectively guide the child in exposures in the home environment. Family accommodation is also an active target in this protocol, because it is believed that young children will have difficulty ending accommodation-seeking behaviors due to the consequences of negative reinforcement.

Marien and colleagues (2009) also note the importance of addressing maladaptive family factors, such as parental psychopathology, that may affect treatment. To do this, the authors suggest addressing parent and child symptoms separately but concurrently, sequentially, or in family therapy. Freeman and Garcia's (2009) manual, *Family Based Treatment for Young Children with OCD: Therapist Guide* is a structured, family-based cognitive-behavioral treatment protocol for children under 8 years of age. The manual adapts traditional exposure and response prevention to appropriately fit the developmental abilities of young children.

For adults, a model of multifamily behavioral treatment (MFBT) is one approach to treating OCD within a group family context (Van Noppen & Steketee, 2003). The goals of the MFBT approach are to alter family patterns of communication and accommodation, increase family support, provide education about OCD and exposure and response prevention, promote empowerment and empathy while decreasing feelings of isolation and confusion, teach self-instruction through ERP homework assignments, and provide strategies to manage symptom reoccurrence. The authors assert that the group context provides opportunities for modeling when challenging irrational thoughts and behaviors. Overall, the research suggests that incorporating family components into traditional CBT-E/RP is beneficial for both children and adults.

## Clinical Implications and Conclusions

Epidemiological studies reviewed in this chapter suggest the lifetime prevalence of OCD is 2%, though more recent studies report prevalence rates as high as 4% in community samples. Accumulated research indicates that OCD interferes significantly with functioning in individuals with the disorder, and more recent studies document the potential adverse impact of OCD on the family. The clinical implications of these effects are amplified as the literature suggests that up to 80% of individuals with OCD had their onset of symptoms in childhood. Therefore, it is not surprising that treatment research literature supports the idea that involvement of the family facilitates positive outcomes. More specifically, the consensus of clinicians treating children is that parental involvement in youth OCD treatment is critical; parents learn to act as the therapy coach in the home setting and encourage the skills learned in treatment. There is also literature suggesting a need for the assessment and treatment of parental psychopathology that may impact outcomes in children.

The empirical literature on OCD has seen marked progress in the past two decades in terms of evidence-based treatment research. Whereas this review has not focused on research on psychopharmacological treatment, this is one of the areas of treatment in which reliable reductions in OCD severity have been identified. Cognitive behavioral treatment (CBT) is the other domain of evidence-based treatment that has been more thoroughly reviewed in this chapter and identified as an important modality of treatment for OCD. There is considerable empirical support for the finding that CBT with Exposure and Response Prevention is the mode of behavioral treatment for OCD with the best outcomes. In this chapter, we have reviewed literature on family involvement in treatment which suggests that various family problems can exacerbate the effectiveness of treatment, as well as, literature that supports the idea that family therapy can facilitate improvements in OCD symptomatology. The target of family treatment may include psychoeducation, family accommodation, or communication training. There is considerable research implicating the importance of assessing and reducing family accommodation in treatment for OCD. The study of accommodation has wide ranging implications for understanding the impact of the family in OCD, as well as, behavior in the family system that can be addressed in CBT for OCD.

While significant progress has been identified in the treatment literature over the past 20 years, the need for further research is indicated. The literature reviewed in this chapter suggests there is also a need for significantly more research on etiological mechanisms, psychometrically sound assessment tools that can be helpful to use with different family members such as siblings, spouses, parents, and children who may have a family member with OCD, and familial relationships and communication patterns. Psychometric research has provided important implications for cognitive behavioral treatment of OCD regarding the impact on domains including social, occupational/school, familial, and emotional. Literature is accumulating to improve the understanding of OCD and to identify treatments with promise for individuals with OCD and their families. However, it is also evident that prior to the widespread dissemination of cognitive-behavioral therapy for individuals with OCD and their families, the clinical implications and conclusions identified in this chapter require further replication and validation. As future research on the impact of the family on OCD continues, it will also be important to consider the fact that the role of the family may vary based on demographic, cultural, and religious considerations.

## References

Abidin, R. R. (1995). Parenting Stress Index (3rd ed.). Odessa, FL: Psychological Assessment Resources.

Abramowitz, J.S., Whiteside, S.P., & Deacon, B.J. (2005). The effectiveness of treatment for pediatric obsessive-compulsive disorder: A meta-analysis. *Behavior Therapy, 36*, 55-63.

Albert, U., Bogetto, F., Maina, G., Saracco, P., Brunatto, C., & Mataix-Cols, D. (2010). Family accommodation in obsessive–compulsive disorder: Relation to symptom dimensions, clinical and family characteristics. *Psychiatry Research, 179*, 204-211.

Amir, N., Freshman, M., & Foa, E. B. (2000). Family distress and involvement in relatives of obsessive-compulsive disorder patients. *Journal of Anxiety Disorders, 14*, 209-217.

Barrett, P.M. (2000). Treatment of childhood anxiety: Developmental aspects. *Clinical Psychology Review, 20*, 479-494.

Barrett, P. M. (2007). *FOCUS: Freedom from obsessions and compulsions using skills (Therapist manual and workbooks)*. Brisbane, Australia: Pathways Health and Research Centre.

Barrett P., Healthy-Farrell, L., & March, J.S. (2004). Cognitive-behavioral family treatment of childhood obsessive-compulsive disorder: A controlled trial. *Journal of the American Academic of Child and Adolescent Psychiatry, 43*, 46-62.

Barrett, P., Farrell, L., Dadds, M., & Boutler, N. (2005). Cognitive-behavioral family treatment of childhood obsessive-compulsive disorder: Long-term follow-up and predictors of outcome. *Journal of the American Academic of Child and Adolescent Psychiatry, 44*, 1005-1014.

Barrett, P.M., Farrell, L., Peris, T.S., & Piacentini, J. (2008). Evidence-based psychosocial treatments for child and adolescent obsessive-compulsive disorder. *Journal of Clinical Child & Adolescent Psychology, 37*, 131-155.

Black, D. W., Gaffney, G., Schlosser, S., & Gabel, J. (1998). The impact of obsessive-compulsive disorder on the family: Preliminary findings. *Journal of Nervous and Mental Disease, 186*(7), 440-442.

Black, D. W., Gaffney, G. R., Schlosser, S., & Gabel, J. (2003). Children of parents with obsessive-compulsive disorder--A 2-year follow-up study. *Acta Psychiatrica Scandinavica, 107*(4), 305-313.

Butler, A.C., Chapman, J.E., Forman, E.M., & Beck, A.T. (2006). The empirical status of cognitive-behavioral therapy: A review of meta-analyses. *Clinical Psychology Review, 26*, 17-31.

Calvocoressi, L., Lewis, B., Harris, M., & Trufan, S. J. (1995). Family accommodation in obsessive-compulsive disorder. *The American Journal of Psychiatry, 152*, 441-443.

Calvocoressi, L., Mazure, C. M., Kasl, S.V., Skolnick, J., Fisk, D., Vegso, S.J., Van Noppen, B.L., Price, L.H. (1999). Family Accommodation of Obsessive-Compulsive Symptoms: Instrument Development and Assessment of Family Behavior. *Journal of Nervous & Mental Disease, 187*, 636-642.

Cartwright-Hatton, S., Roberts, C., Chitsabesan, P., Fothergill, C., & Harrington, R. (2004). Systematic review of the efficacy of cognitive behaviour therapies for childhood and adolescent anxiety disorders. *British Journal of Clinical Psychology, 43*, 421-436.

Cooper, M. (1996). Obsessive-compulsive disorder: Effects on family members. *American Journal of Orthopsychiatry, 66*, 296-304.

de Abreu Ramos-Cerqueira, A. T., Torres, A. R., Torresan, R. C., Negreiros, A. P. M., & Vitorino, C. N. (2008). Emotional burden in caregivers of patients with obsessive-compulsive disorder. *Depression and Anxiety, 25*, 1020-1027.

Diamond, G., & Josephson, A. (2005). Family-based treatment: A 10-year update. *Journal of the American Academic of Child and Adolescent Psychiatry, 44*, 872-887.

Eddy, K.T., Dutra, L., Bradley, R., & Westen, D. (2004). A multidimensional meta-analysis of psychotherapy and pharmacotherapy for obsessive-compulsive disorder. *Clinical Psychology Review, 24*, 1011-1030.

Farrell, L. J., & Barrett, P. M. (2007). The function of the family in childhood obsessive-compulsive disorder: Family interactions and accommodation. In E. A. Storch, G. R. Geffken & T. K. Murphy (Eds.), *Handbook of child and adolescent obsessive-compulsive disorder.* (pp. 313-332). Mahwah, NJ US: Lawrence Erlbaum Associates Publishers.

Farrell, L.J., Schlup, B. & Boschen, M.J. (2010). Cognitive-behavioral treatment of childhood obsessive-compulsive disorder in community-based clinical practice: Clinical significance and benchmarking against efficacy. *Behaviour Research and Therapy, 48*, 409-417.

Fernandez, M. A., Storch, E. A., Geffken, G. R., & Murphy, T. K. (2006). *Family accommodation in pediatric obsessive- compulsive disorder: Examination of youth and parent report.* In L. J. Merlo (Chair), Novel directions in pediatric obsessive-compulsive disorder research.

Flessner, C. A., Berman, N., Garcia, A., Freeman, J. B., Leonard, H. L. (2009). Symptom profiles in pediatric obsessive-compulsive disorder (OCD): The effects of comorbid grooming conditions. *Journal of Anxiety Disorders* 23(6):753-59.

Flessner, C. A., Freeman, J. B., Sapyta, J., Garcia, A., Franklin, M. E., March, J. S., & Foa, E. (2011). Predictors of parental accommodation in pediatric obsessive-compulsive disorder: Findings from the Pediatric Obsessive-Compulsive Disorder Treatment Study (POTS) Trial. *Journal of the American Academy of Child and Adolescent Psychiatry, 50, 716-725.*

Freeman, J.B., Choate-Summers, M.L., Moore, P.S., Garcia, A.M., Sapyta, J.J., Leonard, H., & Franklin, M.E. (2007). Cognitive behavioral treatment for young children with obsessive-compulsive disorder. *Biological Psychiatry, 61,* 337-343.

Freeman, J.B., Choate-Summers, M.L., Moore, P.S., Garcia, A.M., Moore, P.S., Sapyta, J.J. ... Franklin, M.E. (2009). The Pediatric Obsessive-Compulsive Disorder Treatment Study II: Rationale, design and methods. *Child and Adolescent Psychiatry and Mental Health, 3,* 4-19.

Freeman, J.B., & Garcia, A.M. (2009). *Family-Based Treatment for Young Children With OCD* (Workbook and Therapist Guide). New York, NY: Oxford University Press.

Freeman, J.B., Garcia, A.M., Coyne, L., Ale, C., Przeworksi, A., Himle, M. ... Leonard, H.L. (2008). *Journal of the American Academic of Child and Adolescent Psychiatry, 47,* 593-602.

Freeman, J.B., Garcia, A.M., Fucci, C., Karitani, M., Miller, L., & Leonard, H.L. (2003). Family-based treatment of early-onset obsessive-compulsive disorder. *Journal of Child and Adolescent Psychopharmacology, 13,* 71-80.

Geller, D.A., Bierderman, J., Stewart, E., Mullin, B., Martin, A., Spencer, T., & Faraone, S.V. (2003). Which SSRI? A meta-analysis of pharmacotherapy trials in pediatric obsessive-compulsive disorder. *The American Journal of Psychiatry, 160,* 1919-1928.

Ginsburg, G.S., & Schlossberg, M.C. (2002). Family-based treatment of childhood anxiety disorders. *International Review of Psychiatry, 14,* 143-154.

Hibbs, E. D., Hamburger, S. D., Lenane, M., & Rapoport, J. L. (1991). Determinants of expressed emotion in families of disturbed and normal children. *Journal of Child Psychology and Psychiatry, 32,* 757-770.

Hooley, J., & Teasdale, J. (1989). Predictors of relapse in unipolar depressives: Expressed emotion, marital distress, and perceived criticism. *Journal of Abnormal Psychology, 98,* 229-235.

Jacob, M. L., Morelen, D., Suveg, C., Brown, A., & Whiteside, S. P. (2012). Emotional, Behavioral, and Cognitive Factors that Differentiate Obsessive-Compulsive Disorder and other Anxiety Disorders in Youth. *Anxiety, Stress, and Coping, 25, 229-237.*

Jacqueline, M.L., & Margo, T. (2005). Group cognitive-behavior therapy with family involvement for middle-school-age children with obsessive-compulsive disorder: A pilot study. *Child Psychiatry and Human Development, 36*, 113-127.

Keeley, M.L., Storch, E.A., Merlo, L.J., & Geffken, G.R. (2008). Clinical predictors of response to cognitive-behavioral therapy for obsessive-compulsive disorder. *Clinical Psychology Review, 28*, 118-130.

Kreisman, D. E., Simmens, S. J., & Joy, V. D. (1979). Rejecting the patient: Preliminary validation of a self-report scale. *Schizophrenia Bulletin, 5*, 220–222.

Lewin, A.B., Storch, E.A., Merlo, L.J., Adkins, J.W., Murphy, T., & Geffken, G.R. (2005). Intensive cognitive behavioral therapy for pediatric obsessive-compulsive disorder: A treatment protocol for mental health providers. *Psychology Services, 2*, 91-104.

March, J.S., Franklin, M., Nelson, A., & Foa, E. (2001). Cognitive-behavioral psychotherapy for pediatric obsessive-compulsive disorder. *Journal of Clinical Child & Adolescent Psychology, 30*, 8-18.

March, J.S., & Mulle, K. (1998). *OCD in Children and Adolescents: A Cognitive-Behavioral Treatment Manual*. New York, NY: Guildford Press.

Marien, W.E., Storch, E.A., Geffken, G.R., & Murphy, T.K. (2009). Intensive family-based cognitive-behavioral therapy for pediatric obsessive-compulsive disorder: Applications for treatment of medication partial-or nonresponders. *Cognitive and Behavioral Practice, 16*, 304-316.

Mehta, M. (1990). A comparative study of family-based and patient-based behavioural management in obsessive-compulsive disorder. *The British Journal of Psychiatry, 157*, 133-135.

Milne, A. (2008). Summary of 'Behavioral and cognitive behavioural therapy for obsessive compulsive disorder in children and adolescents.' *Evidence-Based Child Health: A Cochrane Review Journal, 2*, 1314-1315.

Merlo, L. J., Lehmkuhl, H. D., Geffken, G. R., & Storch, E. A. (2009). Decreased family accommodation associated with improved therapy outcome in pediatric obsessive compulsive disorder. *Journal of Consulting and Clinical Psychology, 77*, 355-360.

Peris, T. S., Bergman, R. L., Langley, A., Chang, S., McCracken, J. T., & Piacentini, J. (2008). Correlates of accommodation of pediatric obsessive-compulsive disorder: Parent, child, and family characteristics. *Journal of the American Academy of Child & Adolescent Psychiatry, 47*, 1173-1181.

Piacentini J, Jaffer M (1999). Measuring Functional Impairment in Youngsters With OCD (Manual for the Child OC Impact Scale, COIS).

Piacentini, J., Bergman, R. L., Keller, M., & McCracken, J. (2003). Functional impairment in children and adolescents with obsessive-compulsive disorder. *Journal of Child and Adolescent Psychopharmacology, 13*, S61-SS69.

Piacentini, J., Peris, T. S., Bergman, R. L., Chang, S., & Jaffer, M. (2007). Functional impairment in childhood OCD : Development and psychometrics properties of the Child Obsessive-Compulsive Impact Scale--Revised (COIS--R). *Journal of Clinical Child and Adolescent Psychology*, *36*, 645-653.

Pediatric OCD Treatment Study Team (POTS). (2004). Cognitive-behavior therapy, sertraline, and their combination with children and adolescents with obsessive-compulsive disorder: The Pediatric OCD Treatment Study (POTS) randomized controlled trial. *The Journal of the American Medical Association*, *292*, 1969-1976.

O'Leary, E.M., Barrett, P., & Fjermestad, K.W. (2009). Cognitive-behavioral family treatment for childhood obsessive-compulsive disorder: A 7-year follow-up study. *Journal of Anxiety Disorders*, *23*, 973.978.

Rapoport, J.L., & Inoff-Germain, G. (2000). Practitioner review: Treatment of obsessive-compulsive disorder in children and adolescents. *Journal of Child Psychology and Psychiatry*, *41(4)*, 419-431.

Renshaw, K.D., Steketee, G., & Chambless, D.L. (2005). Involving family members in the treatment of OCD. *Cognitive Behavior Therapy*, *34(3)*, 164-175.

Rosa-Alcazar, A.I., Sanchez-Meca, J., Gomez-Conesa, A., & Marin-Martienz, F. (2008). Psychological treatment of obsessive-compulsive disorder: A meta-analysis. *Clinical Psychology Review*, *28*I, 1310-1325.

Stekett, G. (1993). Social support and treatment outcome of obsessive-compulsive disorder at 9-month follow up. *Behavioral Psychotherapy*, *21*, 81-95

Steketee, G. (1997). Disability and family burden in obsessive-compulsive disorder. *The Canadian Journal of Psychiatry / La Revue canadienne de psychiatrie*, *42*, 919-928.

Steketee, G., & Van Noppen, B. (2003).Family approaches to treatment for obsessive-compulsive disorder. *Revista Brasileira de Psiquiatria*, *25*, 43-50.

Stewart, S. E., Beresin, C., Haddad, S., Stack, D. E., Fama, J., & Jenike, M. (2008). Predictors of family accommodation in obsessive-compulsive disorder. *Annals of Clinical Psychiatry*, *20*, 65-70.

Stewart, S.E., Geller, D.A., Jenike, M., Pauls, D., Shaw, D., Mullin, B., & Faraone, S.V. (2004). Long-term outcome of pediatric obsessive-compulsive disorder: A meta-analysis and qualitative review of the literature. *Acta Psychiatrica Scandinavica*, *110*, 4-13.

Stewart, S. E., Hu, Y.-P., Hezel, D. M., Proujansky, R., Lamstein, A., Walsh, C., Pauls, D. L. (2011). Development and psychometric properties of the OCD Family Functioning (OFF) Scale. *Journal of Family Psychology*, *25*, 434-443.

Storch, E. A., Geffken, G. R., Merlo, L. J., Jacob, M. L., Murphy, T. K., Goodman, W. K., . . . Grabill, K. (2007a). Family accommodation in pediatric obsessive-compulsive disorder. *Journal of Clinical Child and Adolescent Psychology*, *36*, 207-216.

Storch, E. A., Geffken, G. R., Merlo, L. J., Mann, G., Duke, D., Munson, M., et al. (2007b). Family-based cognitive-behavioral therapy for pediatric obsessive-compulsive disorder: Comparison of intensive and weekly approaches. *Journal of the American Academy of Child & Adolescent Psychiatry, 46*, 469-478.

Storch, E.A., Lehmkuhl, H., Pence, S.L., Jr., Geffken, G.R., Ricketts, E., Storch, J.F., & Murphy, T.K. (2009). Parental experiences of having a child with obsessive-compulsive disorder: Associations with clinical characteristics and caregiver adjustment. Journal of Child and Family Studies, 18, 249_258.

Storch, E.A., Lehmkuhl, H.D., Ricketts, E., Geffken, G.R., Marien, W., & Murphy, T.K. (2010). An open trial of intensive family based cognitive-behavioral therapy in youth with obsessive-compulsive disorder who are medication partial responders or nonresponders. *Journal of Clinical Child & Adolescent Psychology, 39*, 260-268.

Valderhaug R & Ivarsson T. (2005). Functional impairment in clinical samples of Norwegian and Swedish children and adolescents with obsessive-compulsive disorder. *European Child and Adolescent Psychiatry, 14*, 164 - 73.

Van Balkom, A.J.L.M, van Oppen, P., Vermeulen, A.W.A., van Dyk, R., Nauta, M.C.E., & Vorst, H.C.M. (1994). A meta-analysis on the treatment of obsessive compulsive disorder: A comparison of antidepressants, behavior, and cognitive therapy. *Clinical Psychology Review, 14(5)*, 359-381.

Vande Voort, J.L., & Svecova, J. (2010). A retrospective examination of the similarity between clinical practice and manualized treatment for childhood anxiety disorders. *Cognitive and Behavioral Practice, 17*, 322-328.

Van Noppen, B., & Steketee, G. (2003). Family responses and multifamily behavioral treatment for obsessive-compulsive disorder. *Brief Treatment and Crisis Intervention, 3(2)*, 231-247.

Van Noppen, B., & Steketee, G. (2009). Testing a conceptual model of patient and family predictors of obsessive compulsive disorder (OCD) symptoms. *Behaviour Research and Therapy*. 47, 18-25.

Varni, J. W., Seid, M., Kurtin, P. S. (2001). The PedsQl 4.0:Reliability and validity of the Pediatric Quality of the Life Inventory Version 4.0 generic Core Scales in healthy and patient populations. *Medical Care*. *39*, 800-812.

Vikas, A., Avasthi, A., & Sharan, P. (2011). Psychosocial impact of obsessive-compulsive disorder on patients and their caregivers: A comparative study with depressive disorder. *International Journal of Social Psychiatry, 57*, 45-56.

Watson, H.J. & Rees, C.S. (2008). Meta-analysis of randomized, controlled treatment trials for pediatric obsessive-compulsive disorder. *Journal of Child Psychology and Psychiatry, 49(5)*, 489-498.

Williams, T.I., Salkovskis, P.M., Forrester, L., Turner, S., White, H., & Allsopp, M.A. (2010). A randomized controlled trial of cognitive behavioural treatment for obsessive compulsive disorder in children and adolescents. *European Child & Adolescent Psychiatry, 19*, 449-456.

Wood, J.J., Piacentini, J.C., Southam-Gerow, M., Chu, B.C., Sigman, M. (2006). Family cognitive behavioral therapy for child anxiety disorders. *Journal of the American Academy of Child & Adolescent Psychiatry,45*, 314-321.

*CW Lack*

# About the Authors

**Emily Ach, PhD** is a clinical instructor in the Department of Psychiatry and Behavioral Sciences and the Division of Child and Adolescent Psychiatry at Stanford University School of Medicine. She received her doctorate from The Ohio State University, completing her pre-doctoral training at University of California, Los Angeles and her post-doctoral training at Boston Children's Hospital. Her research interests include child and family adjustment to serious diagnoses and the psychosocial functioning of parents and children following treatment for pediatric cancer.

**Amanda M Balkhi, MS** is a clinical psychology doctoral student in the Department of Clinical and Health Psychology and the Department of Psychiatry at University of Florida. Her research interests include the intersections of anxiety and family factors of child health.

**Natasha L. Burke, MA** is a clinical psychology doctoral candidate at the University of South Florida. She is completing her clinical psychology predoctoral internship at The Warren Alpert Medical School of Brown University and completed her undergraduate and master's studies at New York University. Ms. Burke's research and clinical interests are primarily in child and pediatric psychology, with a specific focus on the psychological comorbidities and sociodemographic factors associated with pediatric obesity treatment and prevention.

**Lauren Craig, MA** is a doctoral student in the counseling psychology program at the University of Oklahoma. A graduate of the University of Central Oklahoma's counseling program, her primary research interests include the impact of athletic identity on student-athlete well-being and performance related concerns and anxiety disorders in the athlete population. Lauren has co-authored multiple scientific publications and has presented her research at numerous conferences.

**Roy Eyal, MD** is a child and adolescent psychiatrist in practice with The Permanente Medical Group of Northern California. He completed medical school at Vanderbilt University School of Medicine, followed by a residency and fewllowshipo in general and adult, and child and adolescent psychiatry at the Neuropsychiatric Institute at UCLA. He is board certified in both psychiatry and child and adolescent psychiatry. Dr. Eyal practices in a general psychiatry clinic, teaches medical students and is currently the president of the Northern California Regional Organization of Child and Adolescent Psychiatry.

**Gary R Geffken, PhD** has been a clinical psychologist on faculty at the University of Florida for 27 years. His primary appointment is in Psychiatry, where he is Chief of Medical Psychology and Director of the CBT Program for OCD. He has additional academic appointments in Clinical and Health Psychology, Pediatrics, and School Psychology. He provides clinical services to children and adults. Dr. Geffken has been a PI and Co-PI on numerous grants and contracts, as well as having authored or coauthored over 200 published scientific studies, abstracts and/or chapters primarily in pediatric and clinical child psychology, and family issues of children. He has also co-authored two books. An educator of healthcare professionals, Dr. Geffken is a site visitor for APA's Committee on Accreditation and has held leadership roles for continuing education for health care professionals at state and national levels, earning a Distinguished Service Award from UF's College of Medicine. Dr. Geffken previously served as President of the Florida Psychological Association, where he received the Distinguished Psychologist Award from his colleagues.

**Linda Herbert, PhD** is an Assistant Professor in the Department of Psychology & Behavioral Health at Children's National Medical Center. She is the Director of the Division of Allergy and Immunology's psychosocial clinical program, for which she coordinates outpatient consultation and therapy services. Dr. Herbert is a member of the Education Working Group for FARE (Food Allergy Research & Education), and regularly speaks at child health community events and national conferences. Dr. Herbert's research interests include the identification of medical and psychosocial factors related to food allergy management and the development of clinical interventions for youth with food allergies and their families.

**Micah Highfill, BA** is a graduate student in school psychology at the Univeristy of Central Oklahoma. She also studies applied behavioral analysis and plans on integrating the two within the school environment.

**Alisa M Huskey, BA** is a graduate student in in experimental psychology at University of Central Oklahoma. She is primarily interested in conducting research investigating the physiological systems and evolutionary underpinnings of psychopathological behavior, particularly PTSD and complex PTSD.

**Marni L. Jacob, PhD** is a licensed psychologist and postdoctoral fellow in the Department of Pediatrics at the University of South Florida. Dr. Jacob's clinical and research activities focus on anxiety disorders, with a particular emphasis on obsessive-compulsive disorder and obsessive-compulsive spectrum disorders. She works with children, adolescents, and adults and specializes in cognitive-behavioral treatment, including exposure therapy for anxiety and phobias, exposure and response prevention for OCD, and habit reversal training.

**Rachel L. (Katz) Juerhing, PhD** is a pediatric psychologist at St. Louis Children's Hospital. She completed her pre-doctoral internship at the University of Florida and her post-doctoral fellowship at Children's Medical Center Dallas. Dr. Juerhing's research and clinical interests focus on quality of life and psychological characteristics of children and adolescents with diabetes.

**Caleb W Lack, PhD** is an Associate Professor at the University of Central Oklahoma. He is the author/editor of four prior books and over 40 articles and book chapters. Dr. Lack is incredibly proud of the fact that he has never been arrested on any of his trips abroad with Dr. Storch, even when he ran into the mayor's car in Copan, Honduras. Twice.

**Adam B. Lewin, PhD, ABPP** is an Associate Professor of Pediatrics and Psychiatry at the University of South Florida College of Medicine. He is the director of the OCD, Anxiety and Related Disorders Behavioral Treatment Program and also serves as Director of Psychology Training within Pediatric Neuropsychiatry. Dr. Lewin's research and clinical interests focus on OCD, anxiety, Tourette's, trichotillomania, and related disorders. Prior to beginning at USF in 2009, Dr. Lewin completed his graduate studies at the University of Florida's Department of Clinical and Health Psychology. Subsequently, he attended the UCLA Semel Institute for Neuropsychiatry for his psychology residency and fellowship. Dr. Lewin is a board certified child and adolescent psychologist and is the Member at Large for Education and Standards for the American Psychological Association Division 53 – Society for Clinical Child and Adolescent Psychology.

**Dean McKay, PhD, ABPP** is a Professor of Psychology at Fordham University, where he directs the Compulsive, Obsessive, and Anxiety Program (COAP). Dr. McKay is a Fellow of the Association for Psychological Science, the Academy of Clinical Psychology, the American Academy of Behavioral Psychology, the American Academy of Cognitive & Behvioral Psychology, and numerous divisions of the American Psychological Association. In addition, he served as the 2013-2014 President of the Association for Behavioral and Cognitive Therapies. The author or co-author of over 100 peer-reviewed articles, dozens of book chapters, and over a dozen books, Dr. McKay focuses on the widespread applicability and acceptance of cognitive and behavioral methods to a wide variety of problems in the treatment community.

**Sean McMillan, MA** has a master's in forensic psychology from the University of Central Oklahoma. His main research focus is on the expression of psychopathy, with interests in social psychology as well. He plans on pursing a doctorate in clinical psychology in the future.

**Joseph P.H. McNamara, PhD** is an Assistant Professor and Division Chief for Online Education in the Department of Psychiatry at the University of Florida. He is the Clinic Director for the Division of Medical Psychology. Dr. McNamara treats both children and adults, and has received additional training in exposure with response prevention and cognitive behavioral therapy. He has also received advanced training in the treatment of insomnia. His research interests are focused on improving treatment outcomes.

**Melissa S. Munson, PhD** is a postdoctoral fellow in the Department of Psychiatry at the University of Florida. Dr. Munson's clinical and research interests focus primarily on anxiety disorders and the impact of social problems on psychological functioning. She has clinical experience with both children and adults treating a range of psychopathology with a specific focus on the treatment of OCD.

**Erika L Nurmi, MD, PhD** is the medical director of the University of Califiornia, Los Angeles (UCLA) Obsessive-Compulsive Disorder Intensive Outpatient Program, the associate director of the psychiatry residency research track, and a member of the Child and Adolescent Psychiatry Division faculty in the Department of Psychiatry and Biobehavioral Sciences at the UCLA Semel Institute for Neuroscience and Human Behavior. Dr. Nurmi's research focuses the genetic basis of childhood OCD and tic disorders.

**Jennifer M Park, PhD** is a Clinical and Research Fellow in the Child CBT Program at the Massachusetts General Hospital/Harvard Medical School (Department of Psychiatry). Dr. Park completed her undergraduate studies at Amherst College, her master's and doctorate in Clinical Psychology at the University of South Florida, and her predoctoral internship at Massachusetts General Hospital/Harvard Medical School. Presently, Dr. Park is involved with both research and clinical activities; she provides weekly and intensive cognitive-behavioral treatment for children and adolescents with various psychiatric disorders, with a specialized emphasis on obsessive compulsive disorder, obsessive compulsive spectrum disorders (e.g., trichotillomania, hoarding disorder), and anxiety disorders. Her research focuses on the efficacy of behavioral interventions and the mechanisms involved in the treatment of youth with obsessive compulsive spectrum disorders. She is also funded by the Livingston Award for Young Investigators to conduct research regarding the risk factors and clinical characteristics of children and adolescents with hoarding behaviors.

**Erin Rabideau, MS** is a graduate student in Clinical Psychology at Ohio University in Athens, Ohio.

**Adam M Reid, MS** is a Clinical and Health Psychology doctoral student at the University of Florida under the mentorship of Dr. Gary Geffken. Mr. Reid's primary research focus relates to investigating factors that impact treatment outcome, as well as the development of potential augmentation strategies, for pediatric and adult Obsessive-Compulsive Disorder.

**Robert R Selles, MA** is a clinical psychology doctoral student at the University of South Florida. He is interested in the treatment of youth with anxiety and obsessive compulsive spectrum disorders, with a particular focus on factors related to symptom presentation and treatment outcome.

**Ashleigh Steever, BA** graduated from the University of Louisville in 2012 with a degree from the Department from Psychological and Brain Sciences. She conducted research on cultural differences in mental health and health care services with Dr. Williams at the Center for Mental Health Disparities. She also worked as a behavioral assistant for patients with obsessive-compulsive disorder.

**Eric A Storch, PhD** is Professor and All Children's Hospital Guild Endowed Chair in the Departments of Pediatrics, Psychiatry and Behavioral Neurosciences, and Psychology at the University of South Florida. He serves as the Clinical Director of OCD and Anxiety Services at Rogers Behavioral Health – Tampa Bay. Dr. Storch has received over $5,000,000 in research funding, is a Fulbright Scholar, and has published 10 books and over 400 articles. He specializes in the nature and treatment of childhood and adult obsessive-compulsive disorder and related conditions, anxiety disorders, and anxiety among youth with autism. Finally, he is most proud of the fact that he outshot Dr. Lack in a shooting gallery in rural Honduras.

**Michael L Sulkowski, PhD** is an Assistant Professor in the School Psychology Program at the University of Arizona. He also is a Clinical Assistant Professor of Psychiatry in the Psychiatry Department at the University of Arizona. His research focuses on supporting the mental health needs of underserved and highly at-risk populations.

**David Weed, MA** has a graduate degree in psychology from the University of Central Oklahoma. He is currently a Human Factors Research Specialist at the Federal Aviation Administration, Civil Aerospace Medical Institute. His research interests include linguistics, social and evolutionary psychology, human-computer interaction, serious games for learning, and cabin safety. He has presented at multiple conferences nationally and internationally and his most recent published research can be found under the Office of Aerospace Medicine Technical Reports. He can be contacted at David.Weed@FAA.gov.

**Monnica T. Williams, PhD** is the Director of the Center for Mental Health Disparities and Assistant Professor of Psychological and Brain Sciences at the University of Louisville in Kentucky. She conducts research on obsessive-compulsive disorder, African American mental health, ethnic differences, and measurement/scale development. She is also the Clinical Director of the Louisville OCD Clinic, where she treats people with severe cases of OCD and related disorders and trains clinicians in cognitive-behavioral therapies. She has published over 50 scientific articles and is an associate editor for BMC Psychiatry. She is currently on the Scientific Advisory Board of the International OCD Foundation.

**Heather Yardley, PhD** is an Assistant Professor in the Department of Pediatric Psychology and Neuropsychology at Nationwide Children's Hospital. Dr. Yardley's position is primarily to provide psychological services to youth with Type 1 diabetes, other endocrine disorders, and Obsessive-Compulsive Disorder. She is actively involved in the training program as an internship supervisor and director of the pediatric psychology externship. Dr. Yardley's research primarily focuses on treatment adherence in youth with Type 1 diabetes.

# About the Editor

**Caleb W. Lack, Ph.D.** is an Associate Professor of Psychology at the University of Central Oklahoma. A licensed clinical psychologist, he is the author of over 40 articles and book chapters, as well as four prior books: *Tornadoes, Children, and Posttraumatic Stress; Anxiety Disorders: An Introduction; Mood Disorders: An Introduction;* and *Psychology Gone Astray*. He received his doctorate from Oklahoma State University and completed his predoctoral internship at the University of Florida. Dr. Lack has won numerous awards for his innovative teaching and research, including an honorary degree from the Escuela de Psicologicá at the Universidad Dr. José Mataís Delgado in El Salvador.

Outside of the realm of clinical psychology, Dr. Lack also teaches undergraduate and graduate courses on critical thinking, science, and pseudoscience. These recently culminated in the edited, free online text *Science, Pseudoscience, & Critical Thinking* as well as the documentary series *Pseudoscience in Oklahoma* (available at youtube.com/professorlack). He also writes the "Great Plains Skeptic" column on the Skeptic Ink Network (skepticink.com/gps/) and presents frequently on how to think critically about paranormal and supernatural claims.

You can learn more about Dr. Lack by visiting his website at www.calebblack.com and following him on Twitter (@professorlack) or Facebook (facebook.com/professorcaleblack).